India's Defence Security: Intra-regional Dimension

India's Defence Security
Intra-regional Dimension

Col. (Retd.) S. C. Narang

PRASHANT PUBLISHING HOUSE
DELHI-110094

Published by :
PRASHANT PUBLISHING HOUSE
C-34, 28 Foota Road, Gali-3,
West Karwal Nagar, Delhi-110094
Phone : 011-22963970, Mob. : 9810396373
e-mail.: prashantpublishinghouse@gmail.com

India's Defence Security: Intra-regional Dimension
Reserved
First Published 2017

ISBN : 978-81-934253-4-3

PRINTED IN INDIA
Published by Mr. R.K. Jha M/s Prashant Publishing House and Published at H.S. Offset House Press, Delhi.

Contents

Preface

India's national security and defence is equally the responsibility of all its citizens. They must not only study matters military, but also be alive to dangers to India's security, both from external and internal threats. As regards India's parliamentarians and politicians are concerned, their responsibility in this respect is far more.

Indian Defence, broadly speaking, falls into three categories: Land Defence, Naval Defence and Aerial Defence which are executed respectively by the Army, the Navy and the Air Force. These three are the basic props of our security against external threats. But these would not suffice without the Engineering Defences needed to fortify our frontiers. Similarly at the times of emergency our National Cadet Corps (NCC) and Border Security Force (BSF) come handy.

One of the world's largest defense, space and security businesses, Boeing Defense, Space & Security (BDS) develops innovative solutions that address evolving capability requirements. The ability to provide customers with the right solutions at the right time and the right cost drives our worldwide success.

Defence planning is essentially a subset of overall national level planning in the political, economic and social spheres and has to be evolved in the context of global and proximate factors affecting the nation.. It has also to take into account the philosophy and ethos animating the national psyche; in other words the historical and cultural forces which have shaped the collective memory and outlook of the people over the centuries. The Cold War, was a classic example of the factors stated above. There were fundamental philosophical differences between the adversaries – the western bloc, advocating the virtues of free enterprise and its own interpretations of democracy, and the Soviet bloc, equally strongly asserting the merits of the socialist system as the only one genuinely meeting democratic aspirations and assuring social equality and economic well-being of the people as a whole, rather than for a few. Fifty years of the Cold War could not conclude the capitalism-socialism debate, though, in the end, it did push the socialist forces into, perhaps temporary, retreat. This was because the struggle was really for power and domination. "The evil empire" of Ronald Reagan's description may have withered away, but the necessity for the US to target the so called "rogue states" has not disappeared.

The Indian debate on the missile defence is an extension of the larger debate on India's nuclear weapons policy. But as this chapter has argued, it is also about the strategic direction of Indian foreign policy in the coming years. While a lot of attention has been focused in the technical details of the missile defence programme and its utility or disutility for Indian security needs, the debate in India is also about the larger issues that confront Indian foreign policy in the new millennium, More than the technical issues, it is the political ramifications of missile defence that require greater scrutiny.

This book makes an interesting reading for historians, defence and policy analysts, researchers and general readers alike.

—*Editor*

1

Introduction

STRATEGIC VISION

Pandit Nehru's strategic outlook of foreign policy neutrality and sturdy political independence in the first two decades after Independence, has gradually changed to its current U.S-predicated strategic dependence, even political subservience. It is regrettable that in the last four plus decades, India has not produced a single political leader with a strategic vision to enable India to adjust to and be on top of today's rapidly changing geo-econo-political situations in a globalizing world. Notwithstanding lack of statesmanship at the apex, reputed Indian strategic think-tanks have recommended creation of a document defining strategic policy encompassing India's international and regional political, economic (including energy) and military aims and objectives, depending upon its present and future needs. Realistic national security is only possible when strategic policy is explicitly understood by persons in government. But none of the successive union governments over six decades have produced a strategic document, thus effectively compromising national security by their ineffectiveness.

The Defence Spectrum

Defence is a highly specialized area, and a military officer rises to the position of service chief of the army, navy or air force with about 40 years of service experience in his own service. He acquires knowledge of the operational capability of the other two services by inter-services exposure in various courses, in joint exercises and also in the hard arena of active operations. He is responsible for and concerned with the operational capability of his own service and looks to the other two services to receive or provide operational support, depending upon the threat situation or type of operation. But in military conflicts-of-the-future, warfare, hitherto limited to operations concerning land, sea, under-the-sea and air, will include the dimensions of space and cyber space warfare. Thus, for the primary role of effective deployment and operations to protect India's sovereignty and territorial integrity, a service chief should be well-versed in the operational and logistic capabilities of his own service and adequately knowledgeable with respect to those of the other two also. It can safely be said that India has never had a service chief who has fallen short in this respect, whatever his other shortcomings.

In a democratic republic like India in which the military is under the control of an elected government, defence preparedness requires mutual trust between the military and the government. Trust can only come out of direct official, institutionalized, periodic contact and discussions between government and the military. The bureaucracy is a necessary link to assist in their communication, but cannot substitute for direct contact.

However, as noted by Lt Gen Vijay Oberoi, " *Our political leadership is highly uncomfortable in dealing with the military directly and prefers to let the bureaucracy do so.*" Thus the bureaucracy is the *de facto* functional link between the defence services and the political executives of the union government, and has a stake in maintaining the distance between them.

Notwithstanding that a few selected bureaucrats are assigned to study in the Defence Services Staff College, the College of Defence Management and the National Defence College for better understanding and coordination with defence services officers, they cannot be blamed for not knowing the details of the functioning of any of the three services, much less about the issues involved in their integrated functioning in war. At the same time, most politicians are ignorant of the functioning of the defence services and their capabilities, mainly because of their "distance" from the military, whatever the reasons.

INDIA'S DEFENCE PREPAREDNESS

India's economic progress has increased it's say in the world order where India is being considered as an emerging superpower. It's the ninth largest country in world in terms of nominal GDP; India has the third largest purchasing power in the world. This has certainly been reflected its recent imports for the defence industry. In the period 2006 to 2010 India surpassed

China as the world's largest importer of weapons systems, indicating India's intention to modernize its military capabilities and efforts toward making its boundaries secure and projecting its capability to outside world. The crucial issue here is that not only weapon & defence technology imports drain country's foreign exchequer but also increases the dependence of our defence technology on other nations.

India's spending on defence as a share of its GDP has remained relatively steady at 2.5 to 3.0 percent. Consequently, India's defence budget has grown by some 64% (in real terms) since 2001 reaching $36.3 billion in the 2011–2012 and $41 billion in 2012-13 (an increase of 17% from the last year). Approximately 40 percent (some $14.5 billion) is allocated to the defence capital outlay budget, which funds for arms procurements, construction and maintenance & installations additional infrastructure, and other military equipment modernizations.

Indian Air Force has experienced a 6 to 7 percent growth in its share of the capital outlay budget over the past decade, while the Indian Army and Navy have seen their shares decrease. The Air Force also receives the major share, some 40 percent of the current capital outlay budget, while the Army and Navy receive 25 and 20 percent, respectively (the remaining is spent on R&D and military production).

Looking at the defence budget one can discern that around 70% of the budget is utilized for paying for imports and the remaining 30% is used for indigenous capability building, defence research and procurement. This is indicative of our dependence on foreign imports and under allocation of resources for indigenous defence technology development. The argument of indigenous R&D in defence technology is Janus faced. R&D in defence technology is predominantly conducted by, and limited to, the government organizations like DRDO, HAL, NAL etc.; but the efficacy and efficiency of these organizations is deplorable, thereby leaving no other alternative but to procure the required technology from abroad. Contesting this it can also be argued that the resource allocation for defence research is very conservative; in fact budget allocation for defence R&D has decreased from 10,539 crores in 2011-12 to 5,995 crore rupees in 2012-13 (43.11% decrease over the last budget) deeply hampering our indigenous R&D. It seems that indigenous R&D in defence technology is a low priority issue for the government; whereas lack of funds could be a pertinent impediment to the ability of the research organizations to deliver.

Boosting indigenous defence research to come up with advanced defence technology with shorter cycle time requires structural reforms. We not only need to spend more on R&D but also need to improve support infrastructure and be more open minded about public-private-partnership (PPP) in the defence sector. There are many important issues which have to be addressed in this context. It's an imperative to build a quality research network for defence research comprising of government research organizations, universities and other research institutes; defence research is too important to be left for government organizations alone. Why not sponsor defence research projects in competent educational institutions in India? Having spent some time with HAL Bangalore, what comes as a critical observation is the extent to which our government research organizations lack professional management. Research organization need to be managed much more professionally than they are; this will require intensive focus on project management, time-bound objectives and performance dependent appraisals.

For these advancements it is critical to invest more in education and research based infrastructure, such as well-equipped labs, operational with high-speed computational computers and testing facilities, and more industry exposure. Analyzing the present scenario, India currently is home to 50 laboratories all over the country predominantly held by government, most of them under Defence & Research Development Organization (DRDO), while others are associated with Indian Space And Research Organization (ISRO). Labs in other educational institutes such as IITs and IISc seem more associated with commercial based research rather than core defence research. This limits the participation from private sector institutions and educational institutions in coming up with innovative ideas in the field of defence technology development.

To boost indigenous defence research India must look forward to partnership with the private sector. To address the security concerns, government can open up the defence sector to private investment gradually or limit private participation to only domestic private players, but private participation is essential. More vigorous private participation in defence research will not only reduce pressure on the government to allocate resources, but will also bring about more ideas, innovative technologies, timely project completion and as a consequence a more robust indigenous defence development.

Currently there are a number of regulatory barriers for entry of private players, making it difficult for small and medium enterprises (SMEs) to enter the market. This is largely due to the high costs of tendering processes, such as in-country trials and obligations for Transfer of Technology. One of the major impediments is the necessity for No Cost No Commitment Trials which can take several years and consequently small players with sophisticated expertise do not have the resilience to survive this risk. Also the tendering process for defence equipment in India is not transparent; and is replete with procedures and red-tapeism. Such entry barriers discourage prospective foreign or domestic private players to invest in defence R&D in India, as this could lead to irrecoverable sunk costs, and might not lead to any returns in future.

There is a shift in policy stance in this matter. Apprehending the gravity of these issues Ministry of Defence (GOI) released the first ever Defence Production Policy in 2011.

This document greatly emphasizes on indigenous production and advocates relaxation of norms and policies, which earlier inhibited private small and medium enterprises entering into defence sector, instilling confidence in them so as to foster public-private-partnerships. But a lot remains to be done for indigenous defence sector development by duly prioritizing R&D investment and related infrastructure and opening up possibilities for private sector participation in the same.

INDIA'S NEED FOR DECLARATORY STRATEGIC DOCTRINES

India having formalised its "strategic vision" should then spell out in declaratory terms the strategic doctrines the country would follow henceforth. In the last 50 years, India has shied away from declaratory strategic doctrines. Declaratory strategic doctrines are necessary for the following reasons:

- India's strategic intentions are made clear in declaratory form. Ambiguity is the weapon of the weak and the passive. India should move away from ambiguous policies.
- Strategic doctrines should define in unambiguous terms the "red lines" whose crossing or attempts to breach by any country will not be tolerated. These "red lines" should flow from the enunciation of India's national security interests. The use of force and swift retaliation should be declared in these strategic doctrines.
- Strategic doctrines so declared will leave no doubt to potential aggressors or those tempted to stir and generate internal security threats in India as to what India's responses would be.
- Declaratory strategic doctrines are especially necessary for combating terrorism, hijacking and other disruptive activities resorted to by adversaries. Doctrines should spell out that even the roots of terrorism and insurgency from across Indian borders will not be immune from India's retaliatory responses.

- On the practical plane, declaratory strategic doctrines would provide the template on which planning for India's national security apparatus and force-planning and force structures can be configured.
- Declaratory strategic doctrines should therefore essentially reflect India's will to use power both in terms of pre-emptive military operations and launching of offensive operations.

In the realms of Indian military strategy, the absence of declaratory strategic doctrines has been most keenly felt. India's military responses to both external and internal threats, so far, perforce, have been defensive and re-active in nature. Our entire national ethos, political and military mind-sets and tactical thinking have been oriented in defensive terms

Such defensive and reactive policies have had a debilitating impact on India's military preparedness and also on India's intelligence machinery. As soon as the crisis blows over, in the absence of strategic doctrines, combat equipment acquisitions and build-up of strategic needs is shelved. It has also led to neglect of our build-up of force-projection capabilities and the development of our offshore island territories into strong military bases for force projection capabilities.

CHINA AND INDIA TODAY: DIPLOMATS JOSTLE, MILITARIES PREPARE

Just as the Indian subcontinental plate has a tendency to constantly rub and push against the Eurasian tectonic plate, causing friction and volatility in the entire Himalayan mountain range, India's bilateral relationship with China is also a subtle, unseen, but ongoing and deeply felt collision, the affects of which have left a convoluted lineage. Tensions between the two powers have come to influence everything from their military and security decisionmaking to their economic and diplomatic maneuvering, with implications for wary neighbours and faraway allies alike. The relationship is complicated by layers of rivalry, mistrust, and occasional cooperation, not to mention actual geographical disputes.

Distant neighbours buffered by Tibet and the Himalayas for millennia, China and India became next-door neighbours with contested frontiers and disputed histories in 1950, following the occupation of Tibet by Mao's People's Liberation Army (PLA). While the rest of the world started taking note of China's rise during the last decade of the twentieth century, India has been warily watching China's rise ever since a territorial dispute erupted in a brief but full-scale war in 1962, followed by skirmishes in 1967 and 1987.

Several rounds of talks held since 1981 have failed to resolve the disputed claims. During his last visit to India, in 2010, Chinese Premier Wen Jiabao dashed any hopes of early border settlement, stating that it would take a very long time to settle the boundary issue—a situation that in many ways works to Beijing's advantage. An unsettled border provides China the strategic leverage to keep India uncertain about its intentions, and nervous about its capabilities, while exposing India's vulnerabilities and weaknesses, and encouraging New Delhi's "good behavior" on issues of vital concern. Besides, as the ongoing unrest and growing incidents of self-immolations by Buddhist monks in Tibet show, Beijing has not yet succeeded in pacifying and Sinicizing Tibet, as it has Inner Mongolia. The net result is that the 2,520-mile Sino-Indian frontier, one of the longest inter-state boundaries in the world, remains China's only undefined land border. It is also becoming heavily militarized, as tensions rise over China's aggressive patrolling on the line of actual control (LAC) and its military drills, using live ammunition, for a potential air and land campaign to capture high-altitude mountain passes in Tibet.

Over the last decade, the Chinese have put in place a sophisticated military infrastructure in the Tibet Autonomous Region (TAR) adjoining India: five fully operational air bases, several helipads, an extensive rail network, and thirty thousand miles of roads—giving them the ability to rapidly deploy thirty divisions (fifteen thousand soldiers each) along the border, a three-to-one advantage over India. China has not only increased its military presence in Tibet but is also ramping up its nuclear arsenal. In addition, the PLA's strategic options against India are set to multiply as Chinese land and rail links with Pakistan, Nepal, Burma, and Bangladesh improve.

Developments on the disputed Himalayan borders are central to India's internal debate about the credibility of its strategic deterrent and whether to test nuclear weapons again. Being the weaker power, India is far more concerned about the overall military balance tilting to its disadvantage. India sees China everywhere because of Beijing's "hexiao gongda" policy in South Asia: "uniting with the small"—Pakistan, Bangladesh, Nepal, Burma, and Sri Lanka—"to counter the big"—India. When combined with Chinese nuclear and missile transfers to Pakistan and building of port facilities around India's periphery, and a dramatic increase in the PLA's incursions and transgressions across the LAC, the official Indian perception of China has undergone a dramatic shift since 2006, with China now being widely seen as posing a major security threat in the short to medium term rather than over the long term. The Indian military, long preoccupied with war-fighting scenarios against Pakistan, has consequently turned its attention to the China border, and unveiled a massive force modernization program, to cost $100 billion over the next decade, that includes the construction of several strategic roads and the expansion of rail networks, helipads, and airfields all along the LAC. Other measures range from raising a new mountain strike corps and doubling force levels in the eastern sector by one hundred thousand troops to the deployment of Sukhoi Su-30MKI aircraft, spy drones, helicopters, and ballistic and cruise missile squadrons to defend its northeastern state of Arunachal Pradesh, territory three times the size of Taiwan that the Chinese invaded in 1962 and now claim sovereignty over as "Southern Tibet."

Propelled by incidents related to border disputes, Chinese opposition to the US-India nuclear energy deal, India's angst over the growing trade deficit due to perceived Chinese unfair trade practices, potential Chinese plans to dam the Brahmaputra River, and the "war talk" in the official Chinese media in the 2007 to 2009 period (reminding India not to forget "the lessons of 1962"), mutual distrust between the Indian and Chinese peoples is growing. Clearly, China's extraordinary economic performance over the last three decades has changed the dynamics of the relationship. China and India had similar average incomes in the late 1970s, but thirty years later they find themselves at completely different stages of development. China's economic reforms—launched in 1978, nearly thirteen years before India's in 1991—changed their subsequent growth trajectories by putting China far ahead of India in all socioeconomic indices. Both China's gross domestic product and military expenditure are now three times the size of India's; recent surveys conducted by Pew Global Research show a growth in popular distrust, with just twenty-five percent of Indians holding a favorable view of China in 2011, down from thirty-four percent in 2010 and fifty-seven percent in 2005. Likewise, just twenty-seven percent of Chinese hold a favorable view of India in 2011, down from thirty-two percent in 2010, with studies of Internet content showing a large degree of "hostility and contempt for India."

Nor is there much effort to keep these emotions submerged. Reacting to the test launch in mid-April of a long-range Agni-V ballistic missile, dubbed the "China killer" by India's news media, a Chinese daily wryly noted that "India stands no chance in an overall arms race with China," because "China's nuclear power is stronger and more reliable." The unequal strategic equation, in particular the Chinese perception of India as a land of irreconcilable socioreligious cleavages with an inherently unstable polity and weak leadership that is easily contained through proxies, aggravates tensions between the two. In 2008, an official reassessment of China's capabilities and intentions led the Indian military to adopt a "two-front war" doctrine against what is identified as a "collusive threat" posed by two closely aligned nuclear-armed neighbours, Pakistan and China. This doctrine validates the long-held belief of India's strategic community that China is following a protracted strategy of containing India's rise.

India is also responding by strengthening its strategic links with Afghanistan, Tajikistan, Mongolia, Vietnam, and Burma—countries on China's periphery. In testimony to the US Senate in February, James Clapper, the director of national intelligence, noted that "the Indian military is strengthening its forces in preparation to fight a limited conflict along the disputed border, and is working to balance Chinese power projection in the Indian Ocean." That "balance" includes a strategic tilt toward the United States that has also had a damaging effect on Sino-Indian relations. Although leaders from both countries often repeat the ritualized denials of conflict and emphasize burgeoning trade ties, such platitudes cannot obliterate the trust deficit. Few if any of China's strategic thinkers seem to hold positive views of India for China's future, and vice versa. Chinese strategists keep a wary eye on India's "great power dreams," its military spending and weapons acquisitions, and the developments in India's naval and nuclear doctrines. A dominant theme in Chinese commentary in the last decade is that India's growing strength—backed by the United States—could tip Asia's balance of power away from Beijing.

Not surprisingly, bilateral relations between Asia's giants remain, in the words of Zhang Yan, China's ambassador to India, "very fragile, very easy to be damaged, and very difficult to repair." Both have massive manpower resources, a scientific and industrial base, and million-plus militaries. For the first time in more than fifty years, both are moving upward simultaneously on their relative power trajectories.

As the pivotal power in South Asia, India perceives itself much as China has traditionally perceived itself in relation to East Asia. Both desire a peaceful security environment to focus on economic development and avoid overt rivalry or conflict.

Still, the volatile agents of nationalism, history, ambition, strength, and size produce a mysterious chemistry. Neither power is comfortable with the rise of the other. Both seek to envelop neighbours with their national economies. Both are nuclear and space powers with growing ambitions. Both yearn for a multipolar world that will provide them the space for growth and freedom of action. Both vie for leadership positions in global and regional organizations and have attempted to establish a sort of Monroe Doctrine in their respective neighbourhoods—without much success.

And both remain suspicious of each other's long-term agenda and intentions. Each perceives the other as pursuing hegemony and entertaining imperial ambitions. Both are non–status quo powers: China in terms of *territory*, power, and influence; India in terms of *status*, power, and influence. Both seek to expand their power and influence in and beyond their regions at each other's expense. China's "Malacca paranoia" is matched by India's "Hormuz dilemma." If China's navy is going south to the Indian Ocean, India's navy is going east to the Pacific Ocean. Both suffer from a siege mentality born out of their elites' acute consciousness of the divisive tendencies that make their countries' present political unity so fragile. After all, much of Chinese and Indian history is made up of long periods of internal disunity and turmoil, when centrifugal forces brought down even the most powerful empires. Each has its vulnerabilities—regional conflicts, poverty, and religious divisions for India; the contradiction between a market economy and Leninist politics for China. Both are plagued with domestic linguistic, ethno-religious, and politico-economic fault lines that could be their undoing if not managed properly.

In other words, China and India are locked in a classic security dilemma: one country sees its actions as defensive, but the same actions appear aggressive to the other. Beijing fears that an unrestrained Indian power—particularly one that is backed by the West and Japan—would not only threaten China's security along its restive southwestern frontiers (Tibet and Xinjiang) but also obstruct China's expansion southwards. Faced with exponential growth in China's power and influence, India feels the need to take counterbalancing measures and launch strategic initiatives to emerge as a great power, but these are perceived as challenging and threatening in China.

China's use of regional and international organizations to institutionalize its power while either denying India access to these organizations or marginalizing India within them has added a new competitive dynamic to the relationship. In the past decade, India has found itself ranged against China at the UN Security Council, East Asia Summit, the Asia-Pacific Economic Cooperation, the Nuclear Suppliers Group, and the Asian Development Bank. In 2009, China vetoed a development plan for India by the latter in the disputed Arunachal Pradesh, thereby internationalizing a bilateral territorial dispute. In a tit-for-tat response, New Delhi has kept Beijing out of India-led multilateral frameworks such as the Bay of Bengal Initiative for Multi-Sectoral Technical and Economic Cooperation, the India-Brazil-South Africa Dialogue, and the Mekong–Ganga Cooperation forums, and rejected China's request to be included as observer or associate member into the 33-member Indian Ocean Naval Symposium, started by India in 2008.

Resource scarcity has added a maritime dimension to this geopolitical rivalry. As China's and India's energy dependence on the Middle East and Africa increases, both are actively seeking to forge closer defence and security ties with resource supplier nations (e.g., Saudi Arabia and Iran), and to develop appropriate naval capabilities to dominate the sea lanes through which the bulk of their commerce flows. Since seventy-seven percent of China's oil comes from the Middle East and Africa, Beijing has increased its activities in the Indian Ocean region by investing in littoral states' economies, building ports and infrastructure, providing weaponry, and acquiring energy resources. Nearly ninety percent of Chinese arms sales go to countries located in the Indian Ocean region. Beijing is investing heavily in developing the Gwadar deep-sea port in Pakistan, and naval bases in Sri Lanka, Bangladesh, and Myanmar. Whether one calls it a "string of pearls" or a series of places at which China's navy can base or simply be resupplied, that navy is setting up support infrastructure in strategic locations along the same sea lanes of communication that could neutralize India's geographical advantage in the Indian Ocean region. A recent commentary from the official Xinhua news outlet called for setting up three lines of navy supply bases in the northern Indian Ocean, the western Indian Ocean, and the southern Indian Ocean. It stated: "China needs to establish overseas strategic support stations for adding ship fuel, re-supply of necessities, staff break time, repairs of equipment, and weapons in Pakistan, Sri Lanka, and Myanmar, which will be the core support bases in the North Indian Ocean supply line; Djibouti, Yemen, Oman, Kenya, Tanzania, and Mozambique, which will be the core support bases in the West Indian Ocean supply line; and Seychelles and Madagascar, which will be the core support bases in the South Indian Ocean supply line."

For its part, New Delhi is pursuing the same strategy as Beijing and creating its own web of relationships with the littoral states, both bilaterally and multilaterally, through the Indian Ocean Naval Symposium, to ensure that if the military need arises, the necessary support infrastructure and network will be in place. India has also stepped up defence cooperation with Oman and Israel in the west, while upgrading military ties with the Maldives, Madagascar, and Myanmar in the Indian Ocean, and with Singapore, Indonesia, Thailand, Vietnam, Taiwan, the Philippines, Australia, Japan, and the United States in the east. In December 2006, Admiral Sureesh Mehta, then India's naval chief, expanded the conceptual construct of India's "greater strategic neighborhood" to include potential sources of oil and gas imports located across the globe—from Venezuela to the Sakhalin Islands in Russia. The Indian navy currently has a stronger naval presence on the Indian Ocean than does China. It is strengthening its port infrastructure with new southern ports, which allow greater projection into the ocean. Taking a leaf out of China's book, the new focus is to develop anti-access and area-denial capabilities that will thwart any Chinese attempt at encirclement or sea-access denial.

In short, maritime competition is intensifying as Indian and Chinese navies show the flag in the Pacific and Indian oceans with greater frequency. This rivalry could spill into the open after a couple of decades, when one Indian aircraft carrier will be deployed in the Pacific Ocean and one Chinese aircraft carrier in the Indian Ocean—ostensibly to safeguard their respective trade and energy routes.

In turn, India's "Look East" policy is a manifestation of its own strategic intent to compete for influence in the wider Asia-Pacific region. Just as China will not concede India's primacy in South Asia and the Indian Ocean region, India seems unwilling to accept Southeast and East Asia as China's sphere of influence. Just as China's rise is viewed positively in the South Asian region among the small countries surrounding India with which New Delhi has had difficult relations, India's rise is viewed in positive-sum terms among China's neighbours throughout East and Southeast Asia. Over the last two decades, India has sought to enhance its economic and security ties with those Northeast and Southeast Asian nations (Mongolia, South Korea, Japan, Taiwan, Vietnam, Singapore, Thailand, Indonesia, and Australia) that worry about China more than any other major power. As China's growing strength creates uneasiness in the region, India's balancing role is welcome within the Association of Southeast Asian Nations (ASEAN) in order to influence China's behavior in cooperative directions. While the Southeast Asian leaders seek to deter China from utilizing its growing strength for coercive purposes and to maintain regional autonomy, Indian strategic analysts favour an Indian naval presence in the South China Sea and the Pacific Ocean to counter Chinese naval presence in the Indian Ocean. On maritime security, Southeast Asians seem more willing to cooperate with India than China, especially in the Strait of Malacca.

A key element of India's Pacific outreach has been regular naval exercises, port calls, security dialogues, and more than a dozen defence cooperation agreements. India has welcomed Vietnam's offer of berthing rights in Na Trang Port in the South China Sea, and news reports suggest that India might offer BrahMos cruise missiles and other military hardware at "friendship prices" to Vietnam. The conclusion of free-trade agreements with Singapore, South Korea, Malaysia, Japan, and the ASEAN, coupled with New Delhi's participation in multilateral forums such as the East Asia Summit and the ASEAN Plus Eight defence ministers' meetings, have also reinforced strategic ties. India's determination to strengthen its strategic partnership with Japan and Vietnam, commitment to pursue joint oil exploration with Hanoi in the South China Sea waters in the face of Chinese opposition, and an emphasis on the freedom of navigation are signs of India maneuvering to be seen as a counterweight to Chinese power in East Asia. New Delhi is also scaling up defence ties with Tokyo, Seoul, and Canberra.

The US-India partnership is also emerging as an important component of India's strategy to balance China's power. India seeks US economic and technological assistance. It helps this relationship that India's longtime security concerns—China and Pakistan—also now happen to be the United States' long-term and immediate strategic concerns as well. Both the Bush and Obama administrations have encouraged India's involvement in a wider Asian security system to balance a rising China and declining Japan. Apparently, US weakness—real or perceived—invites Chinese assertiveness. Since the United States does not wish to see Asia dominated by a single hegemonic power or a coalition of states, India's economic rise is seen as serving Washington's long-term interests by ensuring that there be countervailing powers in Asia—China, Japan, and India, with the United States continuing to act as an "engaged offshore power balancer."

The "India factor" is increasingly entering the ongoing US policy debate over China. Asia-Pacific is now the Indo-Pacific, a term underlining the centrality of India in the new calculus of regional power. The 2010 US Quadrennial Defence Review talked of India's positive role as a "net security provider in the Indian Ocean and beyond." India's "Look East" policy, which envisions high-level engagement with "China-wary" nations (South Korea, Japan, Taiwan, Vietnam, Thailand, Indonesia, and Australia), dovetails with the US policy of establishing closer ties with countries beyond Washington's traditional treaty partners to maintain US predominance. The US-Indian strategic engagement, coupled with India's expanding naval and nuclear capabilities and huge economic potential, have made India loom larger on China's radar screen. An editorial in a Shanghai daily last November lamented the fact that "India will not allow itself to stay quietly between the US and China. It wants to play triangle affairs with the duo, and will do anything it can to maximize its benefit out of it. Therefore, China will find it hard to buy India over." The Chinese fear that the Indian-American cooperation in defence, high-tech R&D, nuclear, space, and maritime spheres would prolong US hegemony and prevent the establishment of a post-American, Sino-centric hierarchical regional order in Asia. This tightening relationship, and the possibility that what is presently a tilt on India's part could turn into a full-fledged alignment, is a major reason for recent deterioration in Chinese-Indian relations.

Although these relations remain unstable and competitive, both have sought to reduce tensions. Despite border disputes, denial of market access, and harsh words against the Dalai Lama, leaders in both countries understand the dangers of allowing problems to overwhelm the relationship. Burgeoning economic ties between the world's two fastest-growing economies have become the most salient aspect of their bilateral relationship.

Trade flows have risen rapidly, from a paltry $350 million in 1993 to $70 billion in 2012, and could surpass $100 billion by 2015. Several joint ventures in power generation, consumer goods, steel, chemicals, minerals, mining, transport, infrastructure, info-tech, and telecommunication are in the works. Intensifying trade, commerce, and tourism could eventually raise the stakes for China in its relationship with India. On the positive side, both share common interests in maintaining regional stability (for example, combating Islamist fundamentalists), exploiting economic opportunities, and maintaining access to energy sources, capital, and markets.

Despite ever-increasing trade volumes, however, there is as yet no strategic congruence between China and India. As in the case of Sino-US and Sino-Japanese ties, Sino-Indian competitive tendencies, rooted in geopolitics and nationalism, are unlikely to be easily offset even by growing economic and trade links. In fact, the economic relationship is heavily skewed. The bulk of Indian exports to China consist of iron ore and other raw materials, while India imports mostly manufactured goods from China—a classic example of the dependency model. Most Indians see China as predatory in trade. New Delhi has lodged the largest number of anti-dumping cases against Beijing in the World Trade Organization. India is keener on pursuing mutual economic dependencies with Japan, South Korea, and Southeast Asian nations through increased trade, investment, infrastructure development, and aid to bolster economic and political ties across Asia that will counter Chinese power.

Even as a range of economic and transnational issues draw them closer together, the combination of internal issues of stability (Tibet and Kashmir), disputes over territory, competition over resources (oil, gas, and water), overseas markets and bases, external overlapping spheres of influence, rival alliance relationships, and ever-widening geopolitical horizons forestall the chances for a genuine Sino-Indian accommodation. Given the broad range of negative attitudes and perceptions each country has for the other, it is indeed remarkable that China and India have been able to keep diplomatic relations from fraying. How long this situation can last is more and more uncertain as each country is increasingly active in what would once have been seen as the other's "backyard" and both engage in strategic maneuvers to checkmate each other.

Just as China has become more assertive vis-à-vis the United States, Indian policy toward China is becoming tougher. India's evolving Asia strategy reflects the desire for an arc of partnerships with China's key neighbours—in Southeast Asia and further east along the Asia-Pacific rim—and the United States that would help neutralize the continuing Chinese military assistance and activity around its own territory and develop counter-leverages of its own vis-à-vis China to keep Beijing sober.

CHINKS IN THE ARMOUR: OUR DEFENCE PREPAREDNESS

The defence budget for 2011-12 has been hiked by 11 percent, pegging the allocation at Rs 164,415 crore (from Rs 1,47,344 crores last year), to fuel the rapid modernization of the Army, Navy and the Air Force. The capital expenditure has also been hiked to Rs 69,199 crore. This bring smiles to the defence ministry mandarins, who hope to finalise several important arms deals such as the $10.4-billion contract for 126 combat planes in the next fiscal. This must also come as a big relief to the defence analysts who were increasingly alarmed at the pace of deterioration set in our defence preparedness due to constant mishandling of past few years. The signs of this decay and depleting force levels were too clearly visible even to general public to be ignored any further. An Army Chetak crashed near Nasik killing both the pilots. INS Vindhyagiri sank after colliding with a merchant vessel off Mumbai. An Air Force Mig-21 crashed after taking off from Gwalior.

Our force levels have indeed been a cause of concern for some time now. None other than the Parliamentary standing committee on defence and CAG have consistently pointed out depleted force levels of our armed forces and the level of technological obsolescence that has marred India's defence preparedness. Today the Indian Air Force is guarding the country with only 32 flying squadrons when it must have 39. And it has 300 pilots less than what it needs to fly the aeroplanes. The MiG 21s, which is the mainstay of our fighters, has already out lived their life and now busy taking the lives of our young pilots. In fact the fleet level of Mig-21 is likely to reduce to six from 13 squadrons that we are required to maintain. Other fleets such as MiG 27s and Mirage 2000 too are due for major upgradation. Any notions about superiority of MiG-29, which was thought to be one of India's most potent weapons, was dispelled by Defence Minister in Parliament when he made the stunning disclosure that the MiG-29 is structurally flawed. Military aviation in particular is driven by technology. Technologies are getting outdated faster than the full utilization of aircraft. Therefore fleet replacements and technological updates are not only a constant necessity but also has long gestation period, hence need to be anticipated in time so that preparedness level is not compromised. Thanks to the lack of foresight, today we are saddled with aircraft, technology and assorted inventory that is more than four decades old and its effectiveness in present day war theatre is suspect.

The army is equipped with some 3,340 main battle tanks like Vijayanta,T-55, T-72, and PT-76 tanks. More than 1500 of these tanks are obsolete and night blind. One former Army Chief revealed that 80 per cent of India's tanks were night blind as against Pakistan where 80 per cent of tanks are night battle capable. Basic weaponry like automatic rifles and ammunition takes forever to reach the forces. Only 250 out of 400 originally purchased Bofors Guns are available for operational deployment. The 130 mm guns held in the inventory are of Second World War vintage and more than 90 % Air Defence artillery is obsolete. Army has not inducted new guns since Bofors were purchased. Today Indian Army has 11300 less officers than what it needs. This shortage is mostly in Lt Col and below ranks, which are the active fighting element of the force. Every year about 600 to 700 officers request for early retirement due to rising frustration levels with the state of affairs in the organization.

The Indian Navy is no better. Delays and upgrades that take forever have meant that a frontline submarine is today waiting to be put to water for years. The Sixth Report of the Parliamentary Standing Committee on Defence reported that out of an accepted force level of 138 ships, the best strength our Navy achieved in last 63 years is 120 ships. The Six Scorpene Submarines, which were earlier scheduled to be delivered to Navy from 2012 have been delayed till 2015. The Ministry itself has acknowledged that induction of submarine has not kept pace with the de-induction schedule. In addition the aircraft carrier Gorshkov that was due for induction in August 2008 is not likely to be delivered by Russia even in December 2012 and will get further delayed. With Vikrant already de commissioned and Viraat due for major repairs, today India will have to go to war without a fully serviceable aircraft carrier. Our submarine fleet comprises of 10 Russian Kilo-class, four German HDW and two virtually obsolete Foxtrot submarines whereas China boasts of 57 attack submarines, 12 of them are nuclear powered. The CAG report highlighted that if India were to go to war against Pakistan at this moment, it will have to make do with only seven to eight submarines, which is less than Pakistan's 12 or so submarines, which include three spanking new French Agosta-90B vessels. The Naval Aviation arm stands depleted to its 26% of its assets. HAL promised to deliver 120 indigenously built Dhruv helicopters to Navy. Selection of the ALH was done with a view to promote indigenization and to standardize the types of helicopters. Induction of Dhruv was to begin by 1991 but there was a slippage of ten years in the development of the helicopter by HAL and even today Navy has received only 6 out of 120 helicopters it needed and even these 6 helicopters are yet to prove their operational capabilities. It is a matter of concern that the country could not achieve a force level that was accepted by Cabinet way back in 1964. Today our Navy is short by 1461 officers.

Our indigenous defence research, development and production were aimed at providing some degree of self-reliance to the defence needs but 63 years later they have failed the nation on this count. While our scientists working in these laboratories have indeed rendered yeoman's service to the nation in missile and nuclear technology, the political and bureaucratic interference and red tapism has ensured that they always under perform to come upto requirements of national defence. What else can explain the inordinate delays in Dhruv, Tejas and Arjun Tank projects? None less than Defence Minister A.K. Antony lamented India's slow pace of defence indigenisation whereby we continue to import 70% of our equipment, inspite of spending huge sums on these PSUs. With private sector not allowed to participate in defence R&D or production, the defence production and research industry has been more of a gravy train for those controlling it. Thousands of Crore Rupees have been spent and we are yet to receive helicopters, ships, submarines and even basic weaponry that DRDO and others were mandated to provide to replenish depleted force levels. In spite of the delays, the armed forces continued to pay the agencies huge amount of money under government directives-money that could have otherwise been used for procurement of equipment to retain war preparedness.

Complicated acquisition procedures put in place for defence procurement by successive governments has also played their part in slowing down the acquisition process. As per AK Anthony, last year more than Rs 7000 crs were returned by armed forces as unspent. Procedural delays and lack of clarity to deal with market forces are main reason. Bofors scandal has forced our top leadership to adopt a pessimistic approach to procurement. A new system for procurement that has been put in place is fraught with in built lacuna of paying more to be seen to be honest!!! According to this system, known as Foreign Military Sales, the government of country manufacturing weapon system negotiates the price for us with the manufacturer. Now onwards another country will decide what is good for Indian defence needs and what is the price that India must pay for it !! This itself proves the lack of understanding of Defence matters by those who have been responsible for it.

As they say, Defence Minister's fetish for a clean image is costing India 125 percent more for buying half the equipment. This system has already started failing. The Howitzer guns shortlisted for purchase under FMS programme from USA failed 12 out of 18 essential QRs of the Indian Army but the government is still keen to acquire them because it makes the deal look clean in public perception! Incidentally the much-tainted Bofors won us Kargil because it was a weapon system, which emerged meritorious because it followed a selection process, which laid down stringent technical QRs.

The biggest area of concern though, is the degradation in military values and ethos of the armed forces personnel as a result of prolonged disappointment of armed forces personnel. Systematic down gradation in successive pay commissions has eroded self-esteem, dignity and respect in lower ranks of the armed forces. The increasing use of armed forces in law and order duties has exposed the lower ranks to the glaring disparities between him and his civilian or police counterpart. A large number of civilian employees who follow different ethos and norms of public dealings are employed by military Organizations such as Military Engineering Services, Directorate General of Rehabilitation, National Cadet Corp, Defence Estate, Defence Audit and Canteen Stores Depots.

The lack of accountability of these personnel and other unscrupulous practices adopted by them rubs off on the military personnel working alongside them, straining the fabric of military values. Today a military commander is helpless against his civilian subordinates for any violation of working conditions. The decision-making amongst senior rank has been geared more towards staving off present crises rather than meeting the aims of a long term structured plan.

The senior leadership of the armed forces also has to share the blame for failing to keep the government apprised of the shortfalls in time. The Adarsh Society scam has caused incalculable damage to the image of our senior military officers in the eyes of their subordinates. The Adarsh method was disarmingly simple. They simply co-opted in their scam whoever looked like standing in the way. If we judge the strategy by its results, it was spectacularly successful. From just 30-odd members, the eventual group grew to more than a hundred. The scary bit about the scam is not that it happened. It is that in the entire chain, there was not one man who refused to compromise himself. There was not one person whose integrity stood its ground in face of temptation. About the bureaucrats and the ministers, we always knew. The really worrying part is that it went on all the way to at least three service chiefs. Not one whistle-blower in the entire system !!! A sea-facing apartment in Mumbai is worth perhaps Rs 8 crore. For a combined booty of no more than Rs 800 crore, you could buy the entire system. I would not like to be a soldier in our armed forces at this moment. The fellow has just seen Lt Generals being prosecuted for land scam. Now, an admiral and two generals are part of a housing scam. One of the former Army chief wrote letters on his official letterhead to CM of Haryana requesting for allotment of land from CMs discretionary quota-not for the welfare of Army but for his personal use. A Major General in Gujarat praises a Chief Minister only to request him for preferential allotment of plot !! And a soldier is expected to die on their orders. The former chiefs have now graciously offered to return the flats, professing ignorance about the fact that land was meant for martyrs' families. As if that is the only thing wrong about the deal. It was stinking from start to finish and if the chiefs could not smell any of it, the Government has a lot to answer for the kind of persons they select for their top most posts. Merely dispossessing them of their ill-gotten apartment would be no punishment. They need to be handed over exemplary punishment for being unworthy custodians of our trust.

India's war preparedness must always be a matter of concern to all of us, as our nation has displayed tendencies to slip into complacency as soon as a war is over. Was there anything wrong with our defence preparedness 12 years ago when we fought Kargil War?. The root cause of Pakistan's military adventurism in Kargil arose from Pakistan's assessment of perceived weakness in our war preparedness at that time. Having lost more than 500 of our brave soldiers, there was intense debate on the tactics adopted by India to reclaim the heights from the Pak paramilitary forces and Kashmiri insurgents in the sector. Orders were to climb the heights head-on as India could not adopt the tactic of blocking off the supplies to enemy positions without crossing the line of control (LoC). Given this situation, the soldiers had to climb the steep hillocks at night with the enemy firing at them from a height and making them easy targets. Reports suggested that many soldiers bore bullet marks up the neck and above as the enemy picked off their ill-equipped targets. Defence experts were outraged that the soldiers weren't even wearing enough protective equipment before taking up such a dangerous mission. The callous manner in which the investigations were carried out into this where charges and counter-charges flew thick and fast and the issue was politicized, only shows that quality of defence equipment is not on anyone's minds.

For far too long, our defence has been left at the mercy of those who have no idea about it in the name of civilian supremacy. The people of our country are kept happy with ceremonial displays such as Air Force day parade and fly past, The Navy Day celebrations and Navy ball, The RD Parade and

Beating The Retreat. On these occasions, nation see proud soldier ready to lay down his life for the country and an impressive display of military hardware-enough to lead them into a false sense of security and complacency. One wonder how much India has already compromised and how much further it is going to compromise as regard to its sovereignty.

Future wars would be at short notice and therefore would have to be fought with readiness of forces at the start of a conflict. What it signifies is that unlike in the past when long lead times were available for mobilization and preparation for war, the same luxury would not be available in future wars.

The crucial deciding factor would be a vigilant state of defence preparedness both by up-gradation of military equipment and modernization, especially Air Force and Navy. In fact the initial defence and offense in today's war scenario will have to come from the Air Force therefore the nation can not afford any depletion in war waging capabilities of the IAF at any cost. The high tech weapon systems that an Air Force needs to induct,must be anticipated well in time so that adequate time is available to our personnel to be trained and fully acquainted on these machines. Success in war in future would not necessarily go to nations larger in size, population resources and potential, but to the one prepared militarily at the outbreak of hostilities. India must therefore shed its illusions that in every war in future its size and military strength will prevail. War preparedness in its most comprehensive form would be the deciding factor.

With this state of defence preparedness, are we ready to meet the threats?? Do our politicians and bureaucrats really understand how the defence of our nation is to be handled? Most importantly, how long can we leave the sovereignty of our country in the hands of people who have no knowledge of how to protect it ?? Have we really learnt anything from the past and are we prepared for the future challenges?

Its time our country has an autonomous Armed Forces Commission, which is kept, insulated from political and bureaucratic interferences, on the lines of CAG or Election Commission. It is an undeniable fact that India is today what it is, because the Indian Armed Forces have never flinched in sacrificing lives for defending the Indian Republic from both external and internal threats. The Indian soldier fights with what he has and not what he wants. But how long can we continue denying him the equipment that he deserves ?? The poignant words inscribed on the Kohima War Memorial fittingly embody this sentiment. It is inscribed:

"When you go home, Tell them of us

And say.

For theirs Tomorrow, We gave our Today."

We need to ensure that this spirit is not allowed to die at any cost. Even Sri Lanka has acknowledged the contribution of our soldiers in defending that country against terrorists and they have built a memorial for the fallen hero's of IPKF. Why are we in India forgetting our soldier at this critical time ?

DEFENCE PRODUCTION AND SUPPLY

The Defence Production Department created in 1962 and the Department of Defence Supply set up in 1965 were merged in 1984 to constitute the Department of Defence Production and Supplies. Presently, 39 Ordnance factories and eight Defence Public Sector Undertakings (DPSUs) come under this department. The Directorate of Quality Assurance, Air Technical Development and Production (Air), Standardisation, and Exhibition Organisation also form part of this Department.

The Ordnance Factories produce more than 1,500 items of arms, ammunition, equipment and components. Most of these products constitute relatively low to medium technology items. Twenty per cent of the output goes to non-defence customers. Due to the very high cost of production, delivery delays and suspect quality, it has not been possible to meet export targets and, sometimes, even orders given by the Services. Ordnance factories as well as DPSUs need to shed the manufacture of low technology items to the private sector and focus on hi-tech products. They should also be in a position to take up substantial product improvement themselves and not be dependent on DRDO.

Defence Planning Tools

In recent years, defence economics and management techniques have made an important contribution to defence planning. A number of techniques such as Operational Research and Systems Analysis (ORSA), Planning Programming and Budgeting System have been developed to make the planning process more systematic and to maximise the benefits obtained from the given amount of resources. Systems Analysis can assist in developing rational procedures for procurement of new weapons systems. Systems performance at design stage can be evaluated through computer simulation. Planners all over the world are using computerised war-gaming techniques and structure analysis. Prospects exist for a more enlightened approach that can bring together military officers, historians, technologists and quantitative analysts.

In many countries, there is a growing interest in analytical realism, operational relevance and integrated defence planning. In India the Services are far behind in introducing these aids in our defence planning system. The planning directorates in Service Headquarters do not even have data banks which can provide relevant information on a specified subject. Most of the planners have high combat and command qualifications but little clue of the modern techniques.

There is an urgent need to introduce modern planning aids into our planning system. Defence planners should also learn the basic principles and techniques of economic analysis and not leave it to their 'Finance' colleagues.

Management of Defence Budget

A major lacuna in defence planning and implementation has been lack of financial commitment for the Plan period. Financially, the defence plans are treated more as annual plans rather than composite five years plan.

There is a rush to spend the annual capital budget by the end of the financial year since the amount not spent has to be surrendered. In FY 2004-05, the previous government had proposed to institute a non-lapsable Defence Modernisation Fund of Rs 25,000 crore.

This was a long awaited reform in the defence-finance mechanism as budgeted capital expenditure worth thousands of crores was surrendered year after year. However, the new government, being of the view that there are no provisions in the budgetary rules and regulations to carry forward unspent funds for three years, has done away with this reform.

It needs to be pointed out that a similar procedure was being followed in the 1930s and 1940s. The provisions invoked at that time need to be studied carefully and could be used as a precedent. Action should be taken expeditiously to revive the Defence Modernization Fund.

Otherwise, funds earmarked for capital expenditure on an annual basis will continue to lapse, leading to lack of systematic defence preparedness.

In the Revenue Budget, there is a need to include incentives to save and reduce annual maintenance expenditure without adversely affecting operational efficiency. It is also necessary to exploit the increasing domestic industrial capability to support the existing infrastructure and thus reduce maintenance costs and enhance the quality of maintenance.

Human Resources Management

The development of human resources must keep pace with the modernisation of the armed forces so that new, state-of-the-art equipment can be optimally exploited by well trained and motivated soldiers, sailors and airmen. The age profile of military personnel, particularly in the Army, and the age of commanders at battalion and brigade levels needs to be looked into. Currently, a soldier has to serve for 15 to 17 years to earn his pension. When he retires, besides the lifelong pension that has to be paid, a trained individual is lost to the nation. Similarly, while there is a shortage of approximately 14,000 officers, most officers retire in rank of Lieutenant Colonel or Colonel at the age of 52-54 years when they still have years of productive life ahead though they are no longer fit for active combat.

Innovative measures need to be adopted to reduce the effects of the current national loss on this account. The best method would be to institute a procedure of 'lateral induction" under which both officers and personnel below officer rank can be transferred to central police and paramilitary forces(CPMFs). The colour (active) service of jawans should be reduced to 7-10 years with no pension liability after which the volunteers are transferred to the BSF, CRPF, ITBP, CISF and other such forces. Similarly, the Shipping Corporation of India, National Port Trust and other such maritime organisations can fruitfully employ Naval personnel. Ex-servicemen will be expected to serve in these organisations till superannuation, after which they would be entitled to pension. This will improve the age profile of the Services, provide trained manpower to the CPMFs, ensure productive long-term employment for a large number of trained men till superannuation, and also reduce the pension bill of the Central Government.

The Army should increase the recruitment of Short Service Officers to make up its shortfall. Induction of these officers to the CPMFs after five years of service will improve junior leadership and effectiveness of these forces in internal security and counter insurgency operations.

RECOMMENDATIONS

- Given the fluid strategic environment and the rapid advances in defence technology, there is a need for judicious allocation of the limited budgetary resources. Long lead times are required for creating futuristic Forces, hence the need to make long-term defence planning mandatory. Greater synergy between defence and development plans is required.
- The lack of a cohesive national security strategy and defence policy has resulted in inadequate political direction regarding politico-military

objectives. The Government should prepare a clear national security strategy, defence policy, and review it every 4-5 years.

- In view of the time taken to create the capabilities necessary for facing future threats and challenges, it is essential for the Defence Services to evolve 10 to 15-year perspective plans with the required budgetary support.
- The Chiefs of Staff Committee has not been successful in preparing comprehensive 'integrated defence plans' due to emphasis on single Service planning and constant competition among the Services for a bigger share of resources. The civilian bureaucrats in the MoD do not have the professional expertise to decide on inter-Service priorities. Hence, the early appointment of Chief of Defence Staff (CDS) is essential as he will be the cornerstone for integrated defence and operational planning.

- A non-lapsable Defence Modernisation Fund must be expeditiously created to ensure that allocations are optimally utilised and funds earmarked for capital acquisitions are not allowed to lapse.
- The Revenue Budget of the Services needs to be better managed. Annual maintenance expenditure can be curtailed by greater exploitation of the available public and private sector industrial infrastructure capability and offering incentives to the Services to save.
- To ensure smooth progress towards self-reliance in defence technology, the Government must undertake a periodic performance audit of the DRDO plans and projects. The review should reinforce efforts in areas of success and weed out unproductive projects.
- Ordnance Factories should produce only hi-tech products and shed the production of low-tech items to the private sector.
- Integrated Defence Staff and the Services' perspective planners should acquire expertise in operational research and systems analysis, as also financial planning, for evolving complex integrated defence plans.
- In order to improve the age profile of the Services and simultaneously reduce the pension bill of the Central Government, personnel below officer rank should be transferred to central police and paramilitary forces (CPMFs) after active service of 7-10 years.
- The Army should increase recruitment of Short Service Officers to make up its shortfall. Induction of these officers to the CPMFs after five years of service will improve junior leadership and effectiveness of these forces in internal security and counter insurgency operations.

Defence planning has been neglected for long in India. This has led to ad-hocism in decision-making and adversely affected the modernisation plans of the Services. The key issues needing immediate attention include the need for formal prior approval for five-year defence Plans, better management of the defence revenue and capital acquisition budgets, streamlining of the defence procurement process and better human resources management.

The Government of India should appoint a group of eminent experts to study the present defence planning process, identify the lacunae and grey areas in the process and recommend structural and procedural changes.

The aim should be to streamline defence planning, harmonize it with national development plans, and make the process more responsive in order to deal effectively with the rapidly changing geo-strategic and regional security environment.

CHALLENGES IN DEFENCE PLANNING

Defence planning is essentially a subset of overall national level planning in the political, economic and social spheres and has to be evolved in the context of global and proximate factors affecting the nation.. It has also to take into account the philosophy and ethos animating the national psyche; in other words the historical and cultural forces which have shaped the collective memory and outlook of the people over the centuries. The Cold War, was a classic example of the factors stated above. There were fundamental philosophical differences between the adversaries – the western bloc, advocating the virtues of free enterprise and its own interpretations of democracy, and the Soviet bloc, equally strongly asserting the merits of the socialist system as the only one genuinely meeting democratic aspirations and assuring social equality and economic well-being of the people as a whole, rather than for a few. Fifty years of the Cold War could not conclude the capitalism-socialism debate, though, in the end, it did push the socialist forces into, perhaps temporary, retreat. This was because the struggle was really for power and domination. "The evil empire" of Ronald Reagan's description may have withered away, but the necessity for the US to target the so called "rogue states" has not disappeared.

Many examples can be found of philosophical differences leading to stand-offs, usually with the USA as one of the parties. The USA-Cuba divide is a long-standing one. USA-Venezuela stand-off is just developing and resonating in other Latin American countries. Sometimes the differences are couched in the language of anticipated threats, such as in US-North Korea, or US-Iran relations. The true reasons and underlying causes are buried in verbiage and obfuscation. A more serious rift has developed over the selective and poorly conceptualised US war on terrorism, launched for spurious reasons in Iraq, when the real source of terror was elsewhere and far more complex. Differing religious beliefs and rigidities are often cited as causes but do not sufficiently explain conflicts within the same religion, as between Protestants and Catholics in Northern Ireland or the Shias and Sunnis in Iraq and elsewhere.

Planning for the security and defence of a vast country like India with its particular geographic location, historical experiences and associations, social, ethnic, religious and cultural diversity, political and economic structure and a large, relatively poor, democratically governed population, is a complex and challenging task. It is rendered more so in the context of the national and international situation in the last sixty years or so, embracing post-World War II de-colonisation, partition, the creation of Pakistan and later Bangladesh, conflicts with Pakistan and China, the Cold War and its aftermath, the disintegration of the Soviet Union, the re-definition of NATO's role, and of most recent and decisive significance, the September 11, 2001 terror attack on the United States mainland. This last factor is significant because it resulted in a major re-orientation in US foreign policy.

Strategic Overview

Planning for defence pre-supposes identification of threats and contingencies. Until about five years ago, the strategic situation for India was difficult but relatively clear. Pakistan was a definite threat, conventional, clandestine and nuclear. China was a strategically reducing threat, though its international power, influence and economy were growing. Uncertainties in Bangladesh and Nepal required us to be vigilant for fall-out effects. There were problems in the north-east of insurgent groups exploiting the ethnic ties and jungles in Myanmar, and the destabilising spill-over effects of the activities of the Liberation Tigers for Tamil Eelam(LTTE) in Sri Lanka. The presence in our proximate waters, of non-littoral naval forces in substantial numbers, such as those of the US, which has been traditionally supportive of Pakistan, had to be taken cognisance of. Also the fact that warfare at sea, because of its distinctive characteristics of rapidity of concentration and dispersal of forces, mobility, flexibility and speed of execution, requires a different, longer term approach to threat assessment. Strategically the global situation is now evolving in a manner less inimical to India's interests than in the preceding fifty years. Yet the end of the Cold War did not see any easing of pressures on India. On the contrary, economic sanctions and technology denials were increased so as to coerce India to conform to norms of international behaviour prescribed by dominant world powers, led by the US and the European Union on the one hand and China on the other. The reason was the desire of the P-5, the five permanent members of the UN Security Council, who are also the N-5, the self-certified nuclear powers, to preserve their monopoly power status in the face of India's challenge through the nuclear tests of 1998.

Yet, the re-evaluation of foreign policies by leading powers set off by the September 11, 2001 terrorist attack on the USA, has initiated processes that are, by and large, beneficial to India. An indication of this is the US declaration of seeing India as a strategic partner for the 21st century, and its efforts to legislate exceptions to its domestic laws to allow supply of nuclear materials for peaceful civilian use to India by the cartel operated by the Nuclear Suppliers Group (NSG).

Nearer home, the pathological hostility of the Pakistanis establishment towards India is rooted in its quest for a national identity, which no novel interpretations, distortions or reinventions of sub-continental history seem able to provide. It will be a long time before there can be normal relations with Pakistan because they are influenced more by the internal contradictions and dynamics of the Pakistani state rather than considerations of mutual benefits through good relations. Since the Pakistan army is the self-appointed guardian of the undefined "ideology of Pakistan", normalcy will come when the Army decides it should be so; or the cost-benefit equation alters.

With China, there is perceptible progress on resolving disputes and fostering economic and cultural relations. As for Nepal, Bangladesh, Myanmar and Sri Lanka, there is no significant positive change, and because of shared borders, internal problems in those countries will continue to spill over into India. Instability in Afghanistan remains a cause of concern, especially because of Pakistan's dubious role, and this will have its impact on the pursuit of India's energy and strategic interests in Central Asia.

Non-littoral naval forces in significant numbers are still present in the Indian Ocean, but there is no coercive or inimical intent as in the past. Indeed, the Indian Navy holds regular friendly exercises with them on a routine basis. China's long term plans for a naval presence in the region have to be taken note of. There are ample signs of Chinese maritime interest, starting from building and operating communications facilities in Myanmar to financing and building Pakistan's Gwadar Port on the Makran coast, collaboration in building warships for the Pakistan navy at Karachi shipyard, as well as port building in Sri Lanka. On the western rim of the Indian Ocean, China is vigorously pursuing options in Africa, underlined by the meeting of 49 heads of state/government in Beijing in early November this year.

National Objectives in the Long Term

Planning for defence has to be in the framework of national objectives over a period of decades ahead, even if these are not publicly articulated. USA does not hesitate to state its intention to remain the dominant global technological, space and military power for the foreseeable future and tailors strategic policies accordingly.

China has, by its actions, investments and developments over the years, demonstrated that it intends to be at least the equal of the USA, though with "Chinese characteristics". Pakistan makes no secret of its intention to be "different" from India, and to compete with and undermine India at every opportunity.

India too has shown in various ways that it intends to be in the forefront of nations in every sphere: economic, technological, industrial and human development. What about military capability? Does it wish to have only a capacity to ward off aggression by land and sea? Or does it aspire to play a larger role in the region? If it emerges as the world's third or fourth largest economy in a few years, would a commensurate military role follow? Or are national objectives to be largely achieved by a combination of diplomacy and economic policies? If it aspires for a permanent seat in the UN Security Council, is it prepared for the increased diplomatic and military responsibilities attached? Many of these seemingly philosophical issues require to be debated to facilitate meaningful defence planning for the future.

ORGANISATION FOR DEFENCE PLANNING

Planning for defence involves almost all aspects of government, not only because of the extreme seriousness of the undertaking, but also because a long duration war will require marshalling the total resources of the nation. It can never be presumed that hostilities will always be of short duration, as there is a tendency to do so in the context of India-Pakistan conflicts. Many instances in history illustrate this, for example the US misadventure in Iraq. The US-led coalition forces were injected on the assumption of a quick victory, a warm welcome by Iraqi citizenry and a glorious return home for Christmas. They are still there nearly three years later, as also in Afghanistan, with no indications of an early resolution of the conflicts. Madeleine Albright, the former US Secretary of State has this to say about the US Iraq expedition: "We have damaged our reputation very badly. Iraq may turn out to be the greatest disaster in American foreign policy, which by its very nature means that it is worse than Vietnam.

In this context, it is worth recalling the words attributed to Fredrick the Great: "No war is accidental or unintended. The only thing unintended is the bloodiness and duration of the conflict. Defeat too is unintended".

No rational planning can be done on basis of a worst-case scenario. Apart from being illogical, it is unaffordable, and therefore unachievable. Rather, realistic defence planning requires a thorough and detailed analysis and evaluation of the security environment, threat perceptions, technological assessments, etc. and should result in an integrated defence plan. Such a plan should be linked to national capacity in the civil sector and integrate utilisation of resources such as road transport, civil aviation and technical manpower in a pre-determined manner for war.

British Example Through almost four hundred years of wars and colonial expansion and contraction, the British learnt to restructure their fleets and armies as the situation demanded and finances allowed. This was not done at the cost of contingency planning and military effectiveness, as the rapid mobilisation at the time of the Falklands war in 1982 showed. A major defence costs study, *Front Line First* was initiated in 1994, whereby the entire UK defence organisation was to be reorganised to effect economies, especially at headquarters, with maximum integration of civil and military staff at all levels, enhanced delegation of financial powers and simplification of procedures. Some of the conclusions of the Study could apply equally to Indian defence organisations:

The Ministry of Defence Head Office and other headquarters at all levels were seen as being too large, too top heavy and too bureaucratic. The process of delegating responsibility to individual budgetholders was generally seen as the key to maximising efficiency. There were too many minor rules and regulations that were rigidly applied, and stood in the way of maximising value for money.

There was a need for greater cost consciousnessso that costs could be linked more explicitly to output. Rationalisation of command, training and support structures on a joint Service basis could increase operational effectiveness as well as offer savings. (Huge differences in the size of the three services and the sub-continental geographic spread would make this impractical in India).

Changes were necessary in the culture of the Department, in simplification of working practices and in placing more weight on personal responsibility and accountability. The possible savings envisaged according to the study were:

- Equipment and Logistics-51 per cent.
- Estate and Support Infrastructure – 14 per cent.
- Organisation and Management – 16 per cent.
- Personnel and Training – 19 per cent.

The reduction in Head Office personnel was to be drastic indeed, from 12,700 in 1990, to 5,200 in 1995 and finally to 3,750 by 1998.

The report contains other interesting observations that have relevance for us:

- There is no single body below the Ministerial level with authority and responsibility for the full range of the Department's policy activity and management. (One may ask whether this is feasible or even desirable).
- Align single Service Chief of Staff's responsibility as professional head, with financial responsibility and accountability.

The MoD in UK is a unique *integrated* organisation in the government, as it is both a Department of State, as well as the headquarters of the Armed Forces as a whole. The Study states: "The importance of preserving clear lines of functional responsibility to Ministers for the different aspects of the business remains. We do not believe that this requires parallel, separate, military or civilian hierarchies. It was encouraging that the study found little evidence of this in the existing structure".

United States Experience

Whereas the UK defence organisation has evolved over a considerable period in a measured way, the Defence structure in the United States in its present form is largely a post-World War II creation. Due to the preponderant role of the US armed forces during and after the war (*"military policy was foreign policy"*), its emergence as a SuperPower with a global reach, the requirements of major wars (Korea and Vietnam), the Cold War, numerous smaller military involvements, and because of the possibility of nuclear war, the US defence organisation has become extraordinarily large and complex.

A further impetus for change and streamlining of the US, UK and other European defence organisations, was the creation of the North Atlantic Treaty Organisation(NATO) and the Warsaw Pact and the half-century long nuclear stand-off between the Western and the Soviet blocs.

These changes were brought about by stark necessity and were *politically driven,* often in the teeth of opposition and even sabotage by the civil and military establishments. The fear of a pre-emptive nuclear attack without warning drove the adversaries to demonstrate an organisational capability to retaliate instantaneously and overwhelmingly, and thus hope to deter the attack altogether.

Major organisational changes in the USA, such as the creation of a Joint Chiefs of Staff Committee (JCSC), and a national security set-up were initiated during President Truman's time in 1947. The last major reorganisation was in 1986 under the Goldwater-Nichols Act of 1986.

Changes in UK followed, notably under Prime Minister Margaret Thatcher. It should be remembered that fear of nuclear war was very real in the minds of national leaderships and military planners during the Cold War. Extremely complex and high cost weapon systems were developed and money had to be found by curtailing duplication and waste in the armed forces and in the civilian and military bureaucracies.

Apart from operational considerations, the creation of the Joint Chiefs of Staff (JCS) in the USA and the CDS in the UK were felt to be necessary for budgetary reasons, to clarify lines of control and responsibility, and to facilitate legislative supervision. All democracies require that armed forces be firmly under civil direction and control, but there is also nagging fear that somehow they manage to evade legislative oversight. In mature democracies, these concerns are not necessarily about relative power, but about better financial management of the requirements of the state, and the apportioning of the budgetary pie. The aim is also to forestall military inspired adventures. Sometimes, however, it is the civilian political authority that goads the military into action, as the USA did in Iraq, despite sound advice to the contrary.

Delays, Cost Overruns and Failures

Despite the more evolved and refined systems of defence management in advanced countries, delays, cost overruns and plain failures of major weapons systems are not infrequent.

Here is what the US Government Accountability Office has to say about the Pentagon's failure "to deliver high quality products in a timely and cost-efficient fashion", asserting that future national security is at risk as a result It is "not unusual to see cost increases that add up to tens or hundreds of millions of dollars, schedule delays that add up to years and large and expensive programmes frequently re-baselined or even scrapped after years of failing to achieve promised capability". The GAO also criticised the lack of accountability in the Department of Defence, and that the Pentagon "has never clearly specified who is accountable for what, invested responsibility for execution in any single individual, or even required programme leaders to stay until the job is done."

The UK experience is much the same as far as major defence projects are concerned. For example, according to the National Audit Office major projects report, the current cost estimates for the three latest Astute class nuclear attack submarines (SSNs) has risen from UK Pounds 2.6 billion to UK Pounds 3.5 billion. The project has barely survived "cost overruns and schedule delays, arising from a combination of poor project management, an immature computer-aided design (CAD) tool and a haemorrhaging of skills and experience in the submarine industry".

Planning for a future submarine nuclear deterrent platform is also not very optimistic. Assuming the UK government takes a decision in 2006, the submarine is not likely to be delivered before 2024, which according to the UK Director General Nuclear and Controller of the Navy, Rear Admiral Andy Mathews, "sounds a long way off, but is actually quite a tight timescale for something like this". If this is the fate of defence planning in mature and experienced countries such as in the UK and the USA, is it any surprise that our planning too is beset with inadequacies?

2

Indian Missile Defence Policy and Security Challenges

The global security architecture has been transformed with the U.S. deployment of the first phase of its missile defence system. The United States formally withdrew from the 1972 Anti-Ballistic Missile (ABM) treaty in 2001, which paved the way for the U.S. pursuit of its ballistic missile defence (BMD) programme without any formal restrictions. The United States had deployed six interceptors at Fort Greely in Alaska and four at Vandenberg Air Force Base in California as part of the first phase of its missile defence system in 2004 followed by ten more interceptors in Alaska in 2005. The United States plans to deploy a sea-based antimissile system capable of protecting allies and U.S. troop deployments abroad. Negotiations are currently under way about radar sites and possible defence missile defence emplacements with several European countries.

The initial missile defence capability is expected to yield a fully integrated and layered BMD system, capable of defeating ballistic missiles of all ranges and in all phases of flights. Though the U.S. military has not accorded its missile defence system the status of an operational weapons system because of ongoing development of an array of radars and interceptors, the American missile defence system went on alert in 2006 when North Korea undertook missile tests.

Like most states in the international system, India is also trying to come to terms with the strategic implications of the U.S. decision for its own security. Though it has yet to come up with a coherent policy response, a vigorous debate has been under way in India on the ramifications of the U.S.

BMD for India and what an appropriate Indian response should be. Though this debate has subsided somewhat in light of other developments on the nuclear front, especially the U.S.-India nuclear deal, it brings to the fore some of the fundamental issues facing Indian foreign and security policy.

This chapter is an attempt to examine this debate and to tease out its broader implications for Indian foreign policy. First, the changes in regional and global context as a consequence of the BMD are delineated in brief. This is followed by an examination of India's engagement with the United States on the issue of missile defence over the last few years. Subsequently, the Indian debate on the U.S. missile defence programme and India's response to it is analysed in detail. Finally, the implications of the Indian debate on missile defence for India's nuclear weapons policy and broader foreign policy are examined.

INDO-U.S. ENGAGEMENT ON MISSILE DEFENCE

In one of its swiftest diplomatic moves ever, within hours of the U.S. declaration that it intends to pursue its plans to deploy the first phase of BMD by the fall of 2004, India became one of the few nations in the world to extend its support for the new security architecture being proposed by the United States.

India hailed the U.S. proposals for deep cuts in nuclear arsenals as well as building missile defences as a significant and far-reaching effort to move away from the adversarial legacy of the cold war. India went on to say that it believes "there is a strategic and technological inevitability in stepping away from a world that is held hostage by the doctrine of Mutual Assured Destruction (MAD) to a cooperative, defensive transition that is underpinned by further cuts and a de-alert of nuclear forces."

This was in sharp contrast to the Indian government's position just one year before when in June 2000 the then Indian foreign minister, Jaswant Singh, had made a case against supporting BMD on grounds that it would undermine international strategic stability, adversely affect the global movement towards nuclear disarmament, and might lead to the militarization of outer space. Not unexpectedly, India's dramatic change of stance generated a vigourous discussion in the country. The opposition parties criticized the government for what they called a hasty and premature reaction to the U.S. proposal with India going ahead with its effusive support even before the traditional U.S. allies had reacted to the decision.

Many in the Indian strategic community, the academe and the think tanks also took exception to India's stand. While the debate on a suitable Indian response to the U.S. missile defence programme continues unabated to date, the political fissures generated by the Indian decision in 2001 revealed that, unlike most issues in Indian foreign policy, where there is by and large a political consensus, this issue was highly divisive. The fact that the Indian government of the day apparently did not take other political parties into its confidence did not help matters.

But regardless of the domestic debate, the Indo-U.S. engagement on BMD continued with the visit of U.S. deputy secretary of state Richard Armitage to India a week after India's declaration of support for the U.S. plans. Armitage briefed India on the details of the new strategic framework espoused by the Bush administration via the BMD, and the two sides decided to work together for this new security regime. This visit was also a signal for the United States that India had moved into the orbit of its "friends," who would be consulted on key strategic issues such as missile defence.

This has been followed by various rounds of bilateral and multilateral discussions on missile defence between India and the United States. Moreover, in 2004, as part of a process called "Next Step in Strategic Partnership (NSSP)," India and the United States formally decided to expand their cooperation in the area of civilian nuclear activities, civilian space programmes, and high technology trade as well as agreed to broaden their dialogue on missile defence to promote nonproliferation and ease the transfer of advanced technologies to India. The proposed cooperation under the NSSP progressed through a series of reciprocal steps building on each other, resulting ultimately in the landmark U.S.-India civilian nuclear cooperation pact signed in 2005. Though the United States has also decided to engage Pakistan on missile defence issues, the two states are not involved in cooperation on space and high technology issues.

Most of the Indo-U.S. discussions on missile defence have taken place under the rubric of the Indo-U.S. Defence Policy Group (DPG), the highest policymaking body that gives shape to Indo-U.S. bilateral cooperation. An Indian team visited Colorado Springs to participate in a missile defence simulation, and India also participated in the missile defence conference in Dallas in 2002.

India was a participant in the 2003 multinational missile defence workshop in Japan as well as the 2004 missile defence conference in Germany. India was also invited to the 2005 annual "Roving Sands" air and missile defence exercises in New Mexico.

The Indo-U.S. DPG meetings have continued even after a change of government in India in 2004. This government is led by the Congress Party and is supported from outside by the Left parties, which, while in opposition, have been less than enthusiastic about the Indian support to the U.S. BMD programme, with the Left parties even calling it a renunciation of Indian autonomy in foreign policy. But once in government, the United Progressive Alliance (UPA) government has adopted a cautious attitude towards this issue and has gone beyond the previous government in cultivating its ties with the United States.

As part of the NSSP agreement, the Bush administration gave clearance for a classified technical presentation of the Patriot Advanced Capability (PAC-2) antiballistic missile system to India in February 2005 in response to a request made by India in 2002. This was done after obtaining assurances from India that this technology would not be shared with any other country by India. Patriot, or Phased Array Tracking Intercept of Target, is the foundation of the U.S. Army's integrated air- and missile-defence architecture.

PAC-2 is a long-range, all-altitude, all-weather air defence system to counter tactical ballistic missiles, cruise missiles, and advanced aircraft. The range of the missile is seventy kilometers and it can climb to an altitude of greater than twenty-four kilometers, with minimum and maximum flight times being less than three seconds and three-and-half minutes respectively. While the Indian defence establishment welcomed the U.S. openness with regard to technical details of the PAC-2 system, it views this as an opening towards PAC-3, the latest upgraded version of the antimissile system. PAC-3 was used in Operation Iraqi Freedom, and has a kill rate of more than 95 per cent. There have been reports that the United States might be willing to offer India the advanced version of PAC-2 missiles with the radar system of the latest PAC- 3 so that when Indian is ready, it can upgrade its missile defence capability.

The United States, on its part, made clear that it would welcome continued Indian cooperation on this issue even though the UPA government has been in no hurry to clarify its stand. There is not only a lack of domestic political consensus on this issue, but the Left parties, which constitute a major part of the governing coalition, have been strongly opposed to any Indian entanglement with the U.S. missile defence system. The Indian military, meanwhile, has undertaken a detailed study of the technical, operational, and budgetary aspects of a missile defence system for India and has submitted its recommendations to the government. India has not only signed a defence cooperation framework agreement with the United States in 2005 that commits both sides to expanding "collaboration relating to missile defence," but it has also demonstrated to the world in 2006 its capability to indigenously produce an effective antiballistic missile prototype. Though India's upgraded Prithvi ABM interceptor has a long way to go before it can be deployed, it has been ranked on par with the U.S. Patriot PAC-3 system, Russia's S-300, and Israel's Arrow in its ability to intercept short- and intermediate-range missile. This has led some to conclude that "India is seriously considering integrating some kind of strategic defensive capabilities into its national military posture."

After successfully testing a hypersonic interceptor missile, which brought India a step closer to developing a full fledged missile defence system, has come the announcement that India should expect to have its home-grown militarily usable missile defence system by 2010.

India's central military research and development facility, the Defence Research and Development Organization (DRDO) claims that it has the technology to develop a potent missile shield for the nation.

The ambition is to eventually develop a two-tier ballistic missile defence system that can intercept missiles at both the mid-course and terminal phases. The Advanced Air Defence (AAD-02), as the new interceptor missile is called, is capable of intercepting M-9 and M-11 class of missiles and compares well with the US PAC-3 (Patriot Advanced Capability). In fact, it is being touted as superior to PAC-3 in interception, range and altitude.

However, with the U.S.-India nuclear pact taking center stage since 2005, discussion of missile defence has taken a backseat in Indian policy discourse but not before exposing the fault lines dividing the Indian foreign policy establishment.

THE GREAT INDIAN NUCLEAR DEBATE

Examining the Indian missile defence debate closely, one should have little difficulty in classifying the various strands of the debate according to the typology that has been offered in the context of the debate on Indian nuclear policy generally. Three schools of thought can be delineated in the realm of Indian nuclear policy. These have been termed as the rejectionists, the pragmatists, and the maximalists. The rejectionists, while holding that nuclear disarmament is both necessary and desirable, argue that India should have nuclear weapons so long as other states with nuclear weapons do not agree to renounce them. Therefore, in the absence of a global and comprehensive nuclear disarmament, India has no option but to have nuclear weapons for deterrence. The pragmatists argue that India should be a part of the global arms control processes, because a comprehensive global nuclear disarmament of the type India wants is neither desirable nor feasible. By agreeing to be a part of the international nuclear arms control regime, which India has traditionally opposed on the grounds it is discriminatory, India should be able to garner several concessions from the international community, and particularly from the United States.

The third viewpoint of the hypernationalists or hyperrealists wants India to go beyond its "credible minimum" deterrent nuclear posture and to equip itself with an entire range of nuclear weapons capability. They want India to acquire the nuclear capability traditionally associated with "great powers." They want India to have nothing to do with global nuclear disarmament. They also would like India to disassociate itself from the nuclear arms control regime, because in their view, it might constrain India's nuclear weapons capability in the future.

The current debate in India on the issue of missile defence is largely along with some subtle differences. In the missile defence debate, the rejectionists and the maximalists have found themselves on the same side, though for very different reasons. Both have expressed strong objections to India's support for the U.S. BMD plans. For the rejectionists, the U.S. missile defence programme would be the beginning of the end of the entire global nuclear arms control and disarmament architecture.

India, with its traditionally supportive stance for the global disarmament movement, should resist supporting the U.S. plans. The maximalists also argue that India should have nothing to do with the U.S. plans, because in their opinion, this is part of the larger global counterproliferation strategy and it will end up constraining the Indian nuclear weapons capabilities in the future, because India would become little more than a U.S. satellite under the U.S. missile defence umbrella. The pragmatists have supported the Indian government's stance of supporting the U.S. missile defence plans. In their opinion, such a diplomatic posture will not only bring India and the United States closer, but India can also get significant economic and technological benefit from the United States. They also think that while it is inevitable that the United States would go ahead with its missile defence plans anyway, it makes little sense to oppose the U.S. plans when India can benefit from being supportive.

There is no doubt that India's support for the missile defence programme has paid dividends, especially leading to greater cooperation in the highly sensitive area of defence technology. Cooperation with the United States is useful, because it meets India's high-tech requirements for the defence sector. The Indian army has initiated as $5 billion fifteen-year programme to equip its infantry with smart, lighter, and more offensive weapons. The navy needs more than a hundred ships over the next fifteen years as replacements and additions as well as maritime patrol aircraft like the P-3 Orion reconnaissance aircraft. And there are major requirements for the air force and civilian space programme. For the pragmatists, Indo-U.S. cooperation on missile defence opens the way for the broader restructuring of the Indian defence sector with U.S. help.

The "Strategic" Direction of Indian Foreign Policy

However, another subtle debate can be delineated in the missile defence discourse in India. And this is a debate about India's larger foreign policy strategy. Many of those who oppose India's support to the U.S. missile defence programme do so on grounds that such a diplomatic posture might end up antagonizing China. China will respond aggressively, they argue, to the U.S. BMD by substantially shoring up its nuclear force posture. China has made its intentions very clear by arguing that "if a country, in addition to its offensive power, seeks to develop advanced TMD [tactical missile defence] or even NMD [nuclear missile defence], in an attempt to obtain absolute security, and unilateral strategic advantage for itself, other countries will be forced to develop more advanced offensive missiles." It might further enhance its nuclear and missile-related cooperation with Pakistan. All this would further endanger India's security.

Conversely, there are those who argue that India should support BMD precisely because it puts China on the defensive. In their opinion, China has done all it could to adversely affect Indian national security interests. India has this one chance to pay China back in the same coin. And if this entails opting for the U.S. missile defence umbrella, so be it.

These two strands in the Indian foreign policy discourse are not clearly defined as of yet. But they reflect the pressures on the Indian foreign policy as a consequence of the global unipolarity and the raising ambitions of India in the last few years. With the end of the cold war, India has increasingly found that its traditional foreign policy posture of nonalignment has become irrelevant.

As a consequence, it has tried to pursue a "multivector, multidimensional" foreign policy, which basically means trying to improve its relations with the major global powers, including the United States, China, the EU, and Russia. But more than any other state, China looms large over the Indian national security landscape. And the larger Indian foreign policy discourse has come to center more and more on China.

It is in this context that China is seen by many as India's rival for geopolitical primacy in Asia. And as China's global profile has risen in recent years, so has India's apprehensions about China's foreign policy goals vis-à-vis India, notwithstanding a substantial improvement in Sino-Indian relations in the last few years. On the one side are those who would like India to improve its bilateral relations with China even further and to do nothing to derail the process of Sino-Indian détente.

They would like India to make a common cause with China in opposing the U.S. attempts at preserving and enhancing its global hegemony. They would like India and China to stand up for a multipolar international political order, which in their view would be more just and peaceful. And therefore the idea of India cooperating with the United States on missile defence is anathema to the advocates of this foreign policy strategy. For them, India's foreign policy should be attuned to the political realities of South Asia's strategic context, rather than serving as a mere extension of U.S. security policy.

On the other side of this debate are those who argue that India can never come out of the straight jacket of being a mere South Asian power unless it starts countering China more proactively. India will have to compete with China for regional dominance in the near term if in the long term it wants to establish itself as a global player of any reckoning. Moreover, they don't see any threat to the U.S. global preponderance in the immediate future. And therefore there is every reason to cooperate with the United States on missile defence, which would greatly enhance India's strategic clout and sideline China. In this context, India's support for the U.S. missile defence plans is viewed as a major factor that has helped in transforming Indo-U.S. ties in the last few years.

It has been pointed out that China can respond to the U.S. BMD plans in a number of ways. It can accelerate its strategic military modernization programme, it can backtrack on its arms control and nonproliferation commitments, and it can reformulate and alter its nuclear weapons doctrine and posture. Whatever course China may adopt in the future, it is clear that it will have a substantial impact on India.

Those who would like India to be opposed to U.S. missile defence plans point to the negative impact the Chinese reaction to the BMD will have on India's security. Whether China decides to upgrade its nuclear arsenal or goes back on its arms control commitments or alters its nuclear doctrine, India's security situation will be adversely affected. However, those who would like India to cast its lot with the United States argue that China's strategic modernization programme has developed and will continue to develop regardless of the U.S. BMD plans, China's dubious nonproliferation record has already hurt India's security, and China's "no-first-use" nuclear doctrine does not apply to India in any case. And therefore supporting the U.S. missile defence plans can only raise India's strategic profile vis-à-vis China.

While there are few who would like India to chart a completely independent route towards its great power status, the debate as it is evolving in the Indian strategic community addresses the larger strategic framework of the Indian foreign policy. Using the typology of the rejectionists, pragmatists, and hyperrealists, the rejectionists are more or less on the side of keeping China in good humour.

Most of the left-liberal Indian political establishment seems at the moment to be supporting this strand. The pro–United States line is taken by the pragmatists and Indian political right. While it is no coincidence that India enthusiastically supported Bush administration's BMD proposals in 2001, when the National Democratic Alliance led by the Hindu nationalist Bharatiya Janata Party (BJP) was in power, the continuing support for strong U.S.-India ties from the centrist Congress Party leading the ruling coalition at the center is a testimony to the growing salience of pragmatists in Indian foreign policy discourse.

Though Indians have been berated for not thinking strategically on national security issues, the Indian debate on missile defence is about the larger strategic direction of Indian foreign policy, even though the advocates on both sides might not even realize this themselves. How this debate shapes up and resolves itself will to a large extent decide the strategic direction of the Indian foreign policy in the coming years.

THE WORLD REACTS

When the former U.S. president, Ronald Reagan, declared in his famous 1983 "Star Wars" speech that the United States would embark on a long-term research-and-development effort to counter the threat of Soviet ballistic missiles and to make nuclear weapons "impotent and obsolete," few experts believed in the feasibility of a foolproof defence shield. The idea of an antimissile shield, however, came to acquire enough bureaucratic and technological momentum that it continued to survive beyond the Reagan administration. After the end of the cold war, the missile defence programme was seen as an answer to the threat of ballistic missiles from "rogue states" to the United States.

A bipartisan commission headed by the then defence secretary, Donald Rumsfeld, concluded in 1998 that "rogue states" like Iran and North Korea had the capacity to develop and deploy long-range ballistic missile in about five years time with little or no warning.

This finding got further support later in the same year when North Korea actually test-fired a three-stage ballistic missile out over the Pacific, signaling that North Korea might develop weapons capable of reaching Alaska and parts of Hawaii in the next few years.

Support for missile defences gained greater strength, and it became difficult even for the Democrats to dissociate themselves from this programme. This paved the way for the Bill Clinton administration to sign legislation in 1999 promising the deployment of a missile defence system as soon as it was technologically feasible. The George W. Bush administration came to office with a gung ho approach towards missile defences, and the terrorist attacks of September 11, 2001, further entrenched the consensus in their favour.

Not surprisingly, other states in the international system are grappling to adjust to the changing strategic milieu being ushered in by the U.S. missile defence plans. The U.S. withdrawal from the ABM treaty and its pursuit of missile defences in all seriousness will and has already forced many states to reevaluate their strategic options and some major realignments in world politics seem to be in the offing. While Australia has announced its decision to take part in the U.S. missile defence programme, Japan has also given the goahead for deployment of a joint U.S.-Japanese missile defence system aimed at protecting Japan from a North Korean attack.

Though Australia formally joined the missile defence programme in 2004, it has not yet agreed to acquire missile defences. Japan, meanwhile, has formally agreed to collaborate with the United States on a two-tiered missile defence system, comprising the Aegis/SM-3 sea-based midcourse defence and the land-based Patriot (PAC-3) missile. Because of the threat from China's missiles, Taiwan has also expressed an interest in U.S. missile defence plans, and negotiations are under way with the United States for the sale of the PAC-3 air defence system.

Hungary, Poland, and the Czech Republic have also expressed interest in being part of the U.S. missile defence project, and negotiations are currently under way over the establishment of advanced radar stations in these Central European states. Denmark has already acceded to the U.S. request to upgrade its early-warning radar system based at Thule Air Base in Greenland so it can be a part of the proposed U.S. missile defence system. Despite domestic political concerns, Britain has moved much closer to the U.S. position on missile defences in the last few years.

A broader consensus also seems to be emerging in Europe in favour of missile defences, with the Europeans deciding to invest about $3.5 billion in an antitactical ballistic missile defence capability for the Aster air-defence system. The Canadian government, giving in to domestic opposition, has decided not to participate in the U.S. missile defence system. However, this decision will have little practical effect, because Canada has agreed to allow its operators at the North American Aerospace Command Center in Colorado to share information on incoming missiles.

Russia and China have vehemently opposed U.S. missile defence plans, because they are the two states most vulnerable to the deployment of missile defences. Only by exponentially increasing their nuclear arsenal will they be able to render the U.S. missile defences ineffective against them. Russia is planning to deploy theater missile defence and space defence systems.

It is making steady progress in developing not only a missile defence system but also weapons capable of overcoming missile shields. Russia plans to deploy a mobile version of the intercontinental ballistic missile Topol-M, increasing its ability to penetrate missile defences to almost 90 per cent. A new version of Topol-M, the RS 24 intercontinental ballistic missile, has also been tested with the aim of replacing Russia's aging missile force composed of RS-18s and RS-20s. Russian president Vladimir Putin has openly declared his intention to develop advanced nuclear missile systems unavailable to any country and without analogues in the other nuclear powers in the next few years. Russia continues to object to American plans for ten missile interceptors in Poland and a radar system in Czech Republic that the United States says is necessary to defend against a possible missile attack from Iran.

China clearly sees U.S. missile defence plans that would exclude it while covering Japan and Taiwan as U.S. attempts to gain global hegemony and containment of China. Its own programme of strategic force modernization will continue with or without the U.S. missile defence programme. The greatest Chinese worry in this regard is related to the issue of Taiwan, because it would greatly constrain its options vis-à-vis the United States in any future crisis over Taiwan. China has made it clear that it will build as many missiles as it needs to be able to overwhelm Taiwan's missile defence protection.

The effect of the U.S. missile defence programme will also be felt in South Asia. The Rumsfeld Commission had pointed out the growing ballistic missile capabilities of both India and Pakistan, arguing that "it would have direct effect on U.S. policies, both regional and global, and could significantly affect U.S. capability to play a stabilizing role in South Asia." This, in effect, implied that the growing capabilities of India and Pakistan might make it difficult for the United States to intervene in South Asian affairs in the future. Also, though neither India nor Pakistan has a capability to threaten the United States at present, the U.S. missile defence system would protect it from such possibilities in the future.

Some might argue that effective U.S. missile defences would thereby constrain India's attempts to emerge as a global nuclear player of any reckoning. Conversely, it has been suggested that India's engagement with the United States on the issue of missile defence has "come to reflect both an example of, and a means towards, the steady improvement in U.S.-India ties occurring in recent years." India's response to U.S. missile defence plans, in essence, is an act of balancing competing priorities, thereby making it difficult for India to come up with a coherent policy response.

THE SUPPORTERS

A vigourous debate has been going on in India on the implications of India's stand on the U.S. missile defence programme. Those who would like India to back the U.S. pursuit of missile defence have an array of arguments to offer. First and foremost is the argument that India lives in a dangerous neighbourhood facing a range of missile threats. As a study on the spread of ballistic missiles in Asia has pointed out, almost one-third of the thirty-four nations around the world possessing some type of ballistic missile capability are located in Asia. Pakistan remains hostile to India and its missile buildup continues with the help of China. China itself has targeted India with its deployment of several short- and intermediate-range missiles in Tibet. The China-Pakistan nexus on nuclear and missile issues makes India particularly vulnerable in the region. Many other states in India's extended neighbourhood, such as Iran, Syria, and Saudi Arabia, are undertaking their own missile programmes.

Moreover, there are cross-national linkages across the region, with China and Pakistan's proliferation records especially troublesome for India. Transfer of missiles and missile-related items from China and Pakistan to states as far and wide as Syria, Iran, North Korea, Libya, and Saudi Arabia has been a constant feature of the Asian security landscape for quite some time now. India has also been concerned about the continued use of the Indian Ocean by the ballistic-missile submarines of the major powers. Pakistan now enjoys a major lead over India in the development and deployment of missiles, thanks to support from China and North Korea, and this is a major concern for India's security planners.

While India has tried to counter these threats by developing its own missile systems as a deterrent, India is also developing an indigenous antimissile system. India is also planning to purchase the Arrow antimissile system from Israel and examining the possibility of modifying the Russian S-300 surface-to-air missiles in an antiballistic-missile mode. India has already acquired the Barak antimissile system and the Greenpine groundbased early-warning radar system and is in the process of purchasing the Phalcon airborne early-warning system.

Many see an Indian missile defence capability as the only effective way to counter Pakistan's nuclear blackmail. The threat of a nuclear war has prevented India from effectively countering the Pakistan-sponsored low-intensity war in Kashmir.

The 1999 Kargil conflict demonstrated for many the inability of India to come up with an appropriate response to the stabilityinstability paradox operating on the subcontinent that has put India at a strategic disadvantage vis-à-vis Pakistan. A missile defence system would help India blunt Pakistan's "first-use" nuclear force posture that had led Pakistan to believe that it had inhibited India from launching a conventional attack against it for fear of its escalation to the nuclear level. With a missile defence system in place, India would be able to restore the status quo ante, thereby making a conventional military option against Pakistan potent again.

Pakistan, therefore, has been concerned about the growing Indo-U.S. cooperation in the realm of missile defence and especially about the expected sale of Patriot missiles to India. It argues that it will critically imbalance Pakistan's strategic capabilities vis-à-vis India and has taken up its concerns with Washington. India would like to acquire counterproliferation know-how that can help in the destruction of hostile missiles while they are still at the launch pad, because the time taken for a missile launched from the subcontinent to impact on India is less than five minutes. Also, from the perspective of nuclear command and control, India should have the ability to shield its ultimate decision-making authority from a bolt-from-the-blue nuclear strike, either through missiles or a low-level penetration aerial strike.

A missile defence for India's national decision-making apparatus and some part of its retaliatory second-strike capability would make India's no-first-use posture more credible. It would enhance the uncertainties of India's potential adversaries, regardless of the degree of effectiveness of missile interception and would act as a disincentive to their resort to nuclear weapons.

A related issue is the threat of terrorism. India has been one of the worst victims of terrorism for more than a decade now. Islamic insurgents aided and abetted by Pakistan's military have used the domestic political turmoil in the Indian state of Jammu and Kashmir to wage their own war against the Indian government. India believes that despite protestations to the contrary, Pakistan military remains involved in these operations. India fears that a missile threat from the terrorists is a real possibility, especially in the event of a governmental breakdown in Pakistan. Pakistan has been in turmoil for the last few years with rising levels of Islamist militancy and political instability.

The ability of the Pakistani military and intelligence to control its nuclear and missile assets has come under question as has its ability to rein in the militants it had nurtured for decades to fight Pakistan's proxy wars in Kashmir and Afghanistan. Security breakdowns in Pakistani nuclear establishment exemplified by the A.Q. Khan network also do not generate enough confidence in the assurances of the Pakistani government that its nuclear weapons are well secured.

It is instructive to note that when the extremist mullahs call on their followers to take up arms in support of an Islamic jihad, their topmost exhortations have always been the "liberation" of Palestine from Israel and of Kashmir from India along with the annihilation of the United States. India sees itself as a partner of the United States in its desire to prevent the weapons of mass destruction and the means of their delivery into falling in the hands of the terrorists. A major focus of India's missile defence cooperation with the United States is China.

Many in India see China as India's greatest long-term security threat. This is despite recent improvements in Sino-Indian bilateral relations. China is seen by many to have contained India within the confines of South Asia. Indo-U.S. missile defence cooperation would put China on the defensive, and it would enable India to bolster its ties with the United States, because the United States also recognizes the need to contain rising Chinese ambitions. Despite denials by the U.S. government, its BMD capability will inevitably undermine the nuclear deterrence posture of China. Conversely, some have argued that this changing strategic situation might propel India under a U.S. strategic missile defence umbrella, thereby bringing India and the United States closer. Missile defence cooperation between India and the United States, thereby became for many Indians a means of initiating a broad-based strategic partnership with the United States.

The U.S. willingness to share information on missile defence can also be viewed as an indication of America's recognition of India's increasingly significant role in the globalizing world. Some have argued that India should take full advantage of the changing strategic realities and develop a long-term defence relationship with the United States, keeping in mind its technological requirements.

India, in other words, should view the missile defence system and the resulting cooperation with the United States as a vehicle for advanced military technological development, opening the door for joint technological development and data sharing. It has also been suggested in some quarters that India can bargain for some major concessions from the United States such as high-technology transfers and a permanent seat at the UN Security Council in return for its support to the U.S. missile defence programme. It has been argued that the new strategic discourse enunciated by the Bush administration contains many of the principles that India has long espoused, such as the need for reduction of nuclear armaments and a movement away from that nuclear balance of terror. The Indo-U.S. nuclear discourse has undergone a change in the last few years. While the Clinton administration was focused on engaging India within the framework of the Nuclear Non-Proliferation Treaty (NPT) and other arms control measures, the Bush administration has been much more open, even indicating its tacit support for an Indian nuclear posture of a small nuclear arsenal protected by a missile shield. There has emerged a significant convergence of Indo-U.S. interests on the issue of nuclear arms control with the Bush administration's radical approach to arms control and India's attempts to engage with the United States more deeply. As a consequence, rather than focusing on nonproliferation, the United States and India have made more active counterproliferation methods such as missile defence a part of their nuclear dialogue.

In this context, some would also argue that, since there is no real alternative to the changing strategic landscape being ushered in by the United States, India should try to adopt a pragmatic approach and garner political and technological benefits for itself rather than irritate the only global superpower with its criticism. While the U.S. offer of PAC-2 may not be complete answer to India's requirements of a missile defence system, it demonstrates that the United States is now prepared to include India among its "friends," because the Patriot missile technology has so far been shared only with Germany, Israel, Japan, Saudi Arabia, and Taiwan. India, via its engagement with the United States on missile defence, also becomes a part of the new global nuclear framework rather than being an outlaw to the nuclear regime of the Nuclear

Non-Proliferation Treaty, the Comprehensive Test Ban Treaty (CTBT), and the Fissile Material Control Treaty (FMCT). BMD is seen by many as a proof of the failure of the NPT regime and thereby a vindication of India's long-stated position on the unsustainable nature of the regime.

Finally, some in India have also offered a guarded response, arguing that while it is not worthwhile for India to go all out in support of a comprehensive missile defence shield, a limited missile defence that protects some major targets is indeed desirable and can augment Indian security.

The Opponents

The opponents of the Indian support for the U.S. missile defence plan have their own set of arguments for their position. The most powerful of these is the effect of the BMD on China's nuclear force posture and its consequences for Indian security. Given the fact that the U.S. missile defence programme would render the Chinese nuclear deterrent ineffective, China would go all out to expand its nuclear force, both qualitatively and quantitatively.

This would make China an even more potent danger for India than it already is. From a strategic deterrent of about twenty ICBMs, China will move towards a robust nuclear triad dominated by long-range, multiple-warhead solid-fuel systems. China can render ineffective any missile defence system that India might be contemplating by simply augmenting the size of its missile inventories so as to overwhelm India's system through a saturated attack.

Moreover, China already feels under pressure of the U.S. military surrounding it in the name of the global war on terrorism. An Indo-U.S. missile defence cooperation would reinforce Chinese suspicions about collusion between the United States and India to encircle and contain it. This would gravely hurt Sino-Indian relations, which have been put on track with a lot of diplomatic finesse over a long period of time. China might enhance its already-substantial strategic cooperation with Pakistan on nuclear and missile issues, further endangering India's immediate security. India's attempts to match China's nuclear profile will propel Pakistan in the same direction, thereby generating an arms race on the subcontinent.

Moreover, many argue that rather than stabilizing the Indo-Pak security dynamic in the region, an Indian missile defence system would engender worst-case military planning on both sides, because Pakistan's confidence in its nuclear arsenal would erode and India might become prone to more aggressive posturing. An Indian missile defence system can introduce an element of strategic instability in India's relationship with Pakistan, because Pakistan might respond by assuming a more aggressive nuclear posture by lowering its threshold for nuclear use. It would become difficult to control any future conflict with Pakistan, because it might be tempted to make the first nuclear move because of its enhanced concerns that its deterrence vis-à-vis India might not work in the face of India's missile defence capabilities.

It has also been argued that Indian plans for the acquisition of a missile defence system go against the declared Indian nuclear doctrine that emphasizes the use of nuclear weapons to deter a nuclear war as opposed to winning one. With a missile defence capability, India might get tempted towards a risk-taking posture and might view preemption as a viable option with respect to Pakistan.

Those in India who saw missile defence as an effective way to counter Pakistan's blackmailing tactics were disappointed by the U.S. offer to also engage Pakistan on missile defence to maintain strategic stability in the region, because it was less clear what specific benefits India could gain vis-àvis its immediate security needs if both India and Pakistan enjoyed missile defence protection. While India would like the United States to better appreciate its need for some of the advanced weaponry such as the Patriot Advance Capability missile system, the United States has so far given little indication of such an understanding.

As of yet, the United States is only willing to supply to India the older, though upgraded, version of the Patriot missile system. India, however, needs the PAC-3 version, which has better radar and launch speed and the capability to fire sixteen missiles against incoming nuclear threats. There are concerns in India that the "nonproliferation fundamentalists" in the U.S. political and foreign policy establishment would make sure that the Indo-U.S. cooperation in the realm of high technology does not attain its full potential. For those on the Indian left, the U.S. pursuit of BMD is merely a manifestation of its desire to gain maximum security and entrench its states as a global hegemon. The U.S. as well as the Soviet policies during the cold war were competitive, offensive, and clearly aimed at gaining nuclear superiority.

None of the arms control agreements were allowed to hamper the efforts on the part of these powers to achieve nuclear superiority. The only purpose of multilateral treaties like the Partial Test Ban Treaty (PTBT) and the NPT served was to prevent other nuclear powers from rising. The bilateral agreements like the Strategic Arms Limitation Treaty (SALT) and Strategic Arms Reduction Treaty (START) reflected more the pressures emanating from the domestic groups than any sincere desire to control nuclear arms. The superpowers pursued nuclear superiority during the cold war because of the concrete political and military advantages it would have conveyed.

And therefore, the Indian Left argues that India should not give up on its long-pursued foreign goals of opposing any kind of hegemonic ambitions by states. India with its long-cherished tradition of nonalignment in its foreign policy cannot be seen as kowtowing to the United States and thereby compromising its strategic autonomy.

There are many in India who do not see the United States as a reliable partner, especially in light of U.S. anti-India policies during the cold war. Some interpreted India's alacrity in hailing the U.S. missile defence plans as a move towards a sort of strategic dependence on the United States.

There is also a sense that the pursuit of missile defence also signals the end of global nuclear arms control and this could impinge negatively on global and regional security. India has been a strong opponent of the militarization of outer space, and for many, the missile defence system signals its beginning. Others on the right have argued that the U.S. offer of cooperation with India is nothing but a part of larger counterproliferation strategy vis-à-vis India. By offering India to be a part of its missile defence umbrella, the United States would like to prevent the emergence of India as a nuclear weapon state of any major import.

India might be constrained in developing its strategic nuclear force posture as per its security requirements as a quid pro quo to the partnership with the United States on missile defence technologies. It was also pointed out that the nonproliferation bureaucracy in Washington is hardly enthusiastic about engaging India on missile defence and high-technology issues and would dragging its feat in cooperating with India on these issues. Finally, there is also the question of how much India should be investing on missile defence technologies, especially since the BMD is not likely to be effective against up-to-date missiles and countermeasures. A case can be made that India, with its limited resources, might end up cutting its other militaryrelated expenses by spending on a technology that is not yet foolproof. To date, there is no consensus even in the United States on the effectiveness of missile defence technologies.

There remain serious questions about the effectiveness of the Patriot antimissile system as a missile interceptor. In India's case, the Patriot's effectiveness might depend on what it is used for. It can be extremely effective if India wants to use it for shooting down planes. However, if India is looking at countering ballistic missiles, then the Patriot can only hit relatively short-range missiles traveling 150 kilometers or less. Even PAC-3 has never been tested by the United States against longer-range missiles, and this limits its effectiveness.

The defined mission of the Patriot antimissile system in the United States is to provide defence of critical assets and maneuver forces belonging to corps and to echelons above corps against aircraft, cruise missiles, and tactical ballistic missiles. But India is unlikely to use the Patriot with the field forces.

India's requirement is more in the nature of ballistic-missile defence of national command center and retaliatory nuclear forces. The Patriot system, in its present state, is not up to the task of making India's no first-use nuclear posture more credible. At best, the PAC-3 may form a part of multitier ballistic- missile defence architecture, but it cannot be the solution in itself.

Therefore, an argument can be made that the Indian armed forces, which are perpetually short of funds and are pursuing a modernization programme based on the "revolution in military affairs," should place emphasis on the procurement of weapons systems and upgrading of technology that suit their immediate threat assessment rather than on a missile defence system that may or may not work when the time comes.

The debate in India on missile defence is not only an extension of the larger Indian debate on the role of nuclear weapons in India's national security policy but it is also a reflection of the broader debate in the Indian strategic community on the strategic direction of Indian foreign policy. This debate has thrown into sharp relief the contending perspectives shaping the trajectory of Indian foreign and security policy.

NUCLEAR PROLIFERATION POLICIES DURING THE COLD WAR

In the South Asian context, a conflictual bipolar security complex, India and Pakistan's transformational process of emerging as opaque nuclear powers was an example of different motivations, aspirations and ambitions for obtaining nuclear status. While the dominance of *realpolitik* trends over states' nuclear decision-making process is not an entirely surprising phenomena, the evolution of India's approach to the nuclear option is interesting from philosophical and strategic viewpoints.

The genesis of the Indian nuclear policy from a categorical opposition to nuclear weapons in the Nehru era to Pokhran I, India's first so-called Peaceful Nuclear Explosion (PNE) in 1974, signified a discontinuity in New Delhi's post-1947 strategic thinking. What caused this discontinuity? What factor(s) led the country of Mohandas Gandhi, who once labelled nuclear weapons as 'diabolic', to obtaining potential nuclear power status under Indira Gandhi? Do the same factors suffice in explaining Pakistan's motives for developing its own nuclear capabilities in the mid-1980s? While some political scientists emphasised national security considerations in locating the roots of India and Pakistan proliferation policy, others have used an alternative theoretical approach with a greater level of structural balance between domestic, military security and symbolic motives. The latter multi-causal approach, summarised by Scott D. Sagan, is particularly useful in providing an inclusive analysis of nuclear proliferation causes. In this context and through the application of Sagan's explanatory models, the essay attempts to analyse the layers in India and Pakistan's 'nuclear thinking' leading to the development of military nuclear technology. The alternative multi-causal explanation constitutes a practically efficient theoretical framework for the comprehensive understanding of states' hybrid logic for nuclear proliferation.

Opposing the neorealist mono-causal security-oriented analysis (i.e. "the security model"), Sagan's approach considers the domestic and norms aspects as effective factors in triggering military nuclear proliferation, thus offering two additional explanations: "the domestic politics model" and "the norms model." According to Sagan, security model states (either weak or strong) perceive nuclear weapons as an enormously powerful means of deterrence to secure their national security in an anarchic international system, if their regional or trans-regional rival(s) acquire nuclear capability. Strong resourceful states develop their own bomb, while weak states, incapable of proliferation, are obliged to join a balancing alliance with a nuclear power to maintain their security and sovereignty with the promise of nuclear retaliation.

In contrast, the domestic politics model reflects the influence of three main domestic actors on governments' nuclear proliferation policies: first, states' nuclear energy establishments (consisting of scientific institutions and civil companies); second, the military elites (especially in the Air Force branch) as domestic bureaucratic actors; and third, politicians who tend to profit from the nuclear weapons discourse for political parties or individual standing regarding pro-proliferation public opinion.

Therefore, these pro-proliferation actors gain additional influence if nuclear weapons are a positive symbol in states' domestic debates – thus the states proliferate in accordance with the influence of one or more of the aforementioned actors. Finally, in the norms model, states' nuclear policies are pro-proliferation due to 'nuclear symbolism' and the 'nuclear myth': states observe military organisation and advanced weaponry as essential elements in their image as modern and sovereign states. The 'nuclear myth', or symbolic implications of nuclear proliferation (e.g. technological advancement, military might, projection of grandeur, etc), are perceived as a means of forming states' modern identity and enhancing their international prestige. While there seems to be an analytical overlap and theoretical interference between the domestic and symbolic models, Sagan's three models offer an efficient toolbox for examining the deciding factors in India and Pakistan's nuclear policies.

The security-model analysis of Indian nuclear policy prior to Pokhran I can be conducted by analysing India's threat perception at the regional and trans-regional levels. The trans-regional level analysis confirms the gravity of Sino-centrism in India's trans-regional threat perception sphere, and the validity of Sagan's security-model explanation. The dynamics of post-1962 Sino-Indian bilateral relations is the fundamental factor in India's horizontal proliferation policy in the security model.

While the Sino-Indian protracted conflict began in 1953 over territorial claims, the 1962 Sino-Indian war and its disastrous consequences for the non-aligned India moved the Chinese threat factor from the periphery of New Delhi's threat perception circle to its centre, triggering incremental yet significant changes in Indian defence policy and military strategy. The subsequent Indian military reorientation towards re-equipment and operational reinforcement (e.g. the creation of ten mountain divisions designed for warfare in the Himalayas and increasing the Army's manpower ceiling to 825,000) confirms the demise of Nehru's *moralpolitik*-type policies regarding China.

However, the fundamental shift in India's nuclear weapons position occurred when Beijing shocked New Delhi with the detonation of its first nuclear device in October 1964. New Delhi's subsequent reaction to China's nuclear capability demonstrated a paradigm shift in India's previously Nehruvian anti-proliferation policy towards what then Prime Minister Lal Bahadur Shastri reluctantly phrased as India considering "nuclear explosion for peaceful purposes". Compatible with the security-model's two policy scenarios, India's inability to develop its own nuclear weapons forced New Delhi to secure nuclear deterrence by joining a balancing alliance with a nuclear power. Accordingly, when India's request to the United States, the Soviet Union and the United Kingdom for nuclear guarantee was refused, India's only option for deterring a nuclear China and maintaining its national security was to obtain horizontal proliferation on its own, leading to the 1974 PNE.

Similarly, the regional-level analysis indicates the significance of nuclear weapons in India's quest for regional hegemony and security in the South Asian region, although against the much less significant threat of Pakistan. A quick glance at pro-Indian political scientists' analysis of the motivation of India's quest for regional security through nuclear weapons reveals New Delhi's mindset regarding Pakistani conventional threat as well as India's strategic policy manoeuvre to achieve several objectives at once. In the bipolar South Asian security complex, Pakistan was (and is) India's major regional security and strategic concern. In spite of its conventional inferiority to India, Pakistan attacked its greater and more militarily powerful neighbour in 1948, 1965 and 1971. While India's decisive military victory in the 1971 war, and the subsequent disintegration of Pakistan through the independence of Bangladesh, considerably weakened Pakistan, it managed to retain most of its military infrastructures.

The series of Indo-Pakistani military conflicts convinced Indian strategists that Pakistan could use the period of Indian domestic political instability to launch other military attacks on India. In the light of alarming Sino-Pakistani cordial relations, and the presumption of Pakistani will to attack India, India's nuclear proliferation became instrumental in maintaining Indian regional security as well as establishing Indian regional hegemony through deterring Pakistan from future attacks. As Saira Khan formulates, the most efficient war-avoidance strategy for India in such conflictual regional settings was 'deterrence by possession of nuclear weapons.'

Similar to the Indian behavioural pattern for proliferation, but in contrast to India's multi-layered threat perception, the application of the security-model framework on Pakistan's nuclear policy produces a mono-causal explanation: Pakistan's nuclear proliferation was a linear reactionary policy to India's 1974 nuclear detonation. In addition to Indo-Pakistani territorial, ideological and ethnic elements of conflict that have formed the essentials of the South Asian security complex since 1947, the 1971 war and dismemberment of Pakistan reinforced Indo-centrism in Pakistan's threat perception. The war crippled Pakistan's economy and displayed the perceived unreliability of Pakistan's allies (i.e. the United States and China) in the time of crisis. Realising its conventional military inferiority to India, in 1972 President Zulfiquar Ali Bhutto initiated a nuclear policy in pursuit of nuclear weapons. Islamabad's nuclear program, however, gained a critical boost by India's 1974 PNE. Closely resembling the pattern of India's reaction to the 1964 Chinese nuclear test, Pakistan's nuclear policy was decisively directed towards inevitable nuclear proliferation after India's 1974 PNE. Against India's combined conventional military superiority and nuclear weapons capability, Pakistan had to obtain its own nuclear weapons as soon as possible to provide deterrence against the gravest threat to its national security. In this context, with Islamabad's failure to obtain security guarantees from the nuclear powers against a nuclear India, Pakistan had no other option other than to embark on its own nuclear proliferation program.

Applying the domestic-model of analysis on the Indian case clearly exhibits the decisive influence of two of the three domestic actors outlined by the model on India's nuclear decision for horizontal proliferation: nuclear energy establishments (consisting of pro-proliferation scientists and defence laboratories) and politicians eager to enhance their respective parties or/and individual standing in public opinion. Due to the pattern of the civil-military relationship in India where the former utterly dominates the latter, military elites as bureaucratic domestic actors had practically no influence over New Delhi's process of nuclear decision-making. After the Chinese 1964 nuclear test, Homi Bhabba, the head of India's Atomic Energy Commission (AEC), tenaciously lobbied for the allocation of required resources for developing nuclear weapons. Eventually, the AEC leadership's lobbying for proliferation along with pro-nuclear Congress party pressure on the government forced the reluctant Shastri to order the initiation of a classified project to develop technical ability to design and detonate a PNE within a certain timeframe. In spite of Bhabba's successor, Vikram Sarabhai's fierce opposition to any form of nuclear proliferation, the AEC developed an alliance with defence laboratories for lobbying the new Prime Minister Indira Gandhi. In a meaningful coincidence, the dynamics of Indian domestic politics in the early 1970s were defined in terms of economic recession, large-scale riots in various regions and the internal conflict in the ruling Congress party, thus an all-time low domestic support for Gandhi's government. In such dire circumstances, with the Prime Minister acknowledging that a theatrical nuclear explosion could have been a decisive 'political ace' for increasing her standing in public opinion, Gandhi's approval of 1974 PNE is hardly surprising. In a later interview, in spite of her initial denial, Gandhi admitted that the PNE "would have been useful for election". As the result, immediately after the detonation, public support for Gandhi's government and the ruling Congress party increased by one-third, both being "restored to the nation's confidence." Considering the pre-PNE Indian domestic politics dynamics, the influence of AEC, the Prime Minister and the ruling party on nuclear proliferation is evident.

Domestic-model Framework

In contrast, the application of the domestic-model framework on the Pakistani case constitutes the presence of non-political domestic dynamics and a higher level of military influence on the process of Pakistan's pursuit of nuclear weapons. As mentioned earlier, a year after the 1971 war and two years before Pokhran I, Pakistan's former leader Bhutto instructed the country's top scientists to concentrate on the development of nuclear weapons.

Yet, such policies could not be pursued without the involvement of the military institution in the process. Decades of military rule has promoted the Pakistani military as the strongest bureaucratic institution in the country, setting the pattern of the country's civil-military relationship in favour of military control.

However, in spite of the military's vast influence in Pakistan's polity, nuclear decisions were made within a coordinated policy framework consisting of Prime Minister Bhutto, the chiefs of the armed forces, the Foreign Minister and the chief of joint services headquarters. The pro-bomb direction of Pakistani organic nuclear decision-making machinery was maintained even after the fall of Bhutto in 1977. The policy momentum and continuity in the country's pursuit for nuclear weapons in the post-Bhutto era confirms the absence of a domestic politics perspective in favour of the strong presence of a national security perspective: all Pakistani political leaders with different attitudes and policy perspectives maintained the essentials of Bhutto's nuclear policy.

As for the nuclear establishment agency's influence, however, a division in the scholarly literature is detectable: while Kapur introduces I. H. Usmani, chairman of Pakistan Atomic Energy Commission (PAEC) as the most important figure in Pakistan's nuclear decision-making during 1970s, Khan maintains that the scientific institutions' influence was largely barred by the institutionalised military, limiting their range of influence to the lobbying of politicians and military elites in favour of proliferation. Yet, in spite of Kapur's exaggerated emphasis on Usmani's influence, the dominance of the security discourse over Pakistan's nuclear policy process is to such a degree that the domestic model's dynamics echoes the trends of the security model.

Finally, analysis of India's Cold War period nuclear proliferation policy signifies the link between India's quest for obtaining international prestige as a mean of gaining 'great power' status and its pursuit of the absolute weapon. From India's perspective, a direct link between nuclear proliferation and international prestige existed: countries in possession of nuclear weapons enhanced their standing in the international system's power pyramid. Nuclear states, developed or underdeveloped, were (and continue to do so) taken seriously by other members of the international community because of the practical implications of possessing the ultimate weapon. India's perspective regarding nuclear symbolism was formed by observing the impact of China's 1964 nuclear explosion on Beijing's power status and international recognition of Chinese power which followed. In addition, China obtained its seat in the United Nations which had previously been denied. The United States' recognition of China's power demonstrated to India the symbolic importance of nuclear weapons in establishing a state's prestige. Remembering the existence of rivalry between the two states, the Chinese model of enhancing prestige propelled India to embark on a quest for horizontal nuclear proliferation to enhance its prestige, not only in the international context, but in regard to its territorial quarrel with China.

In contrast to India, and in spite of the 'Islamic bomb' rhetoric, Pakistan's nuclear proliferation program did not focus on enhancing the country's international prestige nor did it perceive nuclear weapons as a means of promoting a sense of Islamic nationalism. Reviewing the views of Pakistani scholars, strategists and officials regarding the country's motivations for nuclear proliferation clarifies the symbolic-model inefficiency for explaining the rubric of Pakistani proliferation policy. In an interview with Khan, former Pakistani Foreign Minister Agha Shahi rejected the existence of any considerations of symbolic type in Pakistan's military nuclear program. Similarly, the strategist Ross Masud, the Chairman and Director General of the Islamabad's Institute of Strategic Studies confirmed Shahi's view that the projection of Pakistani grandeur by nuclear weapons "has never been a factor in Pakistan's decision-makers' minds", contributing any enhancement in Pakistani prestige to an unintended "spillover effect". In this context, Pakistan's nuclear policy was fundamentally less concerned about the notion of prestige enhancement than national security. However, as mentioned by Masud, while the Pakistani horizontal nuclear proliferation could produce the prestige dimension, such an outcome could not be regarded as the cause of proliferation but as its secondary consequence. In addition, the much referred notion of the 'Islamic bomb' was in fact more of a rhetorical strategy to attract financial support from wealthy Arab states than a symbol of the Muslim states' international prestige. Therefore, the application of a symbolic-model framework on Pakistan's proliferation policy does not demonstrate the symbolic motive as a primary factor in the country's nuclear weapons development.

After outlining the general theoretical frameworks and their policy implication, the essay discussed India and Pakistan's motivations for horizontal nuclear proliferation according to the security model, the domestic politics model and the symbolic model, respectively. Analysing India's motivations through the security-model framework introduces nuclear China as primary incentive for India's nuclear proliferation and India's thrive for regional hegemony in the South Asia through deterring Pakistan as the secondary motivation.

In contrast, the same model shows that Pakistan's sole concern for deterring India as its primary motivation for nuclear proliferation. In the domestic level, while India's nuclear policy was heavily influenced by leaders' political motivations and nuclear energy establishments lobbying – Pakistan's proliferation policy, witnessing a high level of military influence, lacked a domestic politics perspective and was mostly concerned with security perspective. Finally, while the application of symbolic model on India's nuclear policy confirms the significance of nuclear symbolism in India's quest for international prestige through nuclear proliferation, it demonstrates prestige angle as secondary to security-centric Pakistani proliferation policy.

BALLISTIC AND CRUISE MISSILE PROLIFERATION

In the nuclear delivery front, both India and Pakistan have a series of ballistic and cruise missiles in addition to ground attack aircrafts. The maximum range among India's operational ballistic missiles is 2000 km achieved by Agni-2. India's Agni ballistic missiles are indigenously developed by its own missile defence industry known as *IGMDP*. The maximum range among Pakistan's missiles is by *Hatf V Gauri* which is reported to do over 2200 kms. Pakistan's Hatf missiles are based on North Korean *No-Dong* series of IRBMs. Both Pakistan's *Hatf* and India's *Agni* ballistic missiles are nuclear capable. India has also developed a supersonic cruise missile *BrahMos* which is by far the fastest cruise missile at Mach 2.6 and maximum range of 290 km. It is reported to be nuclear capable but it is not confirmed yet. On the Pakistan side, its *Babur* cruise missile has a reported range of 700 km and a maximum speed of 880 km/h (Mach 0.7). As with India *BrahMos, Babur* is also reported to be nuclear capable but there is no confirmation yet.

The Final Verdict

Both Pakistan and India are almost evenly matched head to head in nuclear and missile fronts, however India has strategic and technological superiority over the conventional forces of Pakistan. Indian Navy is larger in fleet and personnel size with a more varied range of ships including an aircraft carrier while Pakistan's Navy is smaller and has no aircraft carriers. Indian's IAF is equipped with highly capable fighters like 4.5th generation *Su-30*s and 4th gen *Mirage 2000*s which are technologically superior to Pakistan PAF's *F-16*s and *Mirage III*s. Additionally Indian pilots are better trained and more capable in air combat than Pakistani forces as was demonstrated by its various wars with Pakistan or joint exercises with US and UK. In the area of conventional ground forces both the Indian as well as Pakistani Army is well equipped and highly trained to survive in extremities of topography and climate in combat conditions, like wars in the high Himalayas.

If a purely conventional war were to take place between both these countries, India would most likely overpower Pakistan owing to its superior military technology and infrastructure, larger manpower, more territorial area and a strategic advantage in its sea and air forces. It must also be noted that a war between these two countries will matter more than India's conventional superiority as both these nations are nuclear powers on an equal deadlock. India has maintained a 'no first use' nuclear policy in the lines of a similar policy by China while Pakistan does not have any such policy, considering their only hope against India is in nuclear deterrance. It would be risky for India at the present scenario to go into any aggressive war against Pakistan as the repercussions would be serious a nuclear devastation for both countries.

Unfortunately India and Pakistan had adversarial relations since sixty years. After the Mumbai carnage Pakistan is under threat of pre-emptive strikes. Fourth Indo-Pakistan war could be triggered by another terrorist attack anywhere in India. This is a dangerous scenario. India and Pakistan have fought three wars, and war drums for the fourth war are getting louder.

It is in order therefore to comprehend Indian military capabilities, and Pakistan's ability to defend itself. Defense capability is an interplay of economic and military potential. Indian economy is booming, and its GDP growth is in double digits. The global recession has impacted Indian economy, but its defense capability remains intact. Military power and capabilities are sustained by economic and industrial potential. Geography, demography, population, oil resources and reserves, industrial capability including defense production, dollar reserves, self reliance, education, quality of manpower and leadership have a bearing on military power. Seven lakh Indian troops are tied down in Jammu and Kashmir. India has over one hundred billion dollar reserves. The West, Israel and Russia are India's weapon suppliers.

Indian Army has eighteen Corps with 34 Divisions including four Rapid Action Divisions, which would spear head ground offensives. Pakistan Army has ten Corps and twenty five divisions. Indian Army has eighteen Infantry, ten Mountain, three Armoured, and two Artillery Divisions. Besides it has five Infantry, one parachute, thirteen Air Defense, and four Engineering Brigades, designated as independent formations. In addition there are two Air Defense Groups, and fourteen Army Aviation Helicopter units. This is a sizeable force, capable of launching major offensives from several fronts.

The decentralized command structure will be an advantage, as compared to Pakistan's centralized Army command organization. Pakistan Army has an active force of 620,000 well trained personnel, with 528000 reservists, and

150000 para-military troops. Pakistan armed forces are seventh largest in the world. Pakistan Army's doctrine of "Offensive Defense", evolved by General Mirza Aslam Beg was put to test in 1989 in Exercise Zarb-e Momin. The doctrine is to launch a sizeable offensive into enemy territory, rather than wait for enemy strikes or attacks. In case of Indian land offensive Pakistan Army and Air Force will respond with land and air offensives to gain and hold enemy territory. Before embarking on further offensive, gains shall be consolidated. In 1990 the Central Corps of Reserves was created to fight in the desert sectors, where enemy land offensives are expected. These dual capable formations trained for offensive and holding actions are fully mechanized.

Pakistan Army has ten Corps including the newly formed Strategic Corps. The Army has twenty six divisions (eight less than India). Two more divisions were raised as Corps reserves for V and XXXI Corps. Pakistan Army has two armoured divisions, and ten independent armoured brigades. Presently one hundred thousand troops are stationed on the Pak Afghan border to fight terror. Special Service Group-SSG comprises two airborne Brigades i.e. six battalions.

Pakistan Army has 360 helicopters, over two thousand heavy guns, and 3000 APC's. Its main anti-tank weapons are Tow, Tow Mk II, Bakter Shiken and FGM 148 ATGM. The Army Air Defence Command has S.A- 7 Grail, General Dynamics FIM-92 Stinger, GD FIM Red Eye, and ANZA Mk-I, Mk-II, Mk-III and HQ 2 B surface ti air missiles. Radar controlled Oerlikon is the standard Ack Ack weapon system.

The ballistic missile inventory of the Army is substantial. It comprises Ghauri III and Shaheen III IRB'S; medium range Ghauri I and II and Shaheen II, and short range Hatf I- B, Abdali, Ghaznavi, Shaheen I and M -11 missiles. All the ballistic missiles can carry nuclear war heads. Nuclear and conventional weapon capable Babur Cruise missile is the new addition to Pakistan's strategic weapon inventory. Number of ballistic missiles and war heads are almost the same as India has. So there is a parity in nuclear weapons, which is a deterrent.

Indian armor is of Russian origin. Out of 2295 Indian Army's Main Battle tanks, 2235 are of Russian origin. The main battle tanks are; 310 T-90-S Bishsma's (300 are on order), 1925 T-72M Ajeya's.. The T-90 and the T-72 have 125 mm smooth barrel guns. T-72 though old is the backbone of Indian Armor Corp's. 268 Ajeya's have been upgraded with Israeli Elbit thermal imaging systems. 1000 T-72 MBT's are awaiting up-gradation. There have been several instances of T-72's gun barrel bursting. 124 Indian made Arjun (heavy 56 ton) MBT are on order. Sixty Arjun's are in operational service. Arjun's engine overheating problem has not been solved. Arjun has a 120 mm gun, but is unfit or desert operations. Pakistan Army is equally strong in armor, capable of giving a fitting response to any Indian military adventure.

Main Battle tanks Al-Khalid and Al-Zarrar are the backbone of Pakistan's armor Corp's. Both are Pakistan made. Pakistan's tank armory comprises :five hundred Al-Khalid MBT's; 320 Al-Zarrar type 85 II MBT's, 500 Al-Zarrar MBT's; 450 79II AP (Chinese type 81 upgrade, and 570 T-80 UD MBT of Ukranian make. In addition Pakistan has 880 Type 59, which were procured from China in 1970.This makes a total of three thousand six hundred and twenty tanks.

All Pakistani MBT's except T-59's have 125 mm smooth barrel guns. Indian armor offensives in Kashmir, Punjab, and Sind would be effectively challenged by Pakistani armor and mechanized formations, depending on PAF's ability to keep the skies over the battle areas clear of Indian Air Force. India's modern air defense system has Israeli Arrow anti-missile missiles, and 90,000 surface to air missiles-SAM's. India has one hundred nuclear armed ballistic missiles (Agni-1 and Agni II), and Brahmos the new supersonic cruise missile. Indian Army is well trained, equipped and highly professional, and so is Pakistan Army. Air power is likely to play a key, if not a decisive role in any future major or minor India-Pakistan armed conflict. The aim of Indian pre-emptive strikes will be maximum destruction by surprise air attacks, combined with shock commando action. A possibe scenario is; intensive bombing of the target to be followed by attacks by armed helicopters and ground assault by heliborne Commandoes. An overview of Indian Air Force and Pakistan Air Force will help comprehension of IAF's offensive capabilities, and defensive capabilities of Pakistan Air Force.

Indian Air Force has 3000 aircraft including training, transport, helicopters and 800-1000 combat air craft, which operate from sixty air bases, including Farkhor airbase in Tajikistan.. Six hundred IAF's strike and air defense fighters are expected to be operational. Pakistan Air Force has 630 aircraft, which include 530 combat aircraft, with 400 operational at any time. In 1996 India signed an agreement with Russia for the purchase of 90 Su 30 Mk-1 multi-role fighter-bombers. In 2004 a multi-billion licence was signed for building additional 140. 240 Su30-Mk-1's were ordered, 120 are already in service. With a maximum speed of Mach 2.3 and range of 8000 Km with refueling and ability to carry tons of conventional munitions and nuclear weapons, it is a lethal and menacing weapon system for the strike and interception role.

Other IAF's advanced strike and combat aircraft are: 51 Mirage-2000 (of Kargil fame), 60 Mig-29's (for air defense), 250 old Mig-21's (110 have been refurbished with Israeli help), 47 Jaguars and 70 Mig-27's for ground attack. 220 LCA Teja's under manufacture at HAL Bangalore will start entering service in 2010... IAF's fighter pilots are well trained and have out shone American pilots during joint exercises.

Pakistan Air Force has 200 rebuilt Mirage- 3's (for night air defense) and Mirage-5's for the strike role. They can carry nuclear weapons. They have been upgraded with new weapon systems, radars, and avionics. Additionally the PAF has 42 F-16's, 150 F-7's including 55 latest F-7 PG's. Manufacture of 150 JF 17 Thunder fighters (jointly designed) is underway at Pakistan Aeronautical Complex Kamra. The JF -17 Thunder is a 4th generation fly by wire multi-role fighter aircraft. Eight are already in PAF service. An order has been placed with China for the purchase of 36 JF-10, a Mach 2.3 -5th generation multi-role fighter, comparable in performance to the Su-30 Mk-1 with the Indian Air Force. PAF is on Red Alert, and is maintaining full vigil to intercept and destroy IAF intruders.

During the recent air space violation, the IAF intruders were in the sights of PAF's F-16's, but were allowed to escape unscathed to avoid a major diplomatic crisis. PAF pilots and technicians are well trained, high professionals, who will be able to prove their mettle in the future battle with India. A comparison of Indian Navy and Pakistan Navy reveals that Pakistan Navy could inflict substantial damage to the Indian Navy. Indian Navy has 16 submarines; Pakistan Navy has ten, some are brand new. Indian Navy has 27 war ships, Pakistan Navy has ten. Indian Aircraft Carrier Veerat, will be a menace, and must be sunk by submarine or air attacks, if it attempts to block Pakistan's sea lanes or ports. It is hoped that better sense prevails and India desists from invading and attacking Pakistan. If it does, the consequences will be horrible for both the countries.

Manpower and Ground Forces

India has the second largest manpower in its military globally - at 3,773,300 personell (2005), next only to China. Pakistan has a much smaller manpower of 1,449,000 personell which is proportionally higher than India in terms of their population ratios. Pakistan's ground forces are equipped with American or Chinese weapons like FIM 92 Stinger SAMs, BGM-71 TOW anti-tank missiles, T-82 tanks and other equipments. Indian ground forces are equipped mostly by home-made or Soviet technologies like IR guided 9K35 Strela-10 SAMs, 3rd Gen IR guided Nag anti-tank missiles, UAVs and a large inventory of tanks and support vehicles. In terms of numbers and equipments, both Indian and Pakistani ground forces are on an closely equal footing.

Comparison of Air Forces

As of 2006, Indian Air Force (IAF) has over 170,000 personnel and 3,382 aircrafts of which 1,330 are combat aircrafts operating off 61 airbases - making it the fourth largest air force in the world. India's strike fighters consist of Russian and French aircrafts like Mikoyan MiG-29, Dassault Mirage 2000, Sukhoi Su-30 - the last one developed under dual licensing by HAL, India's aerospace industry in Bangalore.

In addition to these, India's air force owns ground attack aircrafts, reconnaissance aircrafts, UAVs and support helicopters - a majority of them either of Soviet or French origin. Pakistan Air Force (PAF) has about 530 combat aircrafts and over 65,000 active personnel, operating out of 9 airbases. Its strike fighters consist of US, Chinese and French fighters like F-16 Fighting Falcon, JF-17 Thunder and Dassault Mirage ROSE-III. It also has transport aircrafts like Lockheed Martin C-130 and Airbus A310, however there are no UAVs or reconnaissance aircrafts in the Pakistani Air Force.

Naval and Sea Based Forces

After the overwhelming losses in the 1971 war against India, Pakistan rapidly increased the size of its naval fleet which doubled in the 1980s after a massive 3.2 billion dollar military and economic aid by US President Ronald Reagan. At present, Pakistan's navy owns over 45 vessels, most of them of US or European origin which include submarines, destroyers, frigates, patrol and mine warfare boats. It operates from its sole naval port in Karachi and naval facilities in UK, USA and France.

It had recently been involved in various humanitarian operations during the 2005 Tsunami in South East Asia. Indian Navy on the other hand, is a three dimensional naval force consisting of missile-capable warships, an aircraft carrier, mine sweepers and a host of marine aircrafts; most of its warships indigenously built in its own dockyards. The navy operates from its major naval bases in Visakhapatnam, Mumbai, Goa and the Andaman Islands. Indian Navy has significant capabilities of being a true blue water Navy and is experienced both in war and peacekeeping operations in the Indian Ocean.

The Nuclear Club

India tested a nuclear bomb in 1974 using materials from Canada and technical help from Soviet Union. However the embargo in heavy water export from Canada after the test stalled India's nuclear ambitions till 1998, when it shocked the world by conducting five nuclear detonations termed as Shakti tests.

The highest yield was by a 48 kiloton staged fusion device, which India claimed was a thermonuclear bomb but seismic data on the tests proved otherwise. In the same year 1998, Pakistan conducted a series of six nuclear detonations in a test termed as Chagai.

The highest yield was reported to be about 25 kiloton from a two stage boosted device. At present Pakistan's nuclear stockpile is slated to be around 30-40 warheads while India possesses 70-100 warheads. The nuclearisation of India and Pakistan became a turning point in the history of conflicts between these two countries with high tensions but no war, not very much unlike the US vs USSR Cold War.

CONCLUSION

In years since the end of the cold war, the increased proliferation of ballistic missile systems and weapons of mass destruction has raised the importance of developing and fielding a capable BMD system for the United States. The fundamental goal of the planned U.S. missile defence programme is to build a layered defence to defend the United States and its forces, territories, allies and friends. Whether the United States will be able to achieve this very ambitious goal remains to be seen.

However, it cannot be denied that the U.S. pursuit of BMD has transformed the global strategic landscape, and India, along with other states, is trying to grapple with its implications. India has been debating the implications of missile defences for its own security for some time now and, though this debate has been overtaken by other developments, the Indian government has struggled to come up with a coherent policy response to the changing strategic parameters ushered in by the missile defence programme of the United States.

The Indian debate on the missile defence is an extension of the larger debate on India's nuclear weapons policy. But as this chapter has argued, it is also about the strategic direction of Indian foreign policy in the coming years. While a lot of attention has been focused in the technical details of the missile defence programme and its utility or disutility for Indian security needs, the debate in India is also about the larger issues that confront Indian foreign policy in the new millennium, More than the technical issues, it is the political ramifications of missile defence that require greater scrutiny.

As the United States proceeds with the deployment of the BMD, this debate can only be expected to intensify. The Indian government will also come under increasing pressure to make its stand clear on this contentious issue. Of course, India's diplomatic efforts will focus on carving out a policy response that enhances its security and its technological and economic interests. But the exact ramifications of the long-term missile defence plans of the United States for India's strategic environment still remain in the realm of speculation. While India has made gradual and steady technological advances in its missile defence programme in the last few years, the Indian government's position remains far from coherent on this issue. Even as it has continued to allow the DRDO and the armed forces to receive briefings from the U.S. teams, the Indian Foreign Minister has been quoted as saying that the question of India's participation in the U.S.-led missile defence system does not arise. At a minimum, it seems that the Indian government does not have a well-thought policy on the issue.

As the major powers reduce their nuclear arsenals missile defence will become increasingly rational. Ultimately, technology will determine whether it will be fully deployed or not rather than arms control considerations. India would not like to be behind in this technological race and the politics of missile defence in India is bound to grow more interesting in the future.

3

Defence Security Policy of India

Have we learned any lessons from our experiences during the Nehru era and in subsequent years? Anyone looking dispassionately at our defence and security policies over the decades would respond only in the negative. India frittered away its militarily advantageous position towards the end of Indo-Pakistan War of 1971 when we failed to exploit the operational situation in the Western Front that could have given us back our territory. This was much like towards the end of 1947-48 Indo-Pak conflict when Indian forces were ordered to stop operations. After the cessation of hostilities in 1971, we allowed Pakistan a victory on the negotiating table when India could have at least forced Pakistan's Prime Minister Zulfikar Ali Bhutto in the Simla Agreement of 1972, to convert the cease fire line into a permanent border as we had over 90,000 Pakistani soldiers in our custody.

Some specious response from Bhutto as to what face will he show to Pakistani public was accepted as a justified explanation. Our politico-bureaucratic psyche apparently is averse to following hard policy choices in pursuit of our well cherished and identifiable national interests. Leeway given to Bhutto then and his single minded pursuit of building an Islamic bomb that was successful has created more obstacles for settling the Kashmir issue favourably from the Indian point of view.

Like Nehru allowed Sheikh Abdullah and his cohorts to travel to Pakistan and exchange views with the Pakistani leadership, we continue to show irrational leniency to the separatist Hurriyat leadership and other hostile and anti-national elements to not only confer with officials of Pakistan's High Commission in New Delhi but also to travel to Pakistan, obviously for purposes that would be contrary to India's national interests.

It is a well known fact that such Kashmiri leaders have met those very leaders who sponsor terrorism both in Kashmir and all over India. It needs to be remembered that Sheikh Abdullah, in what is known as Kashmir Conspiracy case, was charged with treason for arranging to supply arms and explosives sourced from Pakistan as part of a conspiracy against the State. Despite the proof presented to Nehru about the involvement of Sheikh Abdullah in the conspiracy, he got him released and allowed him to Pakistan under the mistaken belief that something good might come out of the visit.

Currently, the present government is again inclined to follow soft policies towards Pakistan based on professions of peace by the newly elected Prime Minister Nawaz Sharif knowing very well that Pakistan's India and Afghanistan policies are dictated by the military and security establishment. Plans by Prime Minister Manmohan Singh to visit Pakistan based on the invitation extended by Nawaz Sharif have not been entirely discarded even as India has been waiting for Islamabad to deliver on the masterminds of 26/11 Mumbai terrorist attacks. It is quite evident that there has been no fundamental change in perceptions of Pakistani establishment that it is only cross-border terrorism that moves India to engage with Pakistan and possibly give some concessions to them especially on Kashmir. While India has somehow managed to handle military and security threats from Pakistan, it is the ever expanding Pakistan-China nexus that presents an invidious and most dangerous threat to India's security. It is only a few years back that the Indian Army started propagating a military doctrine to meet the threat of two front war. In a throwback to the Nehruvian policies, the government was more inclined to handle such threats diplomatically rather than spend additional defence funds for arising and equipping of requisite military formations and necessary air support.

The report 'Non Alignment 2.0: A Foreign and Strategic Policy for India in Twenty First Century' authored by a group of eminent experts, that included a member from National Security Advisor (NSA) Shiv Shankar Menon's staff and where NSA also attended some of the deliberations of the group, while talking about military capabilities has opined that *"we need to be clear about what kinds of offensive capabilities will be useful. The prevailing assumption that we should raise and deploy a 'mountain strike corps' against China is problematic. For it simply risks replicating all the problems with our existing strike corps under worse geographic and logistic conditions."* In short, it is not only the economic burden of raising such forces but the mindset about provoking China redolent of Nehru era persists. The report also talks of instigating an insurgency in our areas after they have been captured by the Chinese forces which conveys a defeatist attitude.

Further, what needs to be noticed is that since 2008 not only PLA has improved its posture in Tibet it has undertaken a number of incursions across the Line of Actual Control. This stance of assertive PLA in Tibet has been made possible by the massive build up of logistic structure in Tibet to include extensive railway network and over 58,000 kilometres of roads. The roads have been built up to Indian borders and have also penetrated Nepal. This would ensure smooth induction of the PLA troops in any contingency. This contrasts with our poor civil and military structure even after a lapse of over six decades. No doubt India has recently embarked on activating its old airfields along Sino-Indian border and the MOD has chalked out a plan for building extensive road net work and other infrastructure facilities but our record in implementing plans and projects has so far been very tardy. Thus the asymmetrical situation with China that existed in past during Nehruvian times and thereafter has not been rectified.

Recent incursions by the PLA in Depsang and Chumar areas of Ladakh sector also reveals the government's disinclination to reveal such incidents along the border to the public which conforms to its past practice of withholding such information from the public lest it may embarrass the government in some manner or the other. Apparently, Foreign Minister Salman Khurshid and later Defence Minister Mr. AK Antony have visited Beijing subsequent to these incidents in April and June 2013 which seemed from all angles as conciliatory gestures to China's aggressive policies in line with appeasement policies of Nehru.

The deficiencies in terms of both military capabilities and defence equipment continue to plague our forces. Shortage of basic wherewithal like ammunition deficiencies, need for improvement of ammunition dumps et al as brought out by the current and previous Army Chiefs, continue to persist. There are large scale voids which have also been described as 'critical hollowness' in the army that includes tanks running out of ammunition, obsolete air defence systems and lack of essential weaponry, and lack of critical surveillance and night-fighting capabilities for infantry and special forces. There is an inadequate HUMINT in the border areas and depth and breadth of ELINT, COMINT and satellite cover for intelligence, surveillance and reconnaissance needs to be enhanced.

There have been some improvements in defence organization, structures and processes but the civil-military relations leave lot to be desired. Similarly, there is a lack of integration and jointness in our armed forces. Even though Naresh Chandra's Task Force in their report recommended the institution of the post of a Chairman Joint Chiefs of Staff, the government has shot down that proposal which in any case was a climb down from the Chief of Defence Staff recommended earlier by a Group of Ministers in 2001. HQ Integrated Defence Staff created for enhancing jointness and integration does not have adequate powers or wherewithal to enforce it. Even NAM 2.0 report has recommended many relevant structural changes in the Ministry of Defence to improve civil-military relations but there seems to be lack of political will to implement such recommendations; the shibboleths of past that military might somehow establish ascendancy over the civil or political set up fail to go away.

There is a strong sense of déjà vu that is palpable in the current political approach to defence and security policies which leaves India vulnerable to China's rising military capabilities and its assertive policies across the Line of Actual Control.

While China has been single mindedly pursuing its long term objectives in Ladakh and Arunachal Pradesh sectors, Indian response to China's strategy remains confused and subdued. Further, Pakistan would be too happy to join China in any adventure against India. While diplomatic approach would be of some help, the government needs to take an urgent action to mitigate the gap in military capabilities along the Indo-Tibetan borders that is becoming wider with the passage of time.

THE NEED FOR A STRATEGIC VISION FOR THE TWENTY FIRST CENTURY

India sadly lacks a 'Strategic Vision'. Vision is defined as 'imaginative insight, statesman like foresight, political sagacity.' 'Strategic Vision' would imply the application of imaginative, statesmanlike foresight and political sagacity by India's political leadership to the nation's national security management and long-range strategic planning to counter both external and internal security threats. Hence 'Strategic Vision' for India would imply the need for :

- Political statesmanship that can have a penetrative foresight of how India can be led to its aspirational goals of being a leading regional and global power.
- Political leadership that can translate India's 'Strategic Vision' into time-bound implementation plans. These implementation plans should incorporate short term, medium term and long term goals.
- Political leadership which is resolute, forceful and determined to direct an integrated national effort towards achieving strategic goals, cutting

through bureaucratic red-tapism and lethargy. National security and strategic implementation should have an over-riding priority over all other national activities.

- Political leadership that is bold and audacious and which will ensure that in the pursuit of India's 'strategic vision', any attempts to thwart it by external or internal threats are met with prompt, decisive and crippling military responses. Power is meant to be used to nip any emerging threats to India's national security.

India's 'Strategic Vision' for the 21st century should incorporate the following goals and components and which should be reflected in appropriate declaratory policies binding across the entire Indian political spectrum:

- India is to be the predominant power in the Indian sub-continent. It already is in terms of size, natural resources and human resources. It has an unbridgeable lead in the sub-continent in terms of economy, industrial development and infrastructure and hi-technology wherewithal. India however is not the pre-dominant military power, as Pakistan has been built up as the 'regional spoiler' state by China in terms of a nuclear weapons and missile arsenal. China has been engaged for the last two decades specifically to arrest India's emergence as the predominant power in South Asia by its proxy efforts through Pakistan.
- India is one of the major powers of Asia, along with China and Japan. To this end India's strategic strengths should be built at an accelerated pace and strategic partnerships evolved to ensure that India becomes a determinant in any regional or global power considerations in political, economic and military terms.

To achieve this ' strategic vision' for the 21st century India needs to develop strategically and in military terms, the following capabilities:

- Military preponderance in both the nuclear and conventional military fields. In terms of levels, it should have an overwhelming military superiority in South Asia and relative parity with China.
- India needs to develop 'force projection' capabilities, especially naval and air. Sizeable air-mobile and naval task forces should be available for rapid deployment in India's area of interest and 'areas of influence'.
- India's naval power should be built to levels which would permit sea-denial if not sea-control in the entire Indian Ocean region.
- Nuclear deterrence strong enough to deter even major powers to attempt political or military coercion i.e., development of an ICBM and

> SLBM arsenal. India after fifty years of being a 'Soft State' needs to get into a resurgent mode befitting her size and resources. The time has come not only to have the will to build up her power attributes but also to learn and have the will to use power.

Political leadership of a very high order and calibre is required to lead India towards the achievement of the 'strategic vision' thus envisioned.

INDIA'S FOREIGN POLICY : THE WILL TO USE POWER

For over half a century, the Indian nation state has continuously been projected as a 'Soft State' by the politicisation of national security issues restraining firm responses. India's political leadership shied away from the use of national power to safeguard India's security or sought soft escape routes. All of them exalted the fig-leaf of non-alignment into a virtue and some of them even justifying it as a well thought out and well deliberated strategy of India's national security. The foreign policy of India continued to reflect these sentiments of the national elite i.e., soft responses to external aggression and proxy wars.

India's responses in this field are more akin to those of the United States in earlier years. Robert E Osgood states : "America's non-political approach to war must also be ascribed to a depreciation of the factor of power in international relations. In order to employ military power as a rational and effective instrument of national policy, a nation must have a foreign policy that is defined in terms appropriate to power." India to this day, shies away from this precept, despite possessing all the attributes of power.

NATIONAL SECURITY ISSUES SHOULD NOT BE POLITICISED

India presents a regrettable phenomenon where political opposition parties, in the absence of any other political issue, tend to politicise national security issues.

In this process and in their zeal to discomfit the ruling party at any cost, they fail to realise the impact it has on the Armed Forces of India – their morale, their will to fight and their entire confidence in the political structure of the Indian nation state is seriously jeopardised. The most recent examples of this politicisation of India's national security issues pertain to the then opposition parties reaction to India's nuclear weaponisation in 1998, their ill-informed criticisms during the Pakistan aggression in Kargil in 1999 and thereafter and their attitudinal problems to the Indian Army operations against the Pakistan sponsored proxy war in Jammu and Kashmir

State. National security issues have hardly been discussed by political parties during Defence budget debates in Parliament.

The parliamentary attendance then presents a sorry spectacle. Yet when grave national crises occur every second politician becomes a master strategist or tactician minus the grasp of the essentials of strategy and the intricacies of military operations and oblivious to the fact that the parliamentarians own strategic incompetence brought about the military aggression in the first place.

India's political leaders need to get together and work out conventions where during a crisis they can discuss the issues away from the glare of publicity and arrive at a consensus on how the Indian nation state has to meet the security challenges that arise.

INDIA'S NATIONAL WILL: THE NEED TO BE BRAVE

National will can be described as the collective will of the Indian people to face and withstand a grave crisis, both nationally and individually. In terms of the latter, this came into a grave focus during the painful crisis of the hijacking of Indian Airlines Flight IC. 814 by Pakistani terrorists to Kandahar in Afghanistan.

By courtesy of the irresponsible Indian media, day in and day out during the period, Indian TV channels projected pathetic images of the near and dear ones of the hijacked passengers. While their agony is well understood but not the wailing and crying and demanding the government to bring back their people at any cost. This put unbearable public pressure on the Indian government to submit to all demands of the hijackers including release of dreaded terrorists of Islamic Jehadi organisations.

India's national will was on a pitiable display during those days. One could contrast this with the people of Israel or Japan or Germany. Those peoples would have remained dignified, composed and determined that irrespective of the personal cost, their country should not buckle down before hijackers demands. It is also a lesson for the Indian government not to buckle down to public pressure which affect India's national image, irrespective of the cost.

Asymmetric threats to India's national security are likely to increase where the Indian public gets more and more targeted. It needs to steel its will, endurance, self-discipline and develop a stoic attitude to bravely face violent attacks, suicide bombings and hijackings. India's political leadership has to prepare the public.

The Indian media has to restrain itself from impulsive sensationalism. India's parliamentarians have to desist from politicising such national security issues. None of them went on the air to advise the affected people to be brave during the crisis and that the crisis has to be faced even at the cost of personal loss.

India's rapidly expanding middle class needs to decide whether they want to make themselves fit to continue as a nation. Probably, the best prescription for this shortcoming is to make National Service in the Indian Armed Forces a compulsory requirement.

It cannot be forgotten that "NATIONAL WILL" is one of the major components in the power-estimation that our enemies make of India's strengths in terms of its national power and military power. India's substantial power attributes in other fields are of no consequence, if India's NATIONAL WILL can be so easily subverted.

INDIA'S NATIONAL HONOUR : THE NEED FOR SENSITIVITY

India's "National Honour" and respect and sensitivity to maintain it should be the essence and epitome of its nationhood. Even amplifying it from dictionary meanings "India's National Honour" would imply "High Respect for India as a Nation"; it would imply "Glory for the Indian Nation" and lastly it would imply "Nobleness of Mind to Uphold India's Reputation".

Examples of how India's 'National Honour' gets compromised at the highest levels are listed below:

- India's national honour is impinged when parliamentarians and legislators reduce the sanctified precincts of parliament and legislatures into street corner squabbles.
- India's national honour is impinged when India's parliamentarians and political parties politicise national security issues.
- India's national honour is impinged when India's political leaders are projected on Pakistan TV mouthing pronouncements detrimental to India's national interests prompted by narrow electoral gains to please narrow religion– based constituencies.
- India's national honour is violated when India displays lack of will to take pre-emptive actions against its enemies who inflict proxy war, terrorism and suicide bombings on the Indian state.
- India's honour is at stake when India expects others to restrain or pressurise its enemies from onslaughts against India by external or internal aggression.

- India's national honour is singed when its political and intellectual elites and the Indian media indulge in criticising and condemning the Indian nation state's policies by imposing western liberalist templates, forgetting that India's contextual environment is different and calls for different solutions.

India's "National Honour" is "indivisible". It cannot be divided by India's politicians on grounds of secularism and pseudo-secularism. It cannot be divided on grounds of majority versus minority.

It cannot be divided on grounds of caste and backwardness. It cannot be argued that the Hindu concept of "National Honour" has to be different from India's Muslims concept of "National Honour". It cannot be argued that the Congress, Leftists and Samajwadi Party's concept of "National Honour" is distinct from the Bharatiya Janata Party's or Shiv Sena's concept of "National Honour".

Conclusion

It needs to be stressed that India's national security and defence is not solely, the duty of the Indian Armed Forces

India's national security and defence is equally the responsibility of all its citizens. They must not only study matters military, but also be alive to dangers to India's security, both from external and internal threats. As regards India's parliamentarians and politicians are concerned, their responsibility in this respect is far more. .

All citizens of India are charged by Article 51-A Clause (c) of India's Constitution "to uphold and protect the sovereignty, unity and integrity of India. Clause (j) of the Fundamental Duties also states "to strive towards excellence in all spheres of individual and collective activity so that the nation constantly rises to higher levels of endeavour and achievement".

INDIA'S NUCLEAR DOCTRINE AND POLICY

India's nuclear policy is underpinned by a categorical and unambiguous commitment to "no first use" of nuclear weapons against nuclear armed adversaries and the non-use of nuclear weapons against non-nuclear weapons states. This is rooted in a deeply ingrained cultural belief that the use of force to resolve inter-state disputes is a repugnant concept.

Even though India was subjected to numerous invasions throughout the second millennium, particularly through the Khyber Pass in the northwest, India's strategic approach continued to be rooted in a philosophy of defensive-defence.1 Offensive strategic concepts such as the Great Game played by the British in Central Asia during the Raj were alien to Indian thinking and were quickly discarded by Jawaharlal Nehru, India's first Prime Minister, in favour of a doctrine of peaceful co-existence.

Independent India's leaders were quick to realise the vast potential of nuclear weapons to stoke political fires and for over 50 years India followed a consistent approach to rid the world of nuclear weapons. Many decades before Presidents Reagan and Gorbachev came to the conclusion that nuclear wars cannot be won and therefore should not be fought, total, universal nuclear disarmament was a key objective of India's foreign policy.

Though India had the potential to develop nuclear weapons since the first nuclear explosion at Pokhran in 1974, India steadfastly refrained from exercising its nuclear option and, despite a deteriorating security environment, chose instead to work for nuclear disarmament. Reflecting a strong strand of Indian public opinion (though never a majority view), Prime Minister Morarji Desai had said in an interview to Barbara Walters of American Broadcasting Company (ABC) that he would never go in for nuclear weapons "even if the entire country is destroyed in their absence." When supreme national security interests eventually dictated that India had no option but to go further down the nuclear road, India adopted a purely defensive no first use nuclear policy. This policy is not only consistent with its strategic culture, but also extremely responsible and mindful of the horrendous destruction that nuclear weapons can cause.

India also opted to develop only a credible "minimum" nuclear deterrent due to the widespread recognition that nuclear weapons are political weapons and not weapons of warfighting and their sole purpose is to deter the use and threat of use of nuclear weapons.

There is a broad national consensus on the development of a credible minimum nuclear deterrent capability and the doctrine of no first use. Minimum deterrence may be defined as "a small force of survivable nuclear weapons (that) would deter an adversary from initiating military action that would threaten a nation's vital interests." India is not looking at establishing any capability beyond this level of deterrence.

The concept of deterrence by denial, rather than deterrence by punishment, is central to Indian strategic thinking. However, by voluntarily renouncing its sovereign right of the first use of nuclear weapons to defeat nuclear threats and to prevent nuclear blackmail, India has made an immense strategic sacrifice and imposed a heavy burden upon itself. The government and key decision-makers recognise that should deterrence ever break down, India will have to pay an enormous price for a nuclear first strike by an adversary before retaliating in kind. Hundreds of thousands of Indian lives will be lost and more than one city may be turned into rubble. Hence, India's no first use doctrine demands a robust, infallible and potentially insuperable nuclear deterrent capability to ensure that India never has to suffer a nuclear strike.

India's May 1998 nuclear tests were followed by many policy pronouncements in rapid succession. In an interview with India Today soon after the nuclear tests, Prime Minister Atal Behari Vajpayee said that there was no need to cover the nuclear explosions "with a veil of secrecy... India now is a nuclear weapons state." On May 27, 1998, Atal Behari Vajpayee, India's Prime Minister, stated in Parliament- suo motu Statement of the Prime Minister in Parliament): "We do not intend to use these (nuclear) weapons for aggression or for mounting threats against any country; these are weapons of self-defence, to ensure that India is not subjected to nuclear threats or coercion. We do not intend to engage in an arms race." On May 29, 1998, the day following Pakistan's nuclear tests at Chagai, Prime Minister Vajpayee announced in Parliament that India had declared a voluntary moratorium on further nuclear testing, was ready to engage in negotiations for an FMCT, had undertaken to exercise stringent export controls on nuclear and missile related technologies as well as those relating to other weapons of mass destruction and had offered to discuss a no first use agreement with Pakistan and other countries, bilaterally or in a multilateral forum.

The government also affirmed that India's nuclear threat perceptions were not country specific. On December 15, 1998, Prime Minister Vajpayee spelt out the principal elements of India's nuclear policy in a statement in Parliament: India's resolve to preserve its nuclear independence, minimum nuclear deterrence, no first use, non-use of nuclear weapons against non-nuclear powers, and a firm commitment to the elimination of nuclear weapons. The Prime Minister also reiterated India's willingness to sign the CTBT and re-stated India's readiness to work towards the successful conclusion of the Fissile Materials Cut-off Treaty (FMCT). At the Non-Aligned Summit in Durban in 1998, the Movement accepted India's proposal for an international conference to arrive at an agreement on a phased programme for the complete elimination of all nuclear weapons. At the Millennium Summit of the United Nations in September 2000, the Indian Prime Minister asserted that India's policy is based on "responsibility and restraint" and that India would continue to press for universal, verifiable nuclear disarmament with undiminished commitment, even while safeguarding "our strategic space and autonomy in decision-making. International peace cannot be divorced from the need for equal and legitimate security for all." Before examining India's draft nuclear doctrine, it would be instructive to take a look at the nuclear doctrines of its two regional neighbours.

CHINA

China's nuclear deterrence doctrine has been in synchrony with its conventional warfighting doctrine. It was initially based on self-defence during the era of "people's war". It gradually shifted to one of minimum nuclear deterrence during the 1960s and 1970s and now appears to have stabilised at limited nuclear deterrence, which includes nuclear coercion. China's limited deterrence may be defined as a concept of "having enough capabilities to deter conventional, theatre and strategic nuclear war, and control and suppress escalation during a nuclear war."

However, China's nuclear force structure reveals capabilities that go well beyond the requirements of minimum deterrence. For minimum deterrence, it would be sufficient for China to have long-range ballistic missiles that are capable of delivering effective nuclear strikes against the other four nuclear powers. China's shorter-range ballistic missiles such as CSS-2s and CSS-5s (1,700-km range) can only be used against its immediate neighbours. Gregory S. Jones is of the view that China clearly has a more complex nuclear policy that does not rule out a nuclear first strike against its neighbours under certain circumstances.

China still continues to insist that it will abide by its doctrine of no first use of nuclear weapons. Sha Zhukang, China's Director-General of Arms Control and Disarmament, reiterated China's no first use policy in March 1999: "Because of our own bitter experience of being blackmailed, we have declared to the world we would never be the first to use nuclear weapons." China also observes a policy of "negative security assurances" implying that it will not use nuclear weapons against non-nuclear countries. However, China has lately added several caveats and qualifications to its professed doctrine. The most important of these is that China's military planners do not consider the use of nuclear weapons on their own territory as violative of their no first use doctrine. Obviously, as China claims Taiwan as its own territory, it would be logical to assume that the Chinese may resort to the first use of nuclear weapons during a war over Taiwan. Similarly, China lays claim to the entire Indian state of Arunachal Pradesh (approximately 90,000 square Kilometres in area) and India would need to vector this factor into its strategic calculations. China is also yet to formally recognise the accession of Sikkim to India.

China's leaders have repeatedly emphasised that the fielding of a NMD system by the US or the deployment of Theatre Missile Defence (TMD) systems by Japan and Taiwan will be considered extremely detrimental to China's national security interests and China will take all steps that are necessary to enhance the effectiveness of its nuclear weapons. Tang Jiaxuan, China's Foreign Minister, has stated that, "The development and research of NMD exerts a negative impact on the global and regional strategic balance and stability...

I wish to point out emphatically that if some people want to include Taiwan in the TMD, then that would amount to an encroachment on China's sovereignty and territorial integrity." Besides unilaterally abrogating some of its nuclear weapons-related treaty obligations, China can be expected to substantially increase the number of ICBMs in its nuclear armoury and also graduate to MIRVs for increasing the number of targets that would be presented to NMD and TMD systems so that its nuclear warheads have a relatively better rate of survival after launch. China may even abandon its decades old no first use commitment and adopt a more aggressive nuclear doctrine. Which way China will ultimately go is at present too close to call, but it is to China's credit that besides India it is the only other NWS that stands for no first use.

PAKISTAN

As Pakistan's military rulers have so often emphasised, Pakistan's rationale for its nuclear weapons is not only to deter the threat of India's nuclear weapons but also to counter India's conventional military superiority. Even during the short interludes when duly elected civilian Prime Ministers have ruled the country, Pakistan's foreign and military policies have been crafted in the army's General Headquarters (GHQ) at Rawalpindi, particularly the policies relating to India. Ever since the inception of its nuclear programme, Pakistan's nuclear weapons have been in military custody and the country's civilian rulers have had no control over them. It is, therefore, no surprise that Pakistan has adopted a first use nuclear doctrine. Its military and political leaders have repeatedly stated that Pakistan would resort to the early use of nuclear weapons in a conventional conflict to prevent its comprehensive military defeat at India's hands and to ensure that its survival as a viable nation state is not threatened.

Among others, Pakistan's rationale for its first use doctrine has been cogently spelt out by Lieutenant General Sardar F. S. Lodhi. Writing in the Pakistan Defence Journal, General Lodhi states:

In a deteriorating military situation when an Indian conventional attack is likely to break through our defences or has already breached the main defence line causing a major set-back to the defences which cannot be restored by conventional means at our disposal, the government would be left with no option except to use nuclear weapons to stabilise the situation. India's superiority in conventional arms and manpower would have to be offset by nuclear weapons...

Pakistan's nuclear doctrine would, therefore, essentially revolve around the first strike option. In other words, we will use nuclear weapons if attacked by India even if the attack is with conventional weapons... Pakistan would use what Stephen Cohen calls an "option enhancing" policy. This would entail a stage-by-stage approach in which the nuclear threat is increased at each step to deter India from attack. The first step could be a public or private warning, the second a demonstration explosion of a small nuclear weapon on its own soil, the third step would be the use of a few nuclear weapons on its own soil against Indian attacking forces. The fourth stage would be used against critical but purely military targets in India across the border from Pakistan - probably in thinly populated areas in the desert or semi-desert, causing least collateral damage... Some weapons would be in reserve for the counter value role.

Brigadier Saeed Ismat of the Pakistan Army also expresses similar views and propounds the first strike doctrine to checkmate an Indian offensive which almost all Pakistani defence analysts appear to believe will be aimed at dismembering Pakistan:

There could be many scenarios (of Indian offensive strikes into Pakistan) but just to illustrate this point, let us visualise if an Indian military invasion came through the Rajasthan desert directed towards the Grand Trunk road near Rahimyar Khan, in a matter of days, India could cut off our north-south communication, divide and dislocate our military forces and divide the country in two.

The capture of this critical space could act as a springboard to launch further manoeuvres of exploitation towards areas in depth. If they choose to limit their objectives, they could consolidate and retain these spaces. This action by itself can cause strategic division and isolation of our forces, leading to ultimate defeat and break up of the nation. In conjunction with (ground) offensives in other areas as well, they could prolong the war and go for our areas in depth. Pakistan's options would have foreclosed - except one! We should have a well defined and declared strategy of using our ultimate choice of nuclear weapons aimed at the destruction of those military forces, which have intruded in our territory.

Pakistan's policy planners and military leaders have always gone out of their way to try to convince India that Pakistan's nuclear threshold is low. Quoting Abdul Sattar (now Pakistan's Foreign Minister), Agha Shahi and Zulfiqar Ali Khan's jointly authored article in Dawn on October 5, 1999, C. Uday Bhaskar has written: "The exigency under which Pakistan may use nuclear weapons is spelt out as: 'Although the precise contingencies in which Pakistan may use nuclear weapons have not been articulated or even defined by the government, the assumption has been that if the enemy launches a war and undertakes a piercing attack to occupy large territories or communications junctions, the weapon of last resort would have to be invoked." This may actually be rhetoric designed to deter India through a doctrine of irrationality rather than a carefully considered policy option that can be executed when the chips are down. If Pakistani military and political analysts think things through, they will be forced to conclude that while Pakistan may initiate a graduated nuclear response, as General Lodhi recommends, and achieve short-term tactical gains, India is likely to retaliate massively as per its declared nuclear doctrine of punitive retaliation and Pakistan would cease to exist as a viable nation state. In an interview with CBS TV in October 2000, General Pervez Musharraf, Pakistan's military ruler, asserted that Pakistan could use its nuclear bomb against India if its security is jeopardised. It is a suicidal policy indeed for Pakistani defence planners and policy makers to glibly talk of initiating nuclear exchanges with India without having an escalation dominance capability and knowing fully well that their country would be wiped out from the map regardless of how much damage their nuclear weapons may cause to India.

INDIA'S POLITICAL GOVERNANCE: THE NEED FOR A QUALITATIVE CHANGE

Good political governance is an imperative requirement of the power attributes of any nation aspiring to be a big power. Power status, decisive political leadership, strategic vision, military preparedness, economic advancement and national cohesion cannot be achieved without good political governance.

The indicators of power potential which foreign countries look for pertaining to India all centre around and are focussed on political stability and good governance.

In India's march towards her future goals of being a major power, the weakest link in that achievement is India's political governance and the quality of her polity. This is not an individual opinion but the general opinion of one and all, namely, contempt for the politicians and their ethical standards. Qualitative change in the polity and political governance of India can only be brought about by a conscious and deliberate effort by political leaders of major political parties. It is they who have to set irreproachable high standards personally and also ensure that party tickets are given to intelligent, mature and dedicated men and women of substance. Leaders of major political parties need to discipline their unruly parliamentarians and legislators.

India's polity should not take it for granted that they are not under scrutiny. Ironically this polity which claims to have a prerogative on national leadership stands paralysed qualitatively. This has a grave effect on India, strategically and militarily.

EMERGING SECURITY CHALLENGES

Even as India grapples with diverse external and internal threats to its security, many new challenges are emerging on the security horizon. Before the dangers evident in them can be addressed, the emerging threats need to be identified and understood. The major emerging threats are outlined below:

- Increasing demands for electric power to meet the requirements of industry and the growing population will make energy security a primary concern. Energy security will be particularly important in future, as fossil fuels will become more and more inadequate for the nation's increasing energy needs. Domestic oil production has been declining while the demand has been rising steadily. Hence, oil will continue to be a strategic resource and the security of India's oil supplies from abroad as well as that of all oil reserves and installations will need to be ensured.
- India's growing population and the likelihood of mass migrations into India, for example from Bangladesh, will threaten the existing food reserves and endanger food security. The nation will find it extremely difficult to cope with successive failures of the monsoon, if they occur, and the consequent famine-like conditions that are likely to prevail. For almost a decade now, the monsoon has been bountiful in most parts of India. Quite obviously, this cannot continue for long and the law of averages will catch up sooner rather than later.
- The ravages of global warming and changing monsoon patterns are likely to deplete India's water sources and threaten water security even as the increasing population, rapid industrialisation and the enhanced requirements of irrigation raise the demand for water. The Tata Energy

Research Institute has estimated that the demand for water will almost double from 564 billion cubic metres (bcum) in 1997 to 1,048 bcum in 2047.14 The situation will be further exacerbated when the Himalayan nation-states begin drawing more water for their own consumption. The amicable sharing of the Ganga River waters between India, Bangladesh and Nepal has already been posing problems. Successive droughts have ravaged some of India's western states during 1999 and 2000 mainly due to groundwater levels having fallen to extremely low levels.

- Information warfare is another emerging threat through which, besides nation-states, non-state actors, individual terrorists and even disgruntled elements within a state can play havoc with a nation's telecom, banking, stock exchanges, power grids, railways and air traffic control infrastructure, besides military communications and networks. The prevention of large-scale damage through a complex cyber-security system requires an inter-departmental approach in concert with industry and private entrepreneurs and can only be undertaken by a duly empowered apex organisation.
- The threats to India's maritime security are increasing exponentially as the world turns more and more towards the exploitation of ocean resources for food, energy and raw materials. This long- neglected aspect needs to be incorporated in the management of national security so that India's ocean resources in its exclusive economic zone (EEZ) are not poached at will by state and non-state actors. Increasing piracy at sea and the possible use of India's island territories by terrorist organisations and for trade in contraband goods are other serious maritime threats.
- Security of the environment is another emerging challenge. The continuing increase in the population will threaten the already depleted forest resources as the area of cultivable land comes under pressure. Also, over exploitation of the oceans may upset the delicate marine balance. Increasing urbanisation is causing its own environmental problems. Soil erosion in some areas, specially in hill states due to the impact of deforestation, and the irreplaceable loss of vital nutrients due to the tendency to harvest three to four crops a year in some other states, will eventually lay waste vast areas of cultivable lands and severely curtail agricultural production.
- In future, the Indian government will have to increasingly plan for the security concerns of the vast Indian Diaspora, particularly the migrant

Indian population employed on temporary work permits in the Gulf countries. The Gulf War in 1990-91 had resulted in the most massive airlift since the Berlin airlift as over 100,000 Indian workforce personnel had to be evacuated from Iraq. The increasing persecution of ethnic minorities of Indian origin in countries like Pakistan will create its own tensions and may force India to intervene in future. The May 2000 coup in Fiji, where the Indian minority was specifically targeted, may be a pointer of the shape of things to come.

Still newer challenges that are emerging include those from organised crime and narco-terrorism. India is flanked by two of the most notorious narcotics producing regions in the world - the Golden Crescent (Afghanistan, Iran and Pakistan; annual production approximately 2,500 tonnes) on the west and the Golden Triangle (Laos, Myanmar and Thailand; 1,500 tonnes) on the east. Money laundering and the issue of fake currency by inimical neighbours are new problems to be contended with. The Asian financial crisis demonstrated that a nation's currency can be undermined through external intervention and its economy can be de-stabilised. The Ministry of Defence (MoD) Annual Report 1995-96 listed several other non-military 'pressures' on the national security environment which could not be ignored. These included "...those relating to trade, intellectual property rights, environment, human rights..." The existing and emerging threats to national security are becoming more and more complex to evaluate and manage in the prevailing era of strategic uncertainty.

Need for a Formal Defence Policy

These threats and challenges to national security require systematic evaluation by an apex body and the formulation of a comprehensive national security strategy to ensure that they are managed well and not allowed to spin out of control. Indian defence analysts have for long lamented the lack of a national security vision and strategy. With his characteristic frankness, K. Subrahmanyam minces no words in bluntly stating that, "It is now well recognised all over the world that India does not have a tradition of strategic thinking... mainly due to the incapacity of our political leaders and top civil servants to take a long-term view of national security. This is compounded by their consequent failure in giving a lead to the armed forces in preparing the country to face its long-term need for defence preparedness." In Brahma Chellaney's view, "The lack of an integrated, long-term national security approach stands out as the biggest failure of nation-building in the half-century that India has been independent. In the absence of such an approach, national security policy-making has been characterised largely by ad hoc decisions to meet new threats and realities." M. D. Nalapat says that national security policy has generally been one of reacting to threats and events and, "A holistic view was avoided as this would have reduced the powers of the separate bureaucracies (in the home and defence ministries especially) dealing with the problem... this uncoordinated response to security threats is a major failing in the system." And, K. N. Daruwalla asks, "Can a country have a military doctrine if it does not posses a strategic one? If your overall objectives and goals are ambiguous and undefined, how can you lay down objectives for your armed forces? How can a military doctrine be embedded in such amorphousness?.... Since the armed forces are required to safeguard national interests, foreign policy objectives should go hand in hand with the development of the military machine." However, Jasjit Singh has expressed the view that, "... the reality also must be recognised that (despite the absence of a formally articulated defence doctrine) the country has managed its defence and military affairs well during the past half century."

Indian policy planners have traditionally fought shy of formally articulating the country's defence and national security policies. Perhaps this reticence owes its origins to an innate sense of refraining from hurting the sensibilities of India's adversaries and neighbours. In its Nineteenth Report, the Estimates Committee had recommended that the country should have a formal National Security Doctrine. When the Standing Committee on Defence (1995-96) in the Tenth Lok Sabha enquired about the action taken on this recommendation, the Defence Secretary replied: "... there is a policy; the only thing is that it is not written down as a separate document and published as such... As a matter of policy we have not published such a document and the Government has not been in favour of publishing a separate document. It is only the United States in my knowledge which annually publishes a document called National Security Doctrine. Non-publication of the document does not mean in any way non-existence of policy." Replying to the debate in the Lok Sabha on the Demands for grants of the MoD, on May 10, 1995, Prime Minister P. V. Narsimha Rao, who was also the Defence Minister, stated: "We do not have a document called India's National Defence Policy. But we have got several guidelines which are followed, strictly followed and observed... This policy is not merely rigid in the sense that it has been written down, but these are the guidelines, these are the objectives, these are the matters which are always kept in view while conducting our defence policy..."

Similarly, the Ministry of External Affairs (MEA) avers in its Annual Report 1998-99 that, "We view foreign policy as an integral part of the larger effort of building the nation's capabilities: through economic development, strengthening social well-being and the quality of life and of protecting India's sovereignty, territorial integrity and security, not only in its defence and economic aspects, but in the widest strategic sense of the term." It says that India's external relations are guided by "well-established principles" which have formed the "basis of our foreign policy for decades" and "enjoy a broad national consensus, thus providing a strong foundation of stability and continuity." However, the report does not spell out what those principles are in specific terms and how they translate into practical execution in furthering national interests and objectives.

It is due to this lack of a long-term national security perspective and the failure to initiate a public debate for the formulation of a national consensus on the vital interests, national security objectives and a synergised national security strategy, that the security pendulum has swung between the interventionist "Indira Doctrine" of the 1970s and 1980s on one end and the conciliatory "Gujral Doctrine" of the mid-1990s on the other. The Indira Doctrine stated that, "India will neither intervene in the domestic affairs of any state in the region, unless requested to do so, nor tolerate such intervention by an external power. If external assistance is needed to meet an external crisis, states should first look within the region (that is, to India) for help." The ill-conceived IPKF intervention in Sri Lanka, as also the stand-off with Nepal on the trade treaty and the successful crushing of the coup in the Maldives could be attributed to the practical application of the Indira Doctrine (dubbed as a "muscular" foreign policy by some non-Indian South Asian commentators). The Gujral Doctrine reflected the recognition that India's policies towards its smaller neighbours within Southern Asia should show greater concern for their security perceptions, instead of sticking to hard-line attitudes that have created tensions in the past. The essence of the doctrine was that India would not insist on reciprocity and would be prepared to go more than half way to improve its relations with its smaller neighbours. Inder Gujral, India's Minister for External Affairs, expected the implementation of his ideas to result in a "fundamental recasting of South Asia's regional relationships... to create a climate of greater confidence and close and mutually beneficial co-operation." The two doctrines would require fundamentally different national security strategies to implement though these would not be mutually exclusive and would even overlap in certain areas. Radically different approaches to national security from decade to decade can only lead to a mismatch between capabilities and intentions and must be resolved through wider national debate.

The closest that government documents in India come to articulating national security and foreign policy objectives are the annual reports of the MoD and the Ministry of External Affairs (MEA). In fact, it was only with the 1997-98 annual report that the MoD for the first time spelt out India's national security objectives. Commenting on this interesting development, Raja Menon wrote recently: "The Annual Defence Report of 1997-98 has many welcome changes and for the first time, the notion of 'sacred territory' has been watered down. In all the previous years the role of the armed forces was depicted purely and solely as the 'defence of our territorial integrity', exhibiting a mindset that was not conducive to understanding coercive diplomacy, the manipulation of risk and the threat of military action."

In its opening chapter entitled "National Security Environment", the Annual Report of 1997-98 stated that India's national security objectives are served by:

- Defending the country's borders as defined by law and enshrined in the Constitution and protecting the lives and property of its citizens against terrorism and insurgencies.
- Promoting further co-operation and understanding with neighbouring countries and implementing mutually agreed confidence-building measures.
- Working with countries of the Non-Aligned Movement to address key challenges before the international community and engaging in co-operative security initiatives such as the ASEAN Regional Forum (ARF).
- Pursuing security and strategic dialogues with major powers and key partners.
- Following a consistent and principled policy on disarmament and international security issues based on universality, non-discrimination and equal security for all.
- Having a secure and effective deterrent against the use or the threat of use of weapons of mass destruction against India.

Post-Pokhran II in May 1998, in the 1998-99 Annual Report, the issue of deterrence against weapons of mass destruction was moved up from the last place to the second place in the national security objectives and was re-worded as follows: "Having a secure, effective and credible minimum deterrent against the use or threat of use of weapons of mass destruction against India. The profile of this deterrent, including accurate and refined delivery systems, will not be circumscribed in range and payload by any outside pressure or influence but will be determined by the country's threat perception at any point of time." Also, a new sub-para on technology control regimes was added: "Insulating the country from the effect of individual or group restrictions on the transfer of material, equipment and technologies that have a bearing on India's security, particularly its defence preparedness.

This involves a greater emphasis on in-house research, development and production of the nation's requirements and recourse to feasible alternative sources." In the 1998-99 Annual Report, in the objective on the country's disarmament policy, the phrase "based on the principles of supreme national interest" has been added after the words "and international security issues". Curiously, the report refers to the territorial dispute with China as a "boundary" dispute. A careful reading of the national security objectives enunciated in the annual reports of the MoD reveals a tendency to mix objectives with policy in some cases and shows that the objectives are mere statements of intent in others.

According to the MoD, "... although there has been no specifically written document called India's National Defence Policy, yet it has been articulated clearly and unambiguously through various policy statements over the years. The policy articulated since independence is as follows:

"That our military capability is to be so directed to ensuring the defence of national territory over land, sea and air encompassing among others the inviolability of our land borders, island territories, offshore assets and our maritime trade routes. Government have repeatedly made it clear that it is not our objective to influence/interfere/dominate (the) region on the basis of military strength."

In a submission made by the MoD to the Standing Committee on Defence, it was stated that the following aspects "fully depict the national security interests":

- Defence of national territory over land, sea and air, encompassing among others the inviolability of our land borders, island territories, offshore assets and our maritime trade routes.
- To secure an internal environment whereby our Nation State is insured against any threat to its unity or progress on the basis of religion, language, ethnicity or socio-economic dissonance.
- To enable our country to exercise a degree of influence over the nations in our immediate neighbourhood to promote harmonious relationship in tune with our national interests.
- To be able to effectively contribute towards regional and international stability.

- To possess an effective out-of-the-country contingency capability to prevent destabilisation of the small nations in our immediate neighbourhood that could have adverse security implications for us.

Though national security interests and objectives have been spelt out in bits and pieces by the Government, in annual reports and while answering the queries of the Standing Committee on Defence, as brought out above, these have tended to change from time to time and have not been subject to direct parliamentary oversight. These policy statements are of a transitory nature and could sometimes even be based on the personal predilections of policy makers who may be in power at a given point in time. A case in point is the question of whether or not China poses a threat to India. It is well known that while the Defence Minister was reported to have named China as India's number one threat, the Minister for External Affairs subsequently ruled out such an assessment. Hence, these transitory policy statements do not amount to a comprehensive, nationally debated approach that is sanctified by parliamentary consensus transcending the political divide.

Brahma Chellaney has written: "... it needs to be recognised that national security is much more than defence policy. The defence of India means the defence of its national interests. National security demands integrated planning and co-ordinated use of India's political, military, diplomatic and scientific resources to advance its core interests... Unfortunately, India lacks a long-term national security strategy despite the pressing problems it confronts. There is no integrated policy-making process that seeks to make specific policies compatible with each other... serious efforts have (not been) made to establish institutionalised methods so that policy-making is driven less by personalities and more by long-term integrated planning. A host of functional inefficiencies continue to burden Indian policy-making constricting any government's ability to manage national security in a prudent, cost-effective and result-oriented manner..."

Even the Kargil Review Committee Report has recommended an overhaul of the present system: "The Committee strongly feels that the Kargil experience, the continuing proxy war and the prevailing nuclearised security environment justify a thorough review of the national security system in its entirety."

It clearly emerges that the manifold existing and emerging external and internal threats to national security demand a comprehensive and mature system for their handling and management.

Present Government policies appear to reflect individual ministerial approaches rather than a holistic integrated approach. Coherence in application can only flow from a synergised national security strategy. Only an all-encompassing national security management system can take into account all the prevalent inter-ministerial, inter-departmental and civil-military diversities. The emerging asymmetric threats require systematic evaluation and meticulous planning, so that long-term projections can be made in respect of military force structures and the development of the necessary capabilities.

Only when a comprehensive national security strategy is formulated to deal with the existing and emerging threats on a long- and mid-term basis, can the responsibilities of the armed forces and concerned government departments be clearly visualised. Based on the security objectives and the responsibilities assigned, the Services can review their organisational and force structures and make recommendations to the government to institute the changes necessary to translate policy into action. The virtues of long-term defence planning cannot be over-emphasised. Ad hoc functioning on a year-to-year basis leads to imperfection in decision-making and tends to result in avoidable waste.

4

Defence Commencement Policy of India

The limited success of the offset policy of 2006 led to its elaborate revision in 2008. India had by now become one of the largest importers of defence equipment, with nearly 70 per cent of its requirements being met by foreign suppliers. The demand of the armed forces also resulted in the high growth of India's defence budget.

During the period 2003-07, it registered the fourth highest growth in real terms amongst the 10 largest military spenders in the world. Therefore, the 2008 policy aimed at the creation of conditions for assisting in the development of a domestic military-industrial complex. The salient changes introduced in DPP 2008 include:

- the introduction of a list of products which would qualify for the discharge of offset obligations (Annexure-VI of the DPP);
- the removal of the requirement for private industry to obtain industrial license to participate in offset programme unless stipulated by the regulations of the Departmental of Industrial Policy and Promotion (DIPP);
- offset credit banking;
- banking of surplus offset credit with a validity period of two years after the conclusion of the relevant contract, and;
- exemption of acquisitions under fast track from offset obligations.

Will the 2008 offset policy facilitate the creation of a military-industrial base in India?

With the defence outlay steadily increasing and with only around 30 per cent of the requirement being met indigenously, emphasis has been laid on utilising the growing sophistication of the domestic industrial base to achieve self-reliance in the defence sector. It is now seen as both a necessity and an increasingly achievable goal.

But the introduction of the 2008 policy in itself is no guarantee that it will contribute significantly to this goal. Offsets though beneficial, come with certain inherent risks. The offset policy, therefore, has to be carefully calibrated to reduce its negative impact and maximise its yield. There is almost complete unanimity among defence economists, who have analysed the impact of defence offsets on the development of the defence industry in various countries, that the process is highly complex and therefore defies easy conclusion.

Their efforts have been stymied primarily by the absence of data relating to offset implementation and the notorious level of secrecy with which defence firms guard such details. Offsets have been termed as "smoke and mirrors", with nobody being sure as to "who benefits". Also, almost all of them have questioned the economic efficiency of offset transactions. Offsets are no free lunches.

They are neither freebies. There is an economic cost to offsets. For instance, in a survey conducted in the UK, it was concluded that "evidence suggests that offsets do cost more than off-the shelf purchase and, not surprisingly, that vendors seek to include most of this premium in the selling price." In a study of defence offset implementation in Belgium, it was estimated that the nation had to pay between 20-30 per cent in increased costs in connection with "offsets tied to its military procurement." Depending on the economic conditions prevalent in the offset applying nation, its industrial base or its capacity to absorb technology, vendors hike the cost of their goods/services to compensate for the inefficiency inherent in the nation seeking offsets. Therefore, an offset implementing nation pays more for the import of defence items than it would otherwise have to do if it did not impose mandatory offset obligations.

Among offsets, mandatory offsets have been further estimated to yield less economic dividends. In view of this, it has been concluded that "there is no good reason for a mandatory offsets scheme" to be introduced, as such schemes "merely shift the initiative away from the purchaser and give suppliers scope for opportunism at the expense of the buyer."

From the above, it is seen that India has opted for the use of an economically inefficient vehicle to promote its domestic defence industry. By opting for the mandatory offset scheme, it has further bartered the leverage buyers have in sale and purchase of competitive goods. Given the overwhelming evidence that offsets are generally not welfare enhancing, implicit in the Indian offset policy is the assumption that it is willing to forsake economy in the acquisition of weapons for the long-term goal of creating a defence-industrial base (which according to existing studies is difficult to achieve) through the induction of technology, co-production, license production, etc., that the policy may compel.

Therefore, the moot question is whether India has carefully calibrated its regulations and put in place a system that can optimise the benefits of an offset policy that in the first place comes at a cost. An analysis of the situation in India, however, reveals that the mandatory offset obligations will yield greater dividends if necessary changes are made in all relevant rules and guidelines that have a bearing on the success of the policy. Some of the extant rules are archaic and were not, in the first place, formulated to encourage the absorption of the benefits that offsets offer. Such rules and procedures that were formulated prior to the incorporation of the policy of offsets (licensing policy requirement for private firms to produce defence items, for instance), it is argued, cannot but reduce the benefits the policy can yield.

DEFENCE PLANNING AND POLICY

As regards the planning process, the Government has taken a number of measures to improve the structure, process and procedure relating to defence planning based on the recommendations of Group of Ministers on 'Reforming the National Security System'. The preparation of Long Term Plans, Five Year Defence Plans and Annual Budgetary proposals have been brought under the newly established Integrated Defence Staff (IDS) to bring about greater inter-service coordination in planning. The IDS also interacts closely with Defence (Finance) in the formulation of Plans and Budgets.

The Government has set up a Defence Acquisition Council headed by the Raksha Mantri and consisting of Raksha Rajya Mantri (s), the three Service Chiefs and Defence Secretary, Secretary (Defence Finance), and Secretary (Defence Production) to assist the Raksha Mantri in taking decisions in the totality of the new planning process, including capital acquisitions and major modernisation projects. The Government has also set up a dedicated institutional structure for defence procurement, the Defence procurement Board, headed by the Defence Secretary for acquisitions on the capital account. Planning processes have been further tightened under budgetary pressures and the need to establish greater synergy and jointness amongst the Armed Forces. This has also necessitated greater coordination in planning and procurement among the three services.

The Ministry in its written note submitted on the current status of the implementation of the 10th Plan has inter alia stated that: "The projections of the Ministry of Defence for the Tenth Defence Plan were reviewed thrice between March 2003 and July 2004 bearing in mind the needs of defence modernization and the likely constraints to the availability of funds for defence in the Tenth Plan. The Ministry of Finance have now agreed in principle to the latest projection made by the Ministry of Defence of Rs. 4,18,101 crore. However, a firm indication of annual outlays for the remaining year of the 10th Plan has not yet been given by the Ministry of Finance.

Meanwhile, in the absence of a formal approval of the allocation for defence in the Tenth Plan, defence planning has been harmonised with the allotments for defence in the annual budgets of the Government. Actual expenditures in 2002-2003 and 2003-2004 were Rs. 55,620 crores and Rs. 60,300 crores respectively. An allocation of Rs. 77,200 crores has been made in the Budget Estimate for 2004-2005 against a projection of Rs. 90,928 crores. About, Rs. 11,000 crores additional funds have been allocated beyond the Budget Estimate for the capital head.

The projected expenditure in 2005-2006 and 2006-2007 are Rs. 1,00,960 crores and Rs. 1,10,251 crores respectively. However, an amount of Rs. 83,000 crores only has been allocated in the Budget Estimate (B.E.) for the current financial year 2005-2006.

While some compromises are inevitable in the absence of a formally approved Plan, every effort has been made to ensure that the annual budgets have been utilized in accordance with the Plan projections of the Ministry of Defence and that any negative impact on ongoing modernization, infrastructure development and procurements of equipment is minimized. Ongoing projects and commitments have been reviewed and prioritized so that the main objective of the Tenth Defence Plan to carry forward the process of modernization of the Armed Forces is not adversely affected. A modest outlay of over Rs. 950 crores has been made for new schemes for the Army. (No increase is being sought)".

In response to a query regarding the existence of a core plan the Ministry though a written reply has inter alia stated that : "There is no formal draft core plan to make up for the delay in the finalization of the Tenth Defence Plan. Meanwhile, in the absence of a formal approval of the allocation for defence in the Tenth Plan, defence planning has been harmonised with the allotments for defence in the annual budgets of the Government. While, indigenous production/Research and Development is being made in accordance with the decisions flowing from the Defence Acquisition Council, defence procurement is being made in accordance with annual acquisition plans for the three services as approved by the Defence Procurement Board. Adequate measures have been taken to minimise any adverse effect on ongoing modernisation schemes. On-going projects and contractual commitments have been reviewed and prioritised to minimise the effect of any shortfall in actual allocation vis-à-vis projections, both in respect of modernisation plans and in essential procurement. Keeping in view, the rising competing demands on limited resources, the budgetary framework has been fine-turned in such a manner to ensure most effective utilisation of Government resources".

While presenting a detailed picture on the entire planning exercise that has been undertaken in the recent past, the representative of Ministry has stated as under:

"In the year 2001-02, projections for the 10th Plan were examined in the Ministry of Defence. These projections were made by the different Services and the Departments. They added up to Rs. 4.97 lakh crore. In January, 2002 the Ministry of Finance indicated the likely availability of Rs. 4.21 lakh crore. So, there was a gap of about Rs. 75,000 crore. Therefore, the Chief of Integrated Defence Staff and Chief of Staff were requested for giving their views. They recommended slightly reduced allocation of Rs. 4.61 lakh crore. In February 2003, in consonance with the recommendations, it was done. The matter was again taken up with the Finance Ministry in March 2003. But we did not have received any response from them thereafter. We had to carry out a review of our projections.

This was because if some scheme was supposed to be sanctioned in the first year of the Plan, it will involve expenditure in the first, second, third years and leading up to the fifth year. If, for the first two years, projected allocations are not utilized, there is no way the original amount, which was projected for the entire five years could be spent in the last three years. It is because in defence acquisition, we are not really buying things off the shelf and paying out for the whole thing.

So, if you take a case of some scheme or project costing Rs. 5,000 crore in five years with simplistic allocation of expenditure of Rs. 1,000 crore each year, and if in the first two years, it is not sanctioned and in the third year it is sanctioned, we are not going to have anything in the first two years, but the expenditure will be Rs.3,000 crore in the remaining three years and not Rs. 5,000 crore. When we received the projects, we reviewed what would be and what would not be sanctioned. Then the revised figures came to something like Rs. 4,18,000 crore as indicated. But they did not give us any annual allocations, not capacity utilization, etc".

On the lessons learnt and the measures that are being implemented to overcome the nagging delays of Defence Planning, the Defence Secretary deposed that : "Presentation of the fourth year Budget is made to the Parliament. As has already been mentioned, there is the Ministry of Defence and there is the Ministry of Finance which are the players in this exercise. The exercise for preparing the plan is undertaken by us well in time, much before the start of the year in which the next Five Year Plan is going to start. For example, for the 11th Plan, to answer your question, we have already started the exercise. For doing that planning as to what would be needed, considering the gaps that is there in the Tenth Plan – if any exercise of this nature is to be undertaken – we might have a wish list; it might represent a large figure. But we still have to have some kind of an indicative figure from the Ministry of Finance saying that we have asked for this much amount, which may not be available, but we can have so much amount at the outer limit, beyond which we cannot go. This kind of an indication is no forthcoming. This is what happened in this current year. If you contrast it with the situation of the Ninth Plan, as the Chairman was enquiring, the Ninth Plan was approved on 1st January, 1998.

Therefore, it was approved in the first year. It was a very major achievement and they indicated a total allocation of Rs. 2,20,000 crore. The Annual Budget, as it took place during those five years if you total up those they came to Rs. 2,43,000 crore. That means the annual allocation was more than the indicative figure of the Plan. That was a situation which was quite in contrast to what is prevalent just now where, firstly, the figure itself was not known to us till December – finally what we wanted and how much they can give. This went till December of 2004. If we were to juxtapose the Tenth Plan indicative figure of Rs. 4,18,000 crore divided by four years, which are known, it is nowhere. There was no relation. Therefore, this figure becomes an academic figure. That is the point that we have been discussing, that is the outlays have to be finalized at the beginning of the plan and secondly Annual Allocation should be conforming to the overall outlay".

Adding further on the issue, the Defence Secretary has also stated that : "As has been mentioned earlier, how initial projections of Rs. 4,97,000 crore was done at the beginning of the Tenth Plan (2001-02).This was also communicated to the Finance Ministry with the break up. They needed it in a particular format. It was given in that format. Subsequently, they had indicated Rs. 4,97,000 crore is too much and we may plan within Rs. 4,21,000 crore. There was a gap of about Rs. 75,724 between the projection and what they had indicated. By that time certain time had elapsed. We were involved in an internal exercise of readjusting. In December 2004 they indicated Rs.

4,18,000 crore, which was what we had projected earlier". Explaining the details of the ongoing measures to formulate the Eleventh Defence Plan and how these initiatives have a bearing on the implementation of annual plan programmes, the Defence Secretary has briefed the Committee : "As I just said, we have started our exercise of preparing the Eleventh Plan which means that the Integrated Defence Staff which gets inputs from all the three Headquarters puts together the long-term perspective plan requirements of each service and makes them into one composite plan called the Defence Plan. It sees whether there is any overlapping of capabilities or whether there is any repetition or commonalties. So, it does such modifications and vetting and then it is projecting that requirement to the Ministry where we see whether it is all right or whether it needs any change or not.. Accordingly, we pass it on to the Ministry of Finance for approval. Of course, we have discussions with the Ministry of Finance because they might also like to understand the details. So, that dialogue is there. Our request is, if the Ministry of Finance were to give its indications well before the start of the first year of the Eleventh Plan, then that would help everybody to know what is going to be the situation during the five years of the Eleventh Plan. Secondly, we do need some kind of a figure to show that this is the total figure and whatever amount it might be would be divided in the five years in this fashion in the Annual Budget so that the Annual programmes can then be fine tuned to adjust to the availability. Otherwise, there is likely to be a mismatch between what we might project and the money availability".

When asked whether the Ministry of Finance had intimated the details of the 10th Plan allocations in time, the Defence Secretary has stated that : "It was towards the end of the third year. This was one part of the problem. The second part, as I said, is annual allocations are nowhere matching even this figure. Therefore, how do we do the Planning? We do not know what will be the figure for the fifth plan. Budget has been submitted for the fourth year. It totals up to Rs. 2 lakh something".

The Ministry of Defence in its written Action Taken Reply on the recommendation of the Committee on long term planning of three Services contained in the First Report on Demands for Grants of the Ministry of Defence for the year 2004-05, has stated as under : "A draft Long-Term Integrated Perspective Plan (LTIPP) covering the 15-year period from the Tenth to the Twelfth Plan (2002-2017) was formulated in June 2004 in consultation with the three Services. Since more than two years of the current Tenth Plan period have already elapsed, a new approach paper has been made formulating a Long Term Integrated Perspective Plan (LTIPP) covering the period from 2007-2022. This Plan is expected to be finalised by the Integrated Defence Staff by the last quarter of 2005."

The Committee are unhappy to note that the Ministry of Finance has failed to finalise the 10th Defence plan even after three years of the plan have passed. Non-finalisation of the 10th Defence Plan at its beginning by the Ministry of Finance has created a great deal of uncertainty about the availability of adequate finance for the acquisition of the vital equipment, modernization, etc. The Ministry of Defence had projected a demand of Rs. 4,97,000 crore in 2001 for the Tenth Plan. However, the Ministry of Finance has given indicative figure of Rs.4, 18,000 crore in December 2004,without any firm commitment. The total allocations in the first four years of Tenth Defence Plan just come to about Rs.2, 76,300 crore which is nowhere near their requirements. This gap between the demand and allocations, has adversely affected the defence planning and our preparedness. The Committee take a serious note of this and want the Government to finalise the Tenth Plan immediately and take steps to utilise the committed amount in full. The Committee would like to be apprised of the fmalisation of the Plan as well as the follow-up steps being taken to utilise the total allocation of the Tenth Plan.

The Committee also observe that due to non-finalisation of the Tenth Plan in time, the long term perspective plan of the Forces has got affected and is presently at the fmalisation stage with a revised plan schedule spanning from 2007-2022. The Committee, while expressing their displeasure over the present situation, recommend that the Ministry of Defence should reorient the plans and strive to adhere to the schedules envisaged. As regard the 11th Plan, the Committee desire that it should be finalised at least an year before the plan period starts.

It is high time that the Government prepared a road map for self-reliance. The Committee strongly feels that India should not be taken as a weapons/ arms market by the global suppliers and action in this direction should be visible by the end of Tenth Defence Plan and 11th Plan should entirely be devoted to self-reliance.

The Committee has also observed that the surveillance capabilities of our forces are in adequate. This is primarily due to non-availability of low-level radar systems with the three services. The Committee feel that all round effort should be undertaken by the Government to ensure that the entire country is covered. The Committee feel that the Ministry should explore all possibilities of acquiring the required radar systems in adequate numbers without any delay.

DEFENCE PLANNING SYSTEM

Before independence, the defence services worked on a system of contract budget. Defence expenditure was pegged at Rs 55 crore per year, which was more than half of the Central Government's revenue. There was no serious threat from outside (except during World War II, when a fresh agreement was signed) and this amount was more than adequate to maintain the establishment.

The savings were not allowed to lapse but put away in the Defence Reserve Fund that was utilised to finance measures for re-equipment of the Defence Services, thus freeing the Government from having to provide fund money greater than the contract amount. Expenditure on defence rose steeply soon after independence. However, there was no planned effort and defence programmes consisted mainly of outright purchases from abroad, drawing heavily on available Sterling reserves. In the late 1950s, some efforts were made to initiate domestic weapons production by the Ministry of Defence when Mr. Krishna Menon was the Defence Minister. The Sino-Indian conflict in 1962 aroused a new defence consciousness in the country. After taking care of immediate postwar requirements, systematic defence planning started in 1964. Defence requirements were assessed on a five-year basis and the First Five Year Defence Plan (1964-69) was drawn up. This plan took into account the resources available and assistance which could be expected from friendly foreign countries. The plan was primarily based on an expansion and modernisation programme considered necessary by each Service in the light of the respective threat perception assessed. It also proposed a defence production base that would gradually reduce the country's external dependence, provide for improvements in border roads and communications, and a modest expansion of DRDO. The Government recognised the imperative need to synergise 'defence' and 'development' instead of planning each on a separate and unrelated level. The MoD emphasised the "inevitable need to harness all resources of the country for the country's defence and for the defence effort to derive full sustenance from the country's economic development plans".

Thereafter, the National Development Council authorised the Chairman of the Planning Commission to review the needs of both development and defence. A Planning Cell was established in 1965 in the Ministry of Defence 'to deal with the wider aspects of defence planning'. The new system was intended to facilitate medium and long-term defence planning and to maintain constant liaison with the Planning Commission and other ministries. It was expected that the MoD would derive maximum advantage from the development effort by being able to place its priorities for consideration along with the overall economic and industrial plans drawn up by the Planning Commission. The experience of the First Five Year Defence Plan showed that the development of weapons and equipment was a long drawn out process. The Government realised that there could be no forward movement in attaining self-sufficiency in weapons and equipment unless these requirements were planned over a reasonably long period, long enough to cover the span of development and production of new weapons systems and other fighting tools.

The inadequacy of foreign exchange reserves was another hindrance in planning and implementation. In order to mitigate some of these drawbacks, the Second Five Year Defence Plan (1969-74) was instituted on a "roll-on" basis. After a year, an additional year was added so that the Defence Services would have before them a revised and updated five-year plan. In this context, the MoD commented: "Opportunity is taken by this annual exercise to take note of and reflect the change in priorities, the shifts in emphasis and the latest concepts and programmes to reorient the plan within the scheme of resources so that the aims and means are most effectively balanced." This system was expected to facilitate the planning of projects that took five years or more and to revise or eliminate projects, depending on the prevailing foreign exchange situation and availability of domestic resources.

For a period of five years, firm assurances were to be given on the availability of resources. This, unfortunately, never happened. In 1971, it was impossible to adhere to the discipline and the pattern of the roll-on plan. Instead of roll-on annual revisions, immediate requirements dominated the Government's attention that pre-empted plan efforts. In its 1971-72 Annual Report, the MoD acknowledged that having a Planning Cell in the ministry was an insufficient and unsatisfactory method of meeting a crisis.

The Planning Cell was not taken seriously in the crucial stages of economic planning and the argument that defence needs would be adjusted in the overall allocation of resources was proved wrong. In 1974, an Apex Group headed by the Union Minister for Planning again suggested that steady long-term defence programmes would be more cost effective and economical rather than fluctuating allocations due to periodic economic and security crises. In order to integrate defence planning with the overall economic planning effort, defence and economic development plans were made co-terminus.

Planning Machinery

Most of the defence planning machinery and planning methodology was developed in the decade 1964-74. The Joint Intelligence Committee (JIC) was established in the Cabinet Secretariat to provide external and internal threat assessments. Inputs for this purpose were to be provided by all Intelligence agencies of the Government. The Service Chiefs were to assess the broad military aims and a strategy, coordinated in the Chiefs of Staff Committee, was to be approved by the Defence Minister. However, this was seldom done. Each Service ended up planning its own force level, choice of weapons and equipment, and build-up of infrastructure. In 1977, the Government formed a Committee for Defence Planning (CDP) to "undertake regular assessments relevant to defence planning in the light of all factors having a bearing on national security and defence". However, this committee could not function smoothly nor meet the desired goals.

Planning units were also established in the Department of Defence Production and DRDO. A Planning and Coordination Cell was created in the MoD to coordinate and compile various plans into a 'Defence Plan' for Cabinet approval. As the bureaucrats in the ministry had no professional knowledge or background, this cell could only compile different requirements without any analysis. In Army Headquarters, the Deputy Chief of Army Staff was made responsible for preparing the Army plan. A Perspective Planning Directorate was established in the late 1970s. Naval and Air plans were prepared in the respective Planning Directorates. Financial considerations, nonexistent at this level earlier, were introduced through Finance Planning Sections attached to these Directorates. In 1986, the Directorate General of Defence Planning Staff (DGDPS), comprising officers from the three Services, DRDO, and Ministries of Defence and External Affairs, was established under the Chiefs of Staff Committee (COSC) to coordinate and harmonise defence planning. Civilian officers from the Ministries probably did not find the job professionally satisfying and were gradually withdrawn, thus leaving the DGDPS a tri-Service set up.

All these measures enabled each Service headquarters to prepare defence plans in a more rational manner. But due to lack of clear political direction and each Service primarily planning for itself, joint planning, coordination between Services and other departmental plans of the MoD, were largely ignored. After the Kargil conflict in 1999, the Group of Ministers (GoM) and later the Cabinet Committee on Security (CCS) approved several reforms. An Integrated Defence Headquarters (IDH) was established and the DGDPS was merged with it. The creation of the post of Chief of Defence Staff (CDS), whose tasks would include ensuring intra and inter-Services prioritisation of defence plans and improvement in joint functioning of the Defence Services, was recommended. The reforms also included establishment of a Defence

Intelligence Agency and creation of Defence Equipment Production, Research and Planning councils in the IDH and MoD, respectively. Unfortunately, the CDS, who would be the cornerstone of integrated operational planning for defence, has not been appointed.

Analysis of the System

Despite several years of planning efforts, defence planning in India is characterised by seesaw bouts of frenzied activity followed by long periods of relative inaction. Five-year defence plans have rarely been formally approved before commencement. The Tenth Defence Plan, now in its third year, is yet to be accorded formal government approval.

Adhocism is the order of the day, leading to knee-jerk responses and haphazard planning, making India a reactive rather than proactive nation in matters pertaining to national security. Whenever India's major adversaries plan a big defence purchase, there is an outcry for similar acquisitions, resulting in piecemeal decisions regardless of long-term impact and overall requirements.

The Defence Forces are forced to follow "a case-by-case" approach to modernisation and procurement of arms, ammunition and equipment to replace obsolescent items, in many cases long after their life cycle is over and they cannot be maintained in a cost effective manner. The Army's Vijayanta tanks, MiG-21s of the IAF, and IL-38 maritime reconnaissance aircraft of the Navy are some examples. Weapons development, procurement and absorption are complex processes. A lead-time of 15-20 years is required to plan and execute major projects. Despite this, for several years, a large amount of the capital acquisition budget has been surrendered. In the prevailing era of strategic uncertainty, the changing nature of warfare demands a judicious mix of threat and capabilities-based forces that can operate efficiently as combined arms, joint Services teams and components of multinational coalition forces.

INDIA'S DEFENCE INDUSTRIAL POLICY

Defence industrial policy in the initial years after independence was guided by the simple phrase called 'self sufficiency'. This was subsequently modified to 'self reliance' in defence production and has become a matter of varied interpretation. While for some it means the ultimate objective of complete non-dependence on imports for defence hardware, for others it means selective self-sufficiency in certain critical technologies. And for some others it is a simple reduction in the ratio of imports to indigenous sources of supply to the armed forces.

However, one can say that India's defence industrial policy broadly consists of three components: (i) maximisation of indigenous manufacturing and production (ii) License production of what could be obtained from abroad and (iii) direct purchase of those equipment not covered by the other two categories but considered essential for ensuring security. Another important unspoken element was that everything, whether indigenous production, license production or direct purchase, was done within the government set-up in line with the general industrial policy. The recent policy change, of course, demonstrates the intention to involve the private sector in defence R&D and production through licensing and the indirect opening of the defence industrial sector to foreign companies through equity participation and the offset arrangement.

The moot question is: was there something wrong with the past policy objectives? On the face of it, the policy components and objectives appear quite sound and logical for a country like India. In simple terms, it means that indigenous production should be maximised; what could not be produced indigenously should be produced under license arrangement; and those that could not be obtained through these two routes should be acquired by direct purchase. A sound policy indeed. But the soundness of a policy has to be judged from tangible outcomes. Arguably, the problems might not have been in the contents of the policy per se. It is due to the nature defence technology and limitations of vision as embedded in the policy.

The policy objective was essentially to substitute imported equipment with indigenous production in the hope of attaining 'self-sufficiency' or 'self reliance'. Unfortunately, the security imperatives of a country translated into defence equipment are like 'moving targets'. Neither the technological capability of the defence sector nor its policy instrument as highlighted above was able to catch up with the targets.

The increasing quantum of defence imports from year to year, the country's inability to upgrade the imported equipment held for significant period under license production, and, indirectly, insignificant defence exports amply testify to this situation. The general industrial policy wherein defence items and their productions were kept strictly within the government set-up further compounded the problem. In this context, two aspects of the policy – indigenous production and license production, merit detailed analysis.

Maximising indigenous production would imply more than one thing. It would mean meeting the quantitative requirements in terms of the existing demands of the armed forces for equipment or items at any point of time. It would also mean increasing the varieties of items and equipment required by them. Most importantly, it would mean the ability to meet the challenges of supplying their ever-changing demands of technology specific equipment and items. India's defence industrial policy has conspicuously failed in this respect. In fact, the implication of this policy is that the country should be able to indigenously produce the challenging demands made by the armed forces. Its logical extension is that defence research and development efforts have to be strengthened through policy focused research and development and adequate resources allocations thereto. It is a known fact that the defence research and development organisation has 50-odd laboratories and establishments. However, its lack of focused research and development is equally well known, though of late it has been able to achieve break-throughs in certain strategic technologies. Moreover, its budgetary allocation has been quite modest even within the overall defence budget and until recently it was part of 'Army Demand'. In fact, the Parliamentary Standing committee on Defence recommended that defence R&D budgetary allocation should be at least 14 to 15 per cent of the total defence budget so that indigenous production to imports in the ratio of 70:30 could be achieved. This recommendation was in line with the projected target of the report of the self-reliance committee entitled '10 year plan for self reliance in Defence systems'. But the fact remains that there is no evidence of adequate policy back-up to attain this desirable but difficult goal. The DRDO does not seem to be suffering from lack of funds per se since only 8 to 10 per cent of its total budget is reported to be spent on fundamental research. Perhaps, the solution to this issue lies somewhere else.

How about production under license, another important pillar of the policy? The normal assumption is that production under license would enable the country not only to acquire the capability to produce a particular equipment or product but also help it gain the technical know-how for subsequent upgradation and further technological innovations. For the last fifty-odd years, India has been producing a number of defence equipment under license. Good examples in this regard are the Vijayanta tank and the MIG series of fighter aircraft. But this does not seem to have helped in the development of the Arjun Main Battle Tank and the Light Combat Aircraft. Moreover, India has not even been able to upgrade certain fighter aircraft held and operated for a long time by its armed forces. Thus, the above assumption is definitely not correct.

A closer examination of license production arrangements reveals certain interesting features. License production arrangements are more of an 'institutional framework' under which various types of contractual agreements could be entered into between the supplier and the buyer. It is not necessarily a proven mechanism of technology transfer as such. It may envisage the setting up of a simple production line or facilities in the buyer country for assembly of the finished parts and components for the final finished product. In such cases, hardly any technology transfer takes place and the supplier does not part with any technical know-how. In fact, the supplier agrees to sacrifice only a small portion of his economic interest. It is also not possible to discern under these circumstances whether the supplier has compensated itself for this marginal loss by way of increasing the cost of the technology or equipment and components thereof. On the other hand, there could be a situation where license production involves an intensive process of technology transfer within and beyond the physical production of the equipment in the host county. This is rare rather than routine. The truth of the matter is that since technology is know-how, it is the function of human understanding. The focus of active mechanisms, implicitly or explicitly, is people. However, the truth is that no foolproof prescription could be given for the effectiveness of technology transfer. It all depends on the nature of technology to be acquired. Perhaps, India has learnt it by the hard way the limitations of licence production for attaining the objective of self-sufficiency or self-reliance in defence production.

The fact that defence technology needs long term investment, its obsolescence is high and economies of scale are difficult to attain unlike in other areas of civilian technology are well known. This is essentially because higher capability tends to drive downward the scales of production. In the context of a limited number of customers, this trend is more regressive. On top of this, contrary to logical expectation, the production of the next generation of an equipment or of a different variant does not bring down the cost of the equipment. It has been the British experience that a new generation could cost between one and a half times to four times of the previous variant. This is due to the fact that production of the next generation is not a simple straight line trajectory work but involves the integration of various systems, which sometimes may involve a number of companies and agencies, that were not partners earlier.

This leads to the conclusion that the policy of maximising indigenous production without a strong R&D policy back-up would not bring tangible results. License production is more of an economic compromise between the supplier and the buyer, and it does not and cannot bring about significant technology transfer without an inbuilt specific and suitable mechanism. Every country at one point of time or the other will attain a saturation level when it comes to supplying certain categories of equipment for its armed forces. Therefore, the ultimate defence industrial policy goal must be to foster defence exports without which it is difficult to sustain the economic base of a country's defence industry.

India's defence industrial policy seems to be lacking in all these important ingredients. Since the industrial base has to be sustained for technological and economic reasons, exports are an essential element of defence industrial policy. This is why many countries and their companies are aggressively competing in the global defence market for exports under different arrangements including license production.

It is reported that way back in 1995, the United States government spent more than $7.6 billion in subsidy to help export defence equipment to sustain the economic base of its defence industry. It is a matter of fact that strategic depth in defence production can be increased only by aiming at being 'internationally competitive' through the policy objective of defence exports. In the absence of such an approach, India's defence industrial policy is unlikely to take off in the foreseeable future.

India on the Path to Vibrant Defence Industry

Every major power aspires to build a vibrant defence industrial base. This status is however not easily attainable. Apart from the United States and to some extent Russia and France, all other countries are in the state of struggling to arrive at such a defence industrial position.

Certain countries like the United Kingdom may be able to attain this, but due to strategic or economic preferences may deliberately choose not to consider the enormous costs involved as against the perceived security requirements. India's aspiration for this is well documented wherein it has publicly pronounced its goal of 'self sufficiency' soon after political independence and now graduating it to 'self-reliance'. The unfortunate part is that India is still far from nearing that level even after fifty years of this laudable policy. One of the identified ongoing policy drawbacks is its weak linkage with the civilian sector of industry.

The thrust of the new policy initiative therefore is participation of the private sector in defence industry for both research and development as well as production purposes. It has also opened up the defence sector to foreign equity participation up to 26 per cent, with the government recently expressing its willingness to consider even up to 49 per cent on case-to-case basis. Together with this is the initiation of the 'offset policy' for major foreign procurement of defence equipment of Rs.300 crores and above. The big question is: will all these initiatives contribute to the growth of a vibrant defence industry in India?

The immediate effect of these initiatives is that significant numbers of licenses have been applied for and issued to major Indian companies for production of varied components and systems. In fact, according to CII sources alone, as of date, more than 140 companies are involved in about 345 defence items/products.

Complete systems/platforms/weapons systems constitute the majority of the licenses issued, which demands higher financial investments and technical capability. This reflects the ambition and confidence of the private sector in their new ventures.

On the other hand, there is a flurry of partnership agreements/collaborative ventures by these industrial companies with major global defence industrial giants from the United States, Western Europe and Israel. This is of course not to ignore the existing and ongoing collaborative projects of Defence Public Sector Undertakings (DPSUs) and Ordnance Factories (OFs) with companies from these countries at the governmental level. An analysis would reveal that India's defence industrial scene now is moving on two distinct parallel lines. The first is equipment and technology emanating from Russia and Eastern Europe, which represent approximately 70 per cent of the country's defence industrial set-up. The new addition is Western technology or modified/upgraded technology through private sector companies that are poised to enter India's defence market. The moot question is: Will these different technologies eventually strengthen India's defence industrial base or add further complexities through highly mixed inventories?

In this emerging situation, a few logical things are bound to happen. First, due to the emerging competition from Western technology largely through the private sector, the Russians or other traditional suppliers are likely to at least scale down their often-repeated business behaviour of project delays, delay in supply of spares and parts, and unwillingness to transfer technology.

Moreover, the tendency to jack up costs midway while implementing agreements may also get tempered with the arrival of new competitors. However, the fact remains that the domination of Russian origin technologies and their grip on the Indian military establishment will sustain for quite some years to come particularly given that they are largely embedded through the defence public sector undertakings and other government agencies. The major positive impact of the new situation is, however, that the government agencies/DPSUs are likely to wake up from their slumber at least in those areas where they are producing items of common use, which can be easily produced at a competitive level by the private sector. This will be the immediate benefit brought in by the private sector.

While the above may be the likely positive impact, it is unlikely that Western technology will be able to easily challenge the existing market structure through the private sector. This is due to the peculiarity of defence technology and its market structure. First, given that control of technology is the essence of the growth and expansion of MNCs, the global Western defence giants may not easily part with high-end technology, whereas the Indian establishment would be looking for sophisticated weapons and equipment to supplement what has already been acquired from existing sources. The private sector's ability to enter the market will depend on its capability to supply the components, parts and sub-systems of the new equipment in the initial period. Secondly, opportunities for the private sector would largely depend on the government decision to opt for higher and complete major systems of Western origin technologies such as the MMRCA.

If such a decision goes in favour of any of the fighter aircraft of western origin, the private sector would definitely have significant scope to capture the market through the offset channel or through normal business dealings. Thirdly, the ability and willingness of Western technology to supplement the defence technology requirements of the armed forces would be the decisive factor.

As of now, the armed forces are already in possession of a certain level of defence technology. What they are looking for is conceptually of a higher level, which would be supplementary in nature to bridge perceived security gaps. Will the western powers through their MNCs be willing to part with this level of technology to fill the gap, which, though may be lower than the high-end strategic technology that they possess? If the answer is in the affirmative, the prospects of their capturing the Indian market are very bright. So is also the market potential for the myriad private domestic defence companies in the next five to ten years.

The challenge for Indian industry as a whole would be the will and ability to integrate the two major technology streams in the coming years. This demands the need for dedicated and focused research leading to the capability to integrate existing systems with incoming systems. While the major platforms may continue to be of Russian/Soviet origin, the genius of Indian industry would be tested in its capability to build armaments and other sub-systems and integrating them at higher levels. This is the core challenge and the capability to do it would eventually make the defence industry genuinely vibrant. This will usher in the 'Indian brand of defence technology' even for export purposes free from possible objections on accounts of violations of intellectual property rights. The role of the Government of India as patron and principal customer shall be very crucial for success in achieving the above objective.

CHIEF OF DEFENCE STAFF (CDS)

The Ministerial Committee on National Security had recommended in February 2001 for the creation of the post of Chief of Defence Staff (CDS). When enquired about the present status in this regard, the Ministry of Defence has stated that the Government had constituted a group of Ministers (GoM) on 17 April 2000 to thoroughly review the national security system in its entirety and in particular, to consider the recommendations of the Kargil Review Committee. The GoM had after careful consideration of various issues formulated a comprehensive Report titled 'Reforming the National Security System'. The GoM had inter-alia recommended establishment of the Chief of Defence Staff (CDS).

The recommendations of the GoM were approved by the Government. The Government have not yet come to decision on the post of CDS. Meanwhile, a number of steps have been taken to promote 'synergy' among the Armed Forces, improve inter service coordination on the one hand the Services and the Ministry of Defence on the other, this would bring about optimal utilisation of resources and strengthen the higher defence management.

Pending a decision on the creation of the post of Chief of Defence Staff (CDS), an Integrated Defence Staff has been set up under a Chief of Integrated Defence staff to the Chiefs of Staff Committee (CISC) to support the Chiefs of Staff Committee and its Chairman in the optimum performance of its roles and functions and bringing together and coordinating several functions common to the Services or involving more than one Service. Tri-Service bodies promoting 'jointness' and 'synergy' among the Armed Forces have also been set up like the Defence Intelligence Agency (DIA), the Strategic Forces Command (SFC) and India's first `theatre' command, the Andaman & Nicobar Command. Individual Service Headquarters have been re-designated as part of the `Integrated Headquarters of the Ministry of Defence'. Administrative and Financial powers have also been delegated from the Ministry of Defence to the Integrated Headquarters to promote expeditious decision-making. These steps are expected to enhance the capabilities of the Armed Forces significantly.

Countries with posts of Chief of Defence Staff or similar or comparable systems include the institutions of the Joint Chief of Staff of the USA, the Chief of Defence Staff of the UK, Chief of Defence Forces of Australia, and the Chief of General Staff of China, amongst others. The Committee on Defence, keeping in view excellent work performed by the armed forces in handling of the rescue and relief operation, in their Action Taken Report on Demands for Grants (2004-05) have recommended that the post of Chief of Defence Staff is very much essential for better management of security.

The Defence Expert also, who appeared before the Committee, while tendering oral evidence has supported the rationale for creating the post of Chief of Defence Staff. During the course of deposition he inter-alia stated as under : "All these benefits are lost because we have not appointed. We have taken time to appoint Chairman of the Chief of Staff Committee. Therefore, that should be done early. We are losing time as well as the benefits of having the integrated staff and planning because we have not appointed Chiefs of Staff Committee Chairman."

The Committee are constrained to note that despite their repeated recommendations in the past for establishment of the Chief of Defence Staff (CDS), Government has not yet come to any decision on the creation of the post even after more than three years has elapsed. The Committee further note that in the existing structure for higher defence management viz. the Chief of Staff Committee had not been able to optimally perform their role and functions in bringing together and promoting coordination amongst the Services.

The Committee feel that keeping in view the security scenario of the country and in order to provide single military advice to the Government and to give administer strategic forces and to enhance the efficiency and effectiveness of the planning process, there is an imperative need to create the post of CDS to provide a focal point for better coordination among the three services in the long term perspective plan in conventional and strategic capabilities, prioritise R & D activities and provide effective coordination leading to the path of self-reliance. The Committee desire that Government should give serious consideration to the recommendations of the Committee.

DEFENCE PROCUREMENT UPDATE

Since the 1960s, the Indian Armed Forces have been the main source of sustenance fuel to the erstwhile USSR and later Russian weapons industry. Over 80 percent of our military hardware is of Soviet origin. In the first 15 years of independent India, no new weapons were procured. The governments then were focusing on the indigenization of the weapon systems. That is why the Indian Army had to fight the 1962 Indo-China war with Second World War era weapons, while the Chinese soldiers were equipped with latest automatic weapons. After the war, New Delhi learnt the tough lesson and turned towards, USSR for the modernization of its forces. Soon all the three services started getting weapons of USSR make. Initially it was a win-win situation for both the countries, as most of the western countries were not willing to sell their modern weapons to India as they considered it close to the Eastern Bloc.

Moreover, western weapon systems were too expensive for the very modest Indian economy. India therefore had to turn towards the USSR which did not ask for hard cash and was willing to sell weapons in lieu of grain, wool, etc.

India also got a reliable friend to strategically distract its enemy, China. USSR seized the opportunity of getting a permanent customer for its weapons industry. It helped to ensure a smooth flow of money to the USSR for the development of the next generation weapons. USSR also got a reliable friend in South East Asia to counter the growing influence of the USA.

But the situation has changed now. The IAF has made a great strategic move by turning towards the West for most of the main weapon platforms.

The main reasons for this shift are:

- Consequent to the 1992 financial reforms, India has evolved as the biggest arms market for companies all over the world. So most of the western countries have been doing serious business with India. This has helped in creating a relationship of trust between India and the western countries.
- India is now a strong economy with an average growth rate of almost 9 percent. Increased Defence budgets allow Indian Armed Forces to go for more advanced, reliable and technologically sophisticated western weapon systems.
- In next 10-15 years, India will procure weapon systems worth $40 billion. All the big daddies in the weapon business want to grab the biggest piece of the cake.
- In the past, India had put all its eggs in the same basket. More than one vendor will remove dependency and competition will force all the competitors to field the best weapons and offer the best possible deal.
- Quality standards of western weapons are far superior than that of Russian make. French Mirage aircraft and Israeli weapon systems have scored their impression on the Indian Armed Forces.
- Indian Armed Forces, especially the IAF, have suffered great losses due to lack of spare parts.

- Russia has given India a difficult time in fulfilling its promises like the transfer of technology of T 90 tanks.
- On most occasions, Russia has been failing to meet the promised deadline of delivery, like Project 11356 Krivak IV class guided missile frigates (built in 2004), Aircraft Carrier Gorshkov and IL 76 aircraft for AWACS. Russia miscalculated the time taken to modernize the IL 76 (for AWACS program) by integrating new engine and avionics that caused the whole program to be delayed by 1.5 years.
- $964 millions Aircraft Carrier Admiral Gorshkov deal was signed in 2004 after long negotiations of six years. About two years ago, Moscow informed that it had miscalculated the length of wiring to be done inside the ship. Moscow demanded more money and raised the total cost of the project to $2.2 billion and then to $2.9 billion. Finally, India agreed to pay $2.2 billion, but Moscow insisted on $2.9 billions. This proved to be the last nail in the coffin.

Due to all these factors, Indian forces are now considering and selecting western weapon systems. The contract for of French Scorpene Submarines and contract of developing Barak-NG Missiles are few examples. New Delhi is so annoyed that on the induction ceremony of the AWACS, Defence Minister AK Antony gave a dressing down to Russian and Israeli ambassadors and asked them to ensure that the defence equipments are delivered on scheduled time. There are couple of follow-on orders that Russia was sure of gettin, but the IAF has favored western platforms. These two orders are aircraft for AWACS system and mid-air refueller aircraft.

India is set to place a follow-on order for three more AWACS systems and is seriously considering American Gulfstream, Brazilian Embraer jets and European Airbus. An official said, "We will replace the IL-76 by a modern aircraft like the Gulfstream or Embraer. Both have an endurance of nine hours-that is close to what the Russian aircraft has". But selecting any of these two aircraft will have the problem of having too many platforms in the inventory, as the IAF will have to maintain separate maintenance line for each type of aircraft. The IAF is already considering Airbus A330 multi-role tanker transport (MRTT) for an order of six more mid-air refuellers as the IAF found MRTT far better than IL-78 in the crucial flight evaluation. In case the IAF selects Airbus MRTT for both the orders then this the issue of having too many platforms in the inventory will be resolved.

Currently the IAF is using IL-76 and IL-78 and their maintenance line is already in place. Selecting Airbus MRTT will require one more maintenance line but this will remove dependency on Russia and send a signal to Moscow that arm-twisting will not be tolerated any more. The IAF is also considering Boeing C-17 Globemaster III as its new heavylift aircraft. C-17 is one of the latest and most modern cargo aircraft that has a capability of taking-off and landing on short runways with 70 tons, whereas IL-76 has a capacity of 45 tons only. Moreover, IL-76 is a thirty year old platform and can be upgraded with more powerful engines, better equipments and avionics, but the old platform has its own limitations. Sources said, "The IAF has selected C-17 as the new heavylift aircraft and is all set to place an initial order of 10 aircraft through the US government's Foreign Military Sales (FMS) route, and may later go in for a follow-on order. The defence ministry is considering the proposal and the first aircraft will be delivered in three years after signing of the contract."

In August this year, India will start the flight evaluation trials for the 197 Light Utility Helicopters LUH. Five competitors for the $3 billion contract are Russian Kazan and Mil, American Sikorsky, Italian Finnmeccanica and European helicopter manufacturers Eurocopter. Last year, Request For Proposal (RFP) was sent to six companies.

Five out of the six companies responded. Bell Helicopters of America backed out of the race due to 50 percent offset clause associated with this contract. Previously, Eurocopter was selected by the armed forces but the contract was cancelled by the Defence Ministry in December, 1997 because Eurocopter had sent the civilian version of the helicopter for field trials.

This time, Eurocopter will be sending the military version of the helicopter and is expected to win the contract. Out of the 197 helicopters, 133 will be given to the Army and the rest will be given to the Air Force to replace their aging fleet of Cheetah and Chetak helicopters that are being used in high altitude conditions in air maintenance roles and for surveillance, as well as search and rescue missions. All these developments are giving the desired results to New Delhi.

Moscow is now on the back-foot and has understood that it will face competition in the market it has been ruling. Russia has indicated that it is ready to look at a downward revision of the price for the Aircraft carrier, Admiral Gorshkov.

Moscow has also resolved the issue of Transfer of Technology of T-90 tanks and has released $64 million for the development of multi-role transport aircraft (MTA). Russia and India signed an agreement in 2007 to develop a 20 ton cargo capacity plane to fulfil futuristic needs of both the countries. Ilyushin design bureau, Irkut Corporation and Hindustan Aearonautics Ltd will develop the aircraft.

Production of the aircraft is expected to begin in about eight years and both the countries will equally share the cost of the $600 million project. India will procure about 45 aircraft and Russia is expected to get 100 aircraft to replace An-12, An-26 and An-32 aircraft. Thus the IAF will have three different maintenance lines for three types of aircraft of different cargo capacity (Boeing c-17, Airbus A330 MRTT and Russian MTA) and will not be dependent on of any particular vendor. IAF will also have the option to switch to any vendor at any time.

INDIA'S ECONOMIC POLICIES

Many early post-independence leaders, such as Nehru, were influenced by socialist ideas and advocated government intervention to guide the economy, including state ownership of key industries. The objective was to achieve high and balanced economic development in India in the general interest while particular programs and measures helped the poor. India's leaders also believed that industrialization was the key to economic development.

This belief was all the more convincing in India because of the country's large size, substantial natural resources, and desire to develop its own defence industries. The Industrial Policy Resolution of 1948 gave government a monopoly in armaments, atomic energy, and railroads, and exclusive rights to develop minerals, the iron and steel industries, aircraft manufacturing, shipbuilding, and manufacturing of telephone and telegraph equipment. Private companies operating in those fields were guaranteed at least ten years more of ownership before the government could take them over. Some still operate as private companies in India.

The Industrial Policy Resolution of 1956 greatly extended the preserve of government. There were seventeen industries exclusively in the public sector. The Indian government took the lead in another twelve industries, but private companies could also engage in production.

This resolution covered industries producing capital and intermediate goods. As a result, the private sector was relegated primarily to production of consumer goods. The public sector also expanded into more services. In 1956 the life insurance business was nationalized, and in 1973 the general insurance business was also acquired by the public sector. Most large commercial banks in India were nationalized in 1969. Over the years, the central and state governments formed agencies, and companies engaged in finance, trading, mineral exploitation, manufacturing, utilities, and transportation. The public sector was extensive and influential throughout the economy, although the value of its assets was small relative to the private sector. Controls over prices, production, and the use of foreign exchange, which were imposed by the British during World War II, were reinstated soon after independence. The Industries (Development and Regulation) Act of 1951 and the Essential Commodities Act of 1955 (with subsequent additions) provided the legal framework for the government to extend price controls that eventually included steel, cement, drugs, nonferrous metals, chemicals, fertilizer, coal, automobiles, tires and tubes, cotton textiles, food grains, bread, butter, vegetable oils, and other commodities. By the late 1950s, controls were pervasive, regulating investment in industry, prices of many commodities, imports and exports, and the flow of foreign exchange.

Export growth in India was long ignored. The government's extensive controls and pervasive licensing requirements created imbalances and structural problems in many parts of the economy. Controls were usually imposed to correct specific problems but often without adequate consideration of their effect on other parts of the economy.

For example, government of India set low prices for basic foods, transportation, and other commodities and services, a policy designed to protect the living standards of the poor. However, the policy proved counterproductive when the government also limited the output of needed goods and services. Price ceilings were implemented during shortages, but the ceiling frequently contributed to black markets in those commodities and to tax evasion by black-market participants. Import controls and tariff policy stimulated local manufacturers toward production of import-substitution goods, but under conditions devoid of sufficient competition or pressure to be efficient.

Private trading and industrial conglomerates (the so-called large houses) existed under the British and continued after independence. The government viewed the conglomerates with suspicion, believing that they often manipulated markets and prices for their own profit. After independence the government instituted licensing controls on new businesses, especially in manufacturing, and on expanding capacity in existing businesses. In the 1960s, when shortages of goods were extensive, considerable criticism was levelled at traders for manipulating markets and prices.

The result was the 1970 Monopolies and Restrictive Practices Act, which was designed to provide the government with additional information on the structure and investments of all firms that had assets of more than Rs200 million, to strengthen the licensing system in order to decrease the concentration of private economic power, and to place restraints on certain business practices considered contrary to the public interest. The act emphasized the government's aversion to large companies in the private sector, but critics contended that the act resulted from political motives and not from a strong case against big firms. The act and subsequent enforcement restrained private investment. The extensive controls, the large public sector, and the many government programs contributed to a substantial growth in the administrative structure of government. Indian government also sought to take on many of the unemployed. The result was a swollen, inefficient bureaucracy that took inordinate amounts of time to process applications and forms. Business leaders complained that they spent more time getting government approval than running their companies. Many observers also reported extensive corruption in the huge bureaucracy. One consequence was the development of a large underground economy in small-scale enterprises and the services sector.

India's current economic reforms began in 1985 when the government abolished some of its licensing regulations and other competition-inhibiting controls. Since 1991 more "new economic policies" or reforms have been introduced. Reforms include currency devaluations and making currency partially convertible, reduced quantitative restrictions on imports, reduced import duties on capital goods, decreases in subsidies, liberalized interest rates, abolition of licenses for most industries, the sale of shares in selected public enterprises, and tax reforms.

Although many observers welcomed these changes and attributed the faster growth rate of the economy in the late 1980s to them, others feared that these changes would create more problems than they solved. The growing dependence of the economy on imports, greater vulnerability of its balance of payments, reliance on debt, and the consequent susceptibility to outside pressures on economic policy directions caused concern. The increase in consumerism and the display of conspicuous wealth by the elite exacerbated these fears. The pace of liberalization increased after 1991. By the mid-1990s, the number of sectors reserved for public ownership was slashed, and private-sector investment was encouraged in areas such as energy, steel, oil refining and exploration, road building, air transportation, and telecommunications. An area still closed to the private sector in the mid-1990s was defence industry. Foreign-exchange regulations in India were liberalized, foreign investment was encouraged, and import regulations were simplified. The average import-weighted tariff was reduced from 87 percent in FY 1991 to 33 percent in FY 1994. Despite these changes, the economy remained highly regulated by international standards. The import of many consumer goods was banned, and the production of 838 items, mostly consumer goods, was reserved for companies with total investment of less than Rs6 million. Although the government had sold off minority stakes in public-sector companies, it had not in 1995 given up control of any enterprises, nor had any of the loss-making public companies been closed down. Moreover, although import duties had been lowered substantially, they were still high compared to most other countries.

Political successes in the mid-1990s by nationalist-oriented political parties led to some backlash against foreign investment in some parts of India. In early 1995, official charges of serving adulterated products were made against a KFC outlet in Bangalore, and Pepsi-Cola products were smashed and advertisements defaced in New Delhi. The most serious backlash occurred in Maharashtra in August 1995 when the Bharatiya Janata Party (BJP—Indian People's Party)-led state government halted construction of a US$2.8 million 2,015-megawatt gas-fired electric-power plant being built near Bombay (Mumbai in the Marathi language) by another United States company, Enron Corporation.

FOREIGN DIRECT INVESTMENT (FDI) IN DEFENCE SPHERE

"Direct foreign investment in Indian defence industries for industrial infrastructure for services, co-development, joint and a production of defence products and components" have been identified by DPP 2008 as a method to discharge defence offset obligations. But in order to encourage investment and transfer of technology to India, it will be important to give foreign defence firms the confidence that they will have greater share in the profits and larger say in the management of the entities they create. Larger stakes should be allowed to foreign firms in such entities whose creation would not have been possible but for these foreign companies. Ironically, Foreign Investment Promotion Board (FIPB) guidelines do not encourage this.

According to the FIPB guidelines, foreign firms that may tie up with Indian entities are allowed only 26 per cent equity in such ventures. The remaining equity has to be owned by Indian entities. The ceiling of 26 per cent is a major impediment to the success of the offset policy. First, foreign firms are reluctant collaborators in any mandatory offset arrangement. Otherwise, these firms would have tied up with Indian entities for the production of defence equipment without any compulsion. But as offsets have been made mandatory in cases involving acquisition over Rs 300 crore, foreign firms can nevertheless be expected to collaborate with Indian firms, as otherwise they will lose the opportunity to profit from the contract that can only be signed with the offset obligation. But, if the created entity has to survive on a long-term basis, the collaborating foreign firm should have a stake in it. This can only come through the creation of attractive prospects for the foreign firms to make greater profit than investments made elsewhere. Therefore, there is a need to make them, not reluctant parties, but willing and enthusiastic partners in JVs by increasing their stake in such collaborations. An example of how higher stakes in companies can help add value to the offset policy is the Boeing purchase of 34 per cent of Aero Vodochody, a Czech firm, as an offset deal. Boeing's subsidiary Ayers bought LET Kunovice, a Czech plane manufacturing firm, with plans to move part of the production line for its own planes to LET.

Second, if the balance of the 26 per cent that a foreign company brings has to be raised by Indian partners, it can lead to many difficulties. Since 26 per cent equity is the upper ceiling that a foreign vendor can invest in India, it has to find an Indian firm that is willing to raise the balance 74 per cent. This raises two difficulties. First, it has to find an Indian partner willing to find resources for this high level of investment. Second, if the foreign firm decides to use a JV as the sole means of fulfilling its 30 per cent obligation under offset, then it will have to find an Indian partner or partners willing to invest more in terms of equity. To illustrate, if a company X enters into a contract for Rs 1,000 crore, it will have to invest Rs 300 crore to discharge its offset obligations. But since a foreign vendor is only allowed 26 per cent equity, to invest Rs 300 crore, it will have to form a JV that involves a total investment of Rs 1,153.8 crore (Rs 300 crore by the foreign vendor and Rs 853.8 crore by the Indian entity or entities). Both the choices are difficult, as is would not be easy to find Indian entities that can make such high investments.

Conversely, increasing the equity may benefit the nation in several ways. Given the above dampeners (arising from the upper ceiling of 26 per cent), it may encourage greater participation by foreign firms in JVs if they have larger share of the equity.

Also, foreign vendors will be reluctant to invest 26 per cent in equity and transfer proprietary technology that may have been developed at high research and development (R&D) cost. There is always a stubborn resistance to transferring technical capability and it can only come at a price as "the transferring country does not simply stand still while its 'beautiful princess' (Williamson, 1983) is shipped abroad and effective competition is created." Therefore, a foreign firm will be less reluctant to grudge competition from an entity established in India in which it has substantial stakes and from whose sales it stands to profit.

Given that comparatively cheap factors of production exist in India, the foreign parent company may even chose to outsource components/items from their Indian JV. Though not in the defence sector, the export performance of Hyundai Motors in India should give India reasons to allow more liberal FDI in the defence sector also.

Second, a foreign firm that invests higher equity will have a stake in the success of the project. It will be more willing to outsource items from India to its other holdings to make the project a success.

Otherwise, there is a danger of the interest of the foreign vendor dissipating once the contract is completed, as without a reason to retain their interests, they will shut shop and return. This point can be illustrated with the instance of armoured personnel carriers purchased by the Philippines Army from the UK. After eight of these were imported from the UK and the remaining 142 were assembled in Philippines, the assembly line was closed, with only minimal offset benefits to the nation. Third, as offset banking has now been allowed, it will give such vendors incentive to accumulate credits for discharging their obligations in future contracts by making value additions and introducing new products.

There should be further transparency in dealing with prospective foreign vendors. At present, GoI does consider higher investments on a case-to-case basis. This concept of case-to-case approach is indeed intriguing to a foreign vendor who in any case finds Indian procedures, bureaucratic control and the penchant for secrecy rather perplexing.

The recent reports that the GoI turned down a joint venture proposal of Mahindra and Mahindra with the British defence giant BAE Systems has not helped convey the right message, coming as these did only weeks after the revised offset procedure was announced.

This rejection has even raised doubts on the seriousness with which India is pursuing its policy to attract foreign investment in the defence sector. Perhaps, GoI may have had strong reasons to reject the proposal. But explaining the reasons to the firms may have limited the damage. There should be more transparency in expressing our views and this will result in increased vendor confidence in the nation.

It may also be difficult to argue that increasing the limits of equity participation for foreign firms will impinge on national security. The only danger perhaps is that such foreign firms may end up buying Indian entities (a view expressed by one of the large Indian entities in response to the questionnaire sent by the author). If this is a serious concern, the problem can be addressed by making it a requirement to obtain the approval of GoI before the takeover of any defence establishment by a joint venture.

DOMESTIC INDUSTRY IN DEFENCE PLANNING

Private entities are answerable to their shareholders and are in the business to make profits, whether in defence or any other sector. Attractive return on investment, more than what can be expected in non-defence sectors, is the only mantra that can make them divert their finite resources to the defence sector. Gestation period is also quite high in defence sector as establishing a defence venture can take more time than other commercial ventures. Therefore, advance information of the acquisition plans of the government can give potential domestic investors the lead time and the opportunity to study the prospects of raising funds and also seek foreign collaborations. This is a necessary precondition for creating the right atmosphere for developing an indigenous defence industry.

At present, private players do not have prior knowledge of the defence plans of the country. Though we have 15-year long-term integrated perspective plan (LTIPP) that flows into the 5-year Services Capital Acquisition Plan (SCAP), which in turn flows into the 2-year roll-on plan for Capital Acquisitions, the acquisition proposals are most often than not guarded as secrets. The Indian domestic industry is not privy to these plans. As a consequence, information is sent to them only when requests for proposals (RFPs) are issued. Potential Indian investors, therefore, lose the lead time that is required to plan and prepare for such large investments.

The solution may lie in sharing with a select group of Indian industries the LTIPP and the SCAPs to the extent they relate to items proposed for acquisition. The argument that revealing in advance what the nation seeks to acquire will be detrimental to national security also does not hold much water. Private companies have been involved in the development of closely guarded defence projects in India. Even those relating to some of the most sensitive projects, find their way into leading arms publications sooner than later. Again, there is no reason to believe that private sector can be less trusted in keeping state secrets than the public sector. In any case, we lose some of our eminent public sector personnel to private sector. Like in the US, we should involve the private sector at the planning stage itself. To ensure secrecy of information, suitable regulations may be put in place, like in the US. If necessary, in very sensitive projects, the information need not be shared.

Defence Items

As argued above, private entities will not embark on any manufacturing venture, defence or otherwise, unless they are confident of reaping dividends from it. Therefore, prudence lies in opening up this sector. Let the market forces regulate the industry. Defence contractors are most often not large. Even large entities source components and subcomponents that make up complex systems from countless small enterprises. In India too, there are thousands of small and medium producers. Several of them do not have licenses as many of the items used in defence equipment also have civilian application. Therefore, the requirement of licenses for the manufacture of defence-related items not only complicates the existing situation but also destroys individual and entrepreneurial initiatives.

Introduce Offset Credit Trading

The 2008 procedure has introduced offset banking. According to the guidelines, offset banking is permissible for a maximum of two-and-a-half years. Given the lead time available from the time RFPs are issued, this time-frame may be around 5 years or even 10 depending on the completion schedule of the project. This is a very positive step and has been very widely welcomed. But the bankable years should not end with the end of the project as "rather than linked to the life of a specific offset project, the technology strategy needs to embrace productive opportunities across the broader economy. Offset policy thus needs to be framed accordingly." It has been estimated that credit transfers account for around 7.5 per cent of all offset transactions and that the banking of offsets has resulted in a trend to permit offset commitments over longer periods of time covering several projects rather than limited to specific projects. This will undoubtedly give confidence to foreign firms hoping to bag Indian contracts get a return for their investment. But this alone is not enough. The most encouraging step will be to introduce offset trading.

Offset trading is the sale of credits accumulated by firms over a defined period. The introduction of this provision will make it possible to sell offset credits to any firm that bags a contract in India and has certain offset obligations to fulfil. It will yield several benefits. First, every prospective firm that is hopeful of bagging any defence contract in India will be assured return on their investment even if they are unsuccessful in securing the contract they may have targeted. It may at least ensure that they may have no losses and also obtain profit in many cases.

This may motivate firms to shed their fears of investing in the military sector in India. Second, India has attractive factors of production. The prospect of offset trading will only increase the willingness of foreign firms to capitalise on these advantages and invest in the defence sector in India. While allowing offset trading, government can also consider prescribing diminishing value to credits over a period of time unless there is value addition to the product.

This will encourage firms to sustain their investments in India over a longer time horizon. Third, a firm that is already discharging its offset obligations can continue producing defence equipment over a longer period of time, hoping to accumulate credits for future contracts. Even if it does not bag the contract it may have hoped to, it will be able to trade the offsets. This policy can lead to a win-win situation for both foreign firms and India. The key to success is the prosperity of all the key stakeholders and hope of future profits for investors. Nothing else will succeed. Success will come from giving foreign firms the incentive to sustain their interests in India by encouraging innovativeness and hope of profits through it.

Directing Offsets

For instance, it has been concluded that the Netherlands and Switzerland have been able to displace jobs in the US through offset arrangements by transferring production facilities to themselves. To achieve this, the two nations exercised careful control to ensure the "precise direction in which offset-resources are steered. Almost never are they aimed at increasing indigenous military production capacity." In the study by Brauer, he has cited Molas-Gallart to argue that Spain had to abandon its dream of an "integrated, comprehensive, indigenous industry to be generated via arms trade offsets." It was also argued that when offsets are bureaucratically mandated and applied to some vaguely specified national interests, net benefits may not exist. Therefore, prescribing a generic list from which offset obligations are to be chosen for implementation may not be the best strategy to serve India's defence needs. This issue deserves further examination.

India is a nation that has a reasonable defence industrial capability. It is more advanced in some areas than in others. For instance, in the field of naval shipbuilding, India has been able to achieve a fair degree of indigenisation and in some cases around 76 per cent. India today is designing stealth frigates and constructing them in Indian yards. But almost all the weapon systems are imported though India has developed and is using many indigenous sensors. Therefore, for instance, the navy should be able to identify areas of high priority such as the weapon systems that it will prefer to produce indigenously and incorporate them in the list. Through this process, the benefits of offset can be channelised into identified areas. For instance, given the plan of the navy for a 160-plus ship force by 2022 from the 145 that it has at present, a prospective vendor will be inclined to invest in identified areas included in the list to: 1) fulfil its offset obligations; 2) accumulate offset credits knowing that orders for the weapons or other naval items will be assured for a known period, given the navy's maritime plan; and 3) be reasonably assured of future orders. Assured of continuing orders, firms will also be inclined to provide value addition over time. To give further impetus to foreign vendors to endeavour towards this goal, a system of procurement through repeat orders, say for 10 years or so, from the same source that had produced indigenously such critical items should be seriously considered. Provision of value addition, etc., can also be made mandatory for such repeat orders. Similarly, critical items for the three services can be compiled and included in the list eligible for discharging offset obligations.

PROGRESS TOWARDS BLUE WATER NAVY

The Navy is an unique arm of the Indian Armed Forces. True to the nature of the seas it sails over, the Navy has vast imagination, tons of potential and patience to wait till it transforms into a true blue water Navy.

The Navy is the only arm of the armed forces that has been trying to remove dependency on foreign vendors and has been encouraging indigenous efforts to become self-reliant. The Navy has its own design bureau that started working on designing small ships like patrol boats, corvettes, etc and kept on honing its design skills.

It has successfully designed 7000 ton class destroyer and is now designing the 44000 ton aircraft carrier. The project, codenamed P-71, started in 2002 with the initially sanctioned amount of

Rs 3,260 crore. The project started gaining momentum in 2006, when the production of warship building blocks began in Cochin Shipyard Ltd. This is the latest technology in building large ships.

The Cochin Shipyard Ltd. has already procured 8,000 tons of steel from SAIL and DRDO. The keel of the Indigenous Aircraft Carrier (IAC) was laid on 28th Feburary, 2009 and it is expected to be handed over to the Navy in 2014. India will become the fifth nation in the world to have the capability of making aircraft carriers. The other four nations are the US, Russia, France and the UK. Among these four, UK is still to produce a ship of 44,000 ton capacity. The IAC will have the capacity of handling 30 aircraft, i.e. Russian Mig-29K, indigenous Light Combat Aircraft and Kamov 31 helicopters.

Indian pilots are already training to fly Mig-29 K in Russia. The deal for 12 Mig-29K fighters and 4 Mig-29K UB operational conversion trainer aircraft. The total deal which includes the aircraft carrier Admiral Gorshkov is worth $740 million. These 16 medium multi-role combat aircraft are being upgraded into dedicated, network-centric information warfare platforms that possess force-multiplier capabilities such as airborne early warning and control. The first batch of four aircraft is expected to be delivered by the end of this year and the rest will be delivered by 2010. It is interesting that all the Mig-29Ks will be here by 2010, but the aircraft carrier Admiral Gorshkov for which Mig-29Ks were bought will not be delivered to India before 2013.

Russians raised the total cost of the aircraft carrier to $2.2 billion and then to $2.9 billion. Though Moscow has agreed to look at the downward revision of the final amount but the aircraft will not be delivered before 2013 against the original deadline of 2008.

Russia has also promised that it will meet the scheduled deadline of delivering three Project 11356 Krivak IV class guided missile frigates.

The frigate has deadweight of 4,000 metric tons and speed of 30 knots. This was a follow-on order placed in 2006 at a cost of $1.6 billion. General Director of the Yantar shipyard, Igor Orlov confirmed that the first ship will be floated out this year, the second one in spring 2010 and the third a little later.

All the three ships will be delivered by 2012 and will be equipped with Brahmos supersonic anti-ship cruise missiles and not the Club-N/3M54TE missiles installed on previous frigates.

Defence Acquisition Council (DAC) has given in-principle approval to the Navy's proposal of construction of four more Kolkata class destroyers.

The follow-on order will be given to Mumbai based Mazagaon Dockyards Limited under the project name "Project 15B". MDL is currently constructing three Kolkata class destroyers under "Project 15A" and is expected to start the delivery (one each year) starting from 2010. Subsequently, the MDL will start working on Project 15B. The MDL has given an order for navigational equipments, based on the Consilium Selux radar, for three destroyers at a cost of $4.6 million. With a 6,800 ton displacement, these vessels will be able to cruise with a speed of 30+ knots.

They will have advanced stealth features and will be armed with Brahmos missiles and Israeli Barak air-defence missile systems. They will also be equipped with 'Nagin' active towed array radar and 'Humsa-NG' hull mounted radar. In total, the Navy will have seven Kolkata class destroyers.

The Navy's design chief, Rear Admiral MK Badhwar informed that the cost of each destroyer being built under Project 15-A is Rs. 3800 crore taking the total cost of the project to Rs. 11,000 crore. Project 15-B should be logically cheaper. Project 15-A is taking longer than expected as it incorporated significant changes and upgrades compared to its predecessor, Project 15-Delhi Class destroyers. But Project 15-B will have fewer design challenges; it will differ from Project 15-A only in weaponry and sensors. The MDL thinks that if the order is placed by end-2009, the first 15-B destroyer will be commissioned in the mid-2015 as the design and planning will take about 1.5 years, and once the design is finalized, the first ship should roll out in about four years.

Under another indigenous project, follow-on order of four more Shivalik class guided missile stealth frigates has been approved by the government.

The MDL is currently building the first batch of the frigates that are expected to be delivered to the Navy by 2012. Consequently, the MDL will start constructing the next batch of four frigates. GE LM 2500 gas turbines will be used to power the frigates. Earlier this year, the US State Department gave "stop all work" instructions to GE as these engines are dual-use power plants.

They can be used on civilian as well as military vessels. For this reason, these were listed in the US Munitions List and did not require any export license from State Department's Directorate of Defence Trade Controls (DDTC).

However to be able to use the turbine on a military vessel, GE needed to obtain Technical Assistance Agreement (TAA) from the State Deptartment. After the "stop all work" instruction, GE applied for TAA from the Political-Military Bureau at the State Department and obtained the same on March 12th, 2009. That brought the work on the Shivalik class frigates back on track.

The MDL and other shipyards are looking for larger orders to reduce the cost and construction time of the ships, but the Navy has its own problems. The Navy gives smaller orders of 3-4 ships because construction delays by the shipyards make the design outdated by the time the ship is rolled out.

In 2012, the Navy will start inducting a number of new vessels of different types, but the real challenge that it is going to face will be with its underwater arm. The Navy has 16 submarines-10 Russian Kilo Class, 4 German HDW class and 2 Russian Foxtrot class.

By 2016 the Navy will be left with about 50 percent, or even less of its current submarine strength. In October 2005, New Delhi signed a contract with French companies DCN-Thales and MDL to build 6 Scorpene submarines in MDL. Now the MDL is constructing hulls for the submarine but there is nothing to fit in them as French companies are asking for virtually double the money to supply the critical components. The MDL has sent a proposal to the Cabinet Committee on Security to approve the additional funds.

This will cause a huge price escalation and delay of at least two years. The Navy was expecting to receive the submarines (one each year) from 2012, but now it is not possible before 2014. The Navy is hoping to cover this delay by getting a quick approval for its Project-75 for additional six submarines. The Navy is looking for more stealth features, Air-Independent Propulsion (AIP) system and land attack capabilities in the new submarines. Pakistan has already strengthened its submarine arm by induction of three Agosta class French submarines, one of which has AIP system and is now looking to acquire three advanced Type-214 AIP-equipped submarines from Germany. China already has a strong fleet of 60+ submarines with 10 of them being nuclear powered. China also has at least one Xia-class and 2 Jin-class SSBN submarines. Indigenous nuclear submarines, Advance Technology Vehicle, will be launched later this year but will not be delivered to the Indian Navy before 2013.

The Navy hopes to receive Russian 12,000 ton Akula-II class nuclear powered submarine on a 10-year lease this year. This will strengthen its depleting submarine fleet to an extent, but New Delhi has to give a serious thought to the Navy's future requirements keeping our hostile neighbors in mind.

5

India's Nuclear Security Policy

On March 26-27, 2012, Seoul is hosting the 2nd Nuclear Security Summit (NSS). The first summit was held in Washington on April 13, 2010. India is participating in the Seoul summit, just as it did in the first summit. In fact, India was one of 47 participant countries at the April 2010 NSS. It had actively participated in all the preparatory Sherpa meetings for the 2010 NSS. In these Sherpa meetings, the participant countries decided the communiqué and the work plan of the 2010 NSS.

On January 16-17, 2012, India is also holding the 3rd Sherpa meeting for the Seoul NSS. This is the first time that India will be holding a Sherpa meeting as part of the NSS. India did not hold any Sherpa meetings in the run-up to the 2010 NSS. Does the holding of the Sherpa meeting demonstrate that India has started playing a proactive role in the NSS process? India has been an active participant in the summit process, but is proceeding it cautiously. Organizing the Sherpa meeting should not mean a major departure from India's nuclear security policy, which has been marked by cautious activism.

For years, neither the Indian strategic community nor the Indian government paid serious attention to the problem of nuclear terrorism. Like many other countries, India believed that nuclear terrorism is a remote reality. At the end of the Cold War, the Western world was concerned about Soviet nuclear materials falling into wrong hands, especially of terrorists. Later, the growing threat posed by terrorist networks such as the Taliban and al Qaeda led to a global campaign to deny such networks materials which may be used for the development of Weapons of Mass Destruction (WMD). The 9 11 attacks made a section of the international community highly apprehensive of WMD terrorism, especially its nuclear version. Even though India was long a victim of terrorism sponsored from the outside, only the post 9 11 Western campaign influenced the Indian decision making apparatus to review its quiescent and sceptical policy vis-à-vis nuclear security.

Interestingly, the Indian government joined almost all the international initiatives without hardly any debate in the country. Joining these initiatives may have been discussed or debated within the government among different department and agencies. A large section of the Indian strategic community became aware of India's joining these initiatives during the 2010 NSS, when the foreign policy establishment briefed the media and the Prime Minister made a statement in Washington.

For nuclear security, the international community has concluded two treaties so far. The Convention on the Physical Protection of Nuclear Material was concluded in 1979, opened for signature in 1980 and entered into force in 1987. This is the only legally binding treaty for the physical protection of civil nuclear energy facilities. India became a party to the treaty in 2002. The Convention was amended to plug the loopholes existing in it, and in July 2005 the Amendment was adopted by the state parties. India ratified the Amendment of the Convention in 2007. However, the Amendment is yet to enter into force because it has not been ratified by two-thirds of its member states.

The second treaty is the International Convention for the Suppression of Acts of Nuclear Terrorism, which was mandated by a 1996 United Nations General Assembly (UNGA) Resolution and adopted by the UNGA in 2005. India signed and ratified this convention in 2006. The Convention entered into force in 2007. This convention intends to facilitate cooperation among member countries to avoid a situation leading to nuclear terrorism.

The Indian government has also expressed support for the *Code of Conduct on the Safety and Security of Radioactive Sources, and supplementary Guidance on the Import and Export of Radioactive Sources.* The Code is reflected in the manuals India has prepared for conducting its nuclear affairs. India is now playing an active and cooperative role in the UN Security Council (SC) Resolution 1540 Committee, although initially, along with other NAM countries, it had expressed reservations about the international law making role of the UNSC. India has also positively approached other legal instruments like Physical Protection of Nuclear Material and Nuclear Facilities, (INFCIRC/225) even before the 2010 NSS. In all the documents India signed for Safeguards, different versions of INFCIRC/225 found place in the agreement.

Though India has supported and adopted the international legal framework for nuclear security, it has adopted a somewhat unique approach towards the institutional framework. Its approach towards the international institutional framework really reflects its policy of cautious activism. Like other NAM countries India supports the centrality of the IAEA. The 2010 Summit documents assign an important role to the IAEA. However, an important role for the IAEA could become possible because of the intense pressure a group of countries, including India, had put during negotiations of the documents that were released during the Washington summit. India also opposed the subsequent move to undermine the IAEA.

As a participant in the 2010 NSS, India supports the summit process and its associated philosophy of voluntarism. It shared the thinking of a group of countries that the Sherpa process should not scuttle the summit process of action and initiative. Along with a group of countries, India opposed the setting up of a monitoring system. India also appears sceptical of multilateralising the Cooperative Threat Reduction or Global Threat Reduction Programme. Despite participating in the Global Initiative to Combat Nuclear Terrorism, India feels that the chairpersonship of the initiative should be democratized and not duopolised by Russia and the US.

If India really wants democratization of the nuclear security institutions and architecture, it may have to take up responsibilities for nuclear security. One leading expert has called upon India to contribute financially to Nuclear Security efforts. Others want India to join the G-8 and contribute to nuclear security and other global issues. And some others want India to play a more constructive role in G-20 and the NAM. A NAM country and a rising economy like India that has a growing relationship with the Western countries can play a balancing game in some difficult situations.

The strategic community in India is also increasingly becoming aware of global nuclear security challenges emanating from Pakistan. For years, oddly, the Indian strategic community was reluctant to openly admit that Pakistani nuclear assets may become a source of nuclear terrorism.

This was because of the apprehension caused by the misinformation campaign of the US non-proliferation community and its clubbing of India with Pakistan and targeting both. Now, however, India and Pakistan have been completely de-linked and the international community has realized the gravity of situation in Pakistan. India should join the international community which is trying to concentrate on Pakistan to promote global nuclear security. It may also hold parleys to include North Korea and Iran in the summit process.

During the Washington NSS, India announced the setting up of a global centre of excellence—Global Center for Nuclear Energy Partnership. Afterwards, India signed an MoU with the US and Japan and received support from France. The UK also appeared to be interested in working with India. India should take the opportunity and showcase this global centre. It should be activated quickly since other such centres are already operational and attracting participation. Already a section of the international media and community has started showing skepticism about this Indian venture.

The government needs to inform the Indian people or at least the strategic community about developments in international bodies and organizations. For this purpose, it should work with research institutes or Non-Governmental Organisations.

In fact, the lack of awareness or knowledge about the subject may be seen in some writings, especially those associated with the military establishment.

In these writings, we do not find any distinction between nuclear security and nuclear safety. After the Fukushima incident, the world is seriously talking about synergizing nuclear security and safety. This synergy is subtle and about an advanced combination of parameters and mechanisms for both the issues. However, in the writings of these analysts, nuclear security is often confused, and is casually replaced with, nuclear safety.

While India may continue its cautious activism, gradually it should begin to play a more active role. India has done a commendable job by erecting a legal framework; it may have to sharpen its institutional efficacy. Apart from activating its centre of excellence, it should also develop a nodal body for nuclear security. The Atomic Energy Regulatory Board (AERB) has been doing highly credible work, though for greater credibility and confidence the creation of an independent body has been sought. The AERB may take up the fragmented nuclear security activities in the future and may become a single body for nuclear security.

INDIA'S DRAFT NUCLEAR DOCTRINE

In April 1998, the Indian government had constituted a Task Force to recommend the establishment of a National Security Council (NSC). The Task Force submitted its report in June 1998 and, in November 1998, the government constituted a three-tier NSC with a full time National Security Advisor and a National Security Advisory Board (NSAB). Although the first task that was planned to be originally entrusted to the NSAB was to conduct a strategic defence review, because of post-Pokhran II compulsions, the NSAB was asked to first formulate India's nuclear doctrine. The NSAB submitted a draft nuclear doctrine paper to the government that was released to the public for wider debate on August 17, 1999. The key features of the proposed nuclear doctrine are reproduced below:

India shall pursue a doctrine of credible minimum deterrence. In this policy of 'retaliation only', the survivability of our arsenal is critical. This is a dynamic concept related to our strategic environment, technological imperatives and the needs of national security. The actual size, components, deployment and employment of nuclear forces will be decided in the light of these factors. India's peacetime posture aims at convincing any potential aggressor that:

- Any threat of use of nuclear weapons against India shall invoke measures to counter the threat; and
- Any nuclear attack on India and its forces shall result in punitive retaliation with nuclear weapons to inflict damage unacceptable to the aggressor.

The fundamental purpose of Indian nuclear weapons is to deter the use and threat of use of nuclear weapons by any state or entity against India and its forces. India will not be the first to initiate a nuclear strike but will respond with punitive retaliation should deterrence fail. India will not resort to the use or threat of use of nuclear weapons against states that do not possess nuclear weapons, or are not aligned with nuclear weapons powers.

The draft nuclear doctrine, while generally following the policy guidelines enunciated by the Prime Minister in Parliament, fleshed out his pronouncements and "provides a broad framework for the development, deployment and employment of India's nuclear forces." The draft paper proposes that India should establish a credible, minimum nuclear deterrent capability comprising sufficient, survivable and operationally ready nuclear forces based on the principle of no first use of nuclear weapons. It emphasises that the level of India's nuclear capability should be consistent with maximum credibility, survivability, effectiveness, safety and security. It provides for the establishment of effective intelligence and early warning systems. It recommends that India's nuclear forces be based on a triad of strategic bombers, land-based ballistic missiles and submarine launched ballistic missiles (SLBMs). Though a sea-based nuclear capability will take many decades to develop, the requirement of SLBMs is considered inescapable due to their relatively lower vulnerability. Nuclear forces that need to survive a first strike have no option but to ensure that at least 50 to 60 per cent of the arsenal is made comparatively invulnerable by being maintained as SLBMs. The draft paper proposes that India's nuclear strike capability be configured to inflict punitive retaliation the consequences of which would be unacceptable to a potential adversary who will therefore be deterred from doing the unthinkable. The doctrine highlights the cardinal supremacy of civilian control over India's nuclear weapons and proposes that the final authority for the release of nuclear weapons must vest with the Prime Minister or his designated successor(s).

The proposed doctrine also rejects the concept of nuclear warfighting and does not, hence, consider it necessary for India to match its nuclear warheads and delivery systems with those of its potential nuclear adversaries. A small number of survivable nuclear warheads and delivery systems that can inflict damage which would be unacceptable to the adversary are considered adequate for the purposes of deterrence. Although the paper has left some ambiguity by not clearly rejecting the need for tactical or battlefield nuclear weapons in India's context, the tenor of the paper and its emphasis on a retaliatory policy appear to rule out any thinking towards tactical nuclear weapons. However, the real distinguishing feature of India's nuclear doctrine is that it is "... anchored in India's continued commitment to global, verifiable and non-discriminating nuclear disarmament..." that has been described as India's national security objective. The use of nuclear weapons is considered "the gravest threat to humanity and to peace and stability in the international system." The doctrine paper clearly points out India's desire to see the world completely rid of nuclear weapons.

As expected, the draft doctrine initiated a major debate in the country about its nuclear policies. Amitabh Mattoo called it "an unapologetic realpolitik articulation of the principal raison d'être of India's nuclear weapons and the requirements needed to lend credibility to the country's deterrent posture." While agreeing with the thrust of India's nuclear policy, he wrote that India's primary quest appeared to be to acquire the strategic autonomy necessary for making independent decisions in an often unfriendly world and to pursue economic and political development without fear of external threats. R. Prasannan called the draft doctrine a wish list attached to the collective speeches of the Prime Minister and his Cabinet colleagues. Bharat Wariavwalla criticised the draft doctrine on the grounds that the definition of minimum deterrence would be very different vis a vis China and Pakistan and, hence, the term is much too loose to pass off as doctrine.

Many analysts and even foreign governments have sought to raise doubts about India's draft nuclear doctrine. It did not help matters that the doctrine was unveiled the week after the Indian Air Force had shot down a Pakistani Atlantique reconnaissance aircraft that had intruded into Indian territory. The US government rejected the Indian desire to develop a nuclear arsenal." The Indian tests also spurred fears of a new Middle East arms race. However, not all Western powers denounced India's attempts to establish a credible weaponised nuclear deterrent. France welcomed the release of India's draft nuclear doctrine as a "logical and indeed wanted step". The most surprising criticism of the draft doctrine is that it conjures up dark visions of a nuclear arms race in Southern Asia. If all nuclear weapons states were to follow a no first use policy, it would be logical to assume that there would gradually be a net reduction in the size of nuclear arsenals - an arms race in reverse! Jasjit Singh offers the following explanation:

The concerns about a potential arms race reflect a perception arising out of the prism of Cold War mind-sets where first strike (and even "launch on warning") was the order of the day. This necessitated large arsenals and potentially pre-emptive strikes with nuclear weapons. The result was the peak of 67,000 nuclear warheads. But China did not follow the same route and relied on minimum deterrence concept with a no first use commitment. There is no evidence that China's nuclear posture led to any arms race. Even in future, China's nuclear arsenal is likely to be dictated by the size of US/Russian arsenals and issues like ballistic missile defences etc. rather than the defensive doctrine of India.

The worst criticism of the draft doctrine has been that opting for a triad of nuclear forces is not indicative of a minimalist posture but of a maximalist one, particularly as sea-based nuclear weapons have been envisaged to form part of the nuclear force. This criticism fails to take into account the fact that the credibility of a nuclear deterrent that is limited to retaliatory strikes only hinges around the ability of the nuclear force to survive a first strike in sufficient numbers to inflict unacceptable punishment in retaliation. Since submarines offer the best survival potential, India has to rely on a small number of SLBMs for credible deterrence. Raja Menon has also criticised the proposed doctrine: "...There is a serious dysfunction between 'minimum deterrence' and a tri-Service arsenal. The two cannot go together, and is (sic) akin to yoking a horse and camel together." However, surprisingly, he finds no use for aircraft-delivered nuclear bombs and states that "to even consider the role of the army in nuclear deterrence, minimum at that, is truly distressing." His hypothesis is that an arsenal for minimum deterrence requires only second-strike weapons, which can only be based on SSBNs.

Some critics have averred that the nuclear threats have not been enunciated and that the draft document does not define the nuclear force levels that India considers "minimum". Others have protested that the costs of India's nuclear deterrent have not been spelt out. The critics of the draft document forget that doctrine defines only a set of beliefs and guidelines on which policy and strategy is based. In the Preamble of the draft paper it is clearly stated in Para 1.6 that "this document outlines the broad principles for the development, deployment and employment of India's nuclear forces." Details regarding the targeting philosophy, nuclear force structures and the finer nuances of command and control cannot be expected to appear in a paper on nuclear doctrine.

The exception in the draft doctrine that India's non-use of nuclear weapons policy against countries that are not nuclear weapons states does not apply if they are militarily aligned with nuclear weapons states, has also been criticised. This exception would include non-nuclear members of NATO and the military allies of the US such as Japan. Rajesh Rajagopalan explains the reasons behind such exceptions:

Two reasons could be suggested for this exception, one practical and the other strategic. The practical reason is that the Negative Security Assurance (NSA) of various nuclear weapons states, around which this non-use policy is based, makes similar exceptions. In fact, the exceptions there are broader and the NSA does not apply to countries that have refused to sign the NPT or are suspected of nuclear weapons ambitions...

The strategic reason... (is that) a good number of non-nuclear countries still host the nuclear arms of nuclear weapons states and share in the command and control infrastructure of nuclear powers. Theoretically, a nuclear attack on India could be mounted by the nuclear forces hosted in third countries. Excluding these countries would mean that no retaliation could be mounted on the bases from where such attacks are launched...

Rajesh Rajagopalan points out that 'minimum deterrence' is mistakenly characterised as doctrine whereas it actually refers to the nuclear force structure. He states that the Indian doctrine is one of 'assured retaliation' and this is to be given effect by a minimalist nuclear force as "an assured retaliation posture is premised on the belief that no one will start a nuclear war if they are assured of a nuclear retaliation, even if it is a weak retaliation. In other words, for an Indian nuclear deterrent to work effectively against China or Pakistan, it is not necessary to threaten them with complete destruction: even retaliating with a few nuclear warheads will create unacceptable costs to both." While the interpretation is no doubt technically correct, it is also true that a policy of assured retaliation, combined with a small nuclear force built on the principle of sufficiency, could overall be characterised as minimum deterrence. However, it is a finely nuanced distinction that must be noted.

Pakistani government spokesmen and scholars have been particularly critical of India's no first use doctrine on the grounds that it is only a declaratory policy and can be easily changed when the need arises. They have failed to take note of the fact that a country's nuclear force structure, command and control system, alert status and its deployment posture are based on its nuclear doctrine. First use doctrines require hair trigger alerts, launch-on-warning and launch-through-attack strategies and elaborate surveillance, early warning and intelligence systems with nuclear warheads loaded on launchers and ready to fire. Nuclear armed aircraft would need to be ready on runway alert, if not constantly airborne as in the case of the erstwhile US Strategic Air Command. India cannot ever resort to any of these measures without Pakistan learning about them almost immediately. What the Pakistanis also forget, or deliberately ignore, is that India has offered to negotiate a mutual no first use treaty with Pakistan that would be binding and verifiable. India's track record of adherence to international treaties has been exemplary. Unfortunately, the same cannot be said of India's neighbours who have violated numerous treaties with impunity, including the NPT and the MTCR.

The charge that India's nuclear doctrine would initiate an arms race in the Southern Asian region is specious and unjustified. China's gradual moves towards a nuclear triad over a period of three and a half decades have not forced India to play "catch up". Even now India does not feel it necessary to match China's 400-plus nuclear warheads, or to follow China and develop multiple independently targetable re-entry vehicles (MIRVs). India has decided to base its deterrent on a small force of survivable nuclear warheads and delivery systems for a retaliatory strike that can inflict punitive damage on a handful of value targets. There is no reason why Pakistan should feel compelled to match India's nuclear warheads and missiles, particularly as it has opted for a first strike doctrine and does not have to worry about the survival of its nuclear forces. With a first use doctrine, even for deterring conventional war Pakistan does not need to match India warhead for warhead and missile for missile. Kenneth Waltz has argued that the distinction between nuclear forces designed for war fighting, that need to be compared with one another, and those designed to deter the use of nuclear weapons, must be clearly understood. Forces designed for deterrence need not match the adversary's nuclear forces as long as they can do unacceptable damage to the adversary with unacceptable damage sensibly defined. Putting it most appropriately, he has said that "more is not better, if less is enough." Hence, those who are raising the bogey of a nuclear arms race in Southern Asia need to review their alarmist views.

It emerges quite clearly that most of the criticism of the proposed nuclear doctrine stems not from any genuine disagreement with India's no first use doctrine and its professed need to establish a credible minimum nuclear deterrent, but from the desire of many Western countries that India should "cap, reduce and eliminate" its nuclear capability and sign the NPT and the CTBT as a non-nuclear weapons state. Since India's nuclear tests and its declaration of the weaponisation of its nuclear deterrent were based on substantial national security interests, the cap, reduce, eliminate mantra is unlikely to now get anywhere.

Efficacy of No First Use

The concept of no first use logically flows out of the current conventional wisdom that the sole purpose of nuclear weapons, if they have a purpose at all, is to deter the use of nuclear weapons. As is well known in nuclear theology, Bernard Brodie had argued many decades ago that the advent of nuclear weapons had fundamentally altered the relationship between war and national policy and that nuclear weapons were so destructive that their only real purpose could be the avoidance of war itself. On the other hand, many other strategists saw nuclear weapons as simply one more addition to a nation's or even a military commander's arsenal, though a very destructive one, and convinced themselves that the use of nuclear weapons could be incorporated into warfighting strategies. Those who saw nuclear weapons as serving a military purpose in real combat naturally opted for first use and pre-emptive nuclear strategies and developed complex warfighting doctrines while the others saw no real purpose except that of deterrence and adopted deterrence strategies, including no first use.

India's declaration of its no first use doctrine has once again focussed international debate on the efficacy of no first use policies, even though India has repeatedly re-iterated that it is willing to negotiate no first use treaties bilaterally or multilaterally with all nuclear weapons states including China and Pakistan. It is often mistakenly believed that the concept of no first use is China's contribution to international peace and stability.

In fact, the no first use formulation goes back to 1925 when the international community concluded a no first use treaty on chemical weapons and toxins in the Geneva Protocol. Though enormous stockpiles of chemical weapons were produced during the Second World War, neither side used them. This was because mutual deterrence continued to operate among the nations that had chemical weapons stockpiles till these were finally delegitimised by the 1993 Chemical Weapons Convention. However, in situations of asymmetry, deterrence did not operate and chemical weapons were used on several occasions: "By the Italians in Ethiopia, by the Japanese against the Chinese and finally by Saddam Hussain against the Iranians." It could be concluded that a no first use policy works best during conditions of mutual deterrence.

A no first use commitment is not merely a verbal or even a negotiated assurance, it can and must be seen to be reflected in the nuclear force structure, the deployment patterns, the types of surveillance assets in place and the state of readiness of a country's nuclear forces. China announced a no first use commitment immediately after its nuclear test in October 1964. In recent years it has diluted this policy by emphasising that such a declaration does not apply to territories that belong to China. While Taiwan falls in this category, so does Arunachal Pradesh in India which China still claims as its own territory. Hence, it can be plausibly stated that China could contemplate the use of nuclear weapons during a war over Taiwan or a border conflict with India in Arunachal Pradesh. The former Soviet Union had also subscribed to the no first use policy. As far back as 1955, the Soviet Union had proposed a no first use pledge by all nuclear weapons states. However, Russia's recently declared military doctrine has withdrawn that pledge and Russia is now committed to a first use nuclear policy even against conventional military threats. Several US thinkers, some of them important former members of the US military establishment such as Robert McNamara and George Kennan, have repeatedly called for a no first use pledge. Despite the end of the Cold War, the US and its NATO allies and friends, including the United Kingdom and France have refused to heed such wise counsel. In fact, the US has said that it would consider the use of its nuclear weapons against chemical and biological weapons and NATO, under US leadership, has developed an "out of area" strategic concept that undermines peace and stability in the international order.

Rooted in its strategic culture as it is, India's no first use doctrine is not a hastily formulated policy designed to win brownie points from the international community after upsetting the non-proliferation apple cart. It is a carefully thought through policy that has taken decades to mature, even if it was not publicly well articulated. Jaswant Singh has written: "No other country has debated so carefully and, at times, torturously over the dichotomy between its sovereign security needs and global disarmament instincts, between a moralistic approach and a realistic one, and between a covert nuclear policy and an overt one." K. Subrahmanyam had written in 1986: "Today the international system is dominated by nuclear dacoits who are refusing to disarm and there is nothing unethical if India were to secure for itself necessary self-protection capabilities to ward off coercive use of nuclear diplomacy... If India is to make a serious intervention in the disarmament debate and contribute to nuclear disarmament, acquiring nuclear capability is a fee that has to be paid." Even during the mid-1980s, defence analysts like General K.

Sundarji and K. Subrahmanyam were advocating a minimum deterrent capability for India and had ruled out the need for tactical nuclear weapons as these were meant for nuclear warfighting - a concept that India did not subscribe to. Hence, minimum deterrence is not a new concept in the Indian context that has been thrust on an unsuspecting nation by the government and the NSAB.

The No First Use Dilemma

Ever since the May 1998 nuclear explosions and the Indian government's advocacy of the doctrine of no first use and a minimum credible deterrent, a major debate has been raging in the strategic community in India on the issue of no first use of nuclear weapons. Many analysts have averred that India has gained nothing and has unnecessarily elected to bear the horrendous costs of a nuclear strike by choosing to adopt a purely retaliatory nuclear policy.

Rear Admiral Raja Menon asks: "Will India... be committed to absorbing a nuclear strike in case deterrence fails?" And answers: "Hardly, because in the event that an intelligence warning of a 'definite' nuclear strike is received, the NCP (National Command Post) will have to consider, among other options, a first launch." To advocate no first use and then consider first use as soon as the alarm bells are sounded would be duplicitous and worthy of the strongest possible condemnation.

It is argued that after all India's no first use doctrine is only a declaratory doctrine and if other nuclear powers are not willing to accept India's offer of a negotiated no first use treaty, why should India subject itself to the ravages of nuclear destruction? It is likely that eventually one or more NWS (including Pakistan) will come around to accepting India's offer of a negotiated bilateral or multilateral no-first-use treaty. Given the groundswell of public opinion against the continuation of nuclear weapons almost all over the world, it may happen sooner rather than later. Meanwhile, some hard questions need to be asked. Is India likely to be faced by situations occasioned by operational realities when it might become necessary for the Indian political leadership to order the first use of nuclear weapons? When will the situation become operationally so critical that India might be forced to do the unthinkable? So, is India's no first use doctrine merely rhetorical nonsense or is it based on sound operational reasoning? These issues pose a strategic dilemma and present a complex challenge that is not at all easy to rationalise.

It is now universally accepted that nuclear weapons are political weapons and not weapons of 'warfighting'. However, the close link between nuclear weapons and a nation's conventional military capabilities is undeniable. If a nation's conventional capability is extremely low vis a vis a nuclear armed adversary, it may be necessary for that nation to adopt an in extremis 'first use' strategy to thwart a conventional military offensive that may threaten to undermine its territorial integrity and lead to its break up. This is the situation that Pakistan finds itself in at present. While India may have no intentions of launching a major conventional offensive into Pakistan, given India's conventional superiority (no matter how slender the edge may be), Pakistan has based its national security strategy on the first use of nuclear weapons to prevent its comprehensive military defeat like in 1971 and, consequently, its disintegration as a nation. It is for this reason that Pakistan does not accept India's offer of a bilateral no first use treaty as a nuclear confidence building and risk reduction measure.

Though overall China's conventional military forces far outnumber India's, due to China's problems in inducting, deploying and logistically sustaining large forces in Tibet, India enjoys a reasonable defensive capability at present and therefore does not need a 'first use' nuclear strategy to deter a conventional Chinese offensive backed by nuclear-tipped ballistic missiles deployed in Tibet. However, India's existing defensive capability is being quickly eroded as China is rapidly modernising its armed forces, raising rapid deployment divisions and improving the logistics infrastructure in Tibet while exhibiting extreme intransigence in resolving the outstanding territorial and boundary dispute with India. If India continues to neglect the upgradation of its conventional military capability and military modernisation by investing the grossly inadequate sum of less than 2.5 percent of its GDP for defence, as it is doing at present, the nation may again have to suffer the ignominy of large-scale military reverses, should China choose to fight even a limited border war after completing its military modernisation by 2005-2010.

While nuclear doctrine must undoubtedly be based on sound theoretical underpinnings, it has to be ultimately tested in the crucible of operational reality. The proponents of a first use strategy for India need to more deliberately ponder the threat scenarios that might justify the unthinkable. Some plausible scenarios are worth considering in this context. Starting at the lower end of conventional conflict with low intensity conflict (LIC) and Pakistan's ongoing proxy war with India, would the use of a Stinger or Unza surface-to-air (SAM) missile by Pakistan-supported mercenary Islamists to bring down an Indian Airlines aircraft over Kashmir Valley justify an Indian nuclear strike? Or, would a pro-active punitive response across the Line of Control (LoC) with massive artillery and air power sustained over a few weeks be more desirable?

In another scenario, would a battalion or even a brigade size attack by the Pakistan army across the LoC, or even Kargil-type intrusions on the Indian side of the LoC, that result in major gains for Pakistan, justify the first use of nuclear weapons by India when their retaliatory use by Pakistan would be a certainty? Or, would a punitive ground and air forces conventional response across the LoC (and perhaps across the international boundary by the IAF) in another sector yield better dividends? After all, it is well known that there are areas on the LoC where Indian forces could be heading for key value objectives in Pakistan Occupied Kashmir (POK) within days of the outbreak of hostilities in Jammu and Kashmir (J&K).

In case such exchanges across the LoC escalate to a larger conventional conflict, as they well might, Pakistan may launch its Army Reserve North (ARN) through the Shakargarh Bulge in the Sialkot sector and threaten to cut off Kashmir's lifeline NH-1A between Pathankot and Jammu. If Pakistan achieved initial success, such an offensive would pose a grave danger to the security of J&K. Would the first use of nuclear weapons be a rational choice for India under such circumstances? Or would it perhaps be more prudent to launch one or more Indian Strike Corps counter-offensives across the International Boundary in Punjab, Rajasthan and Gujarat, as General Harbaksh Singh did in 1965 with Lal Bahadur Shastri as Prime Minister, to make the Pakistanis recoil from their offensive in the Jammu sector? Surely, the launching of sizeable counter offensives into Pakistan's heartland would be a better way to relieve pressure on J&K.

Another option favoured by military analysts is the "zero warning" option in which Pakistan is given the credible capability of launching what may be termed as a "cold start" conventional war due to the proximity of its cantonments to the International Boundary, or by concentrating strike formations under the garb of training exercises. While there may be some merit in the initial military viability of such an option, unless India strengthens its technological intelligence and humint capabilities, what needs to be considered is the "day after" impact of India's counter moves to checkmate such a Pakistani offensive. With the IAF in full flow within hours and army formations closing in rapidly on the ingressing Pakistani units, while also simultaneously sealing the border behind them, the invaders would be hard pressed to ensure their own security and would eventually be destroyed in detail.

International opinion would also be firmly on India's side. Any well prepared army or air force can achieve tactical surprise, as the Egyptians did during the Yom Kippur war against the Israelis in 1973; the acme of military skill lies in being able to sustain the offensive logistically beyond 48 hours and holding on to the initial gains in the face of the adversary's reaction. It should be clear to perceptive observers that Pakistan has learnt the right lessons from its strategic blunder in Kargil during the summer months of 1999 and is unlikely to repeat such hara-kiri in a hurry.

Inherent in an Indian nuclear first strike option, as advocated by the opponents of no first use, is the Pakistani nuclear retaliation that would inevitably follow on Indian cities and military targets. Cities like Jodhpur, Bikaner, Ahmedabad, Jalandhar, Ludhiana and perhaps even New Delhi and Mumbai would be the likely targets of a retaliatory Pakistani nuclear strike. The limited gains that an Indian first strike may achieve and the real possibility of successful Pakistani nuclear retaliation, the resounding answer to the first use nuclear option by India is no. An Indian nuclear first strike would not be justified as the costs of Pakistani retaliation would be prohibitive. Nor would it be operationally expedient. In none of the above scenarios India's survival as a nation-state is likely to be seriously threatened. Various other even more pessimistic scenarios could be considered but the result would be the same.

It clearly emerges that across the entire spectrum of conventional conflict, the first use of nuclear weapons by India does not make sound strategic sense. Besides, a first use doctrine would invite international opprobrium, seriously undermine India's efforts towards total nuclear disarmament and be prohibitively costly to implement. It is not generally well appreciated that a first use doctrine requires a massive investment in surveillance and target acquisition infrastructure by way of satellite and aerial reconnaissance and human intelligence to execute 'launch on warning' and 'launch through attack' strategies, with the nuclear forces being maintained on permanent hair trigger alerts. A first use doctrine also requires quick political decision-making and decentralisation of the control of nuclear weapons to theatre commanders in the armed forces. Hence, such a doctrine is inherently more risky and more likely to lead to the accidental, even unauthorised, use of nuclear weapons.

It would, of course, be far better to mutually negotiate a no first use treaty with adversarial nuclear armed states as that would be the best nuclear risk reduction measure. Russia and China have signed a mutual no first use treaty. In case India's nuclear-armed adversaries continue to be recalcitrant in signing a binding no first use pact, it would be worthwhile for India to consider some essential qualifications to India's unilateral no first use doctrine. The first is to clearly spell out that a nuclear strike on Indian soldiers even within Pakistani territory would be deemed to be a nuclear strike on India and would invite massive punitive nuclear retaliation. The absence of this rider would negate India's conventional edge over Pakistan as the army would be forced to plan on launching only shallow limited objective offensives to avoid risking nuclear strikes on the mechanised spearheads leading India's advance. Only the capability of executing deep offensive strikes can ensure conventional deterrence and present viable policy options to prevent Pakistan's predilection for attempting salami slicing in J&K.

The second caveat should be that even a conventional bombing or missile attack on India's nuclear establishments and nuclear weapons storage sites during war, that results in casualties due to a nuclear explosion or even radiation leaks, would invite a nuclear response.

Though India and Pakistan have signed an agreement on not targeting each other's nuclear facilities, such agreements have little value when war is declared. Also, state-sponsored acts of terrorism or sabotage of India's nuclear establishments and storage sites should also result in nuclear retribution against the sponsoring country. With better surveillance systems and improvements in the intelligence gathering apparatus, it should be possible to accurately determine the identity of the originator of such heinous crimes. Without these inescapable qualifications, with others to be added when necessary, it would be extremely difficult for India to implement a credible no first use doctrine.

Key Features

Even though the draft nuclear doctrine formulated by the NSAB is yet to be formally debated in Parliament, there is a broad national consensus on its central facets. According to Jasjit Singh, the following essential elements constitute the key features of India's nuclear doctrine:

Firstly, India's nuclear weapons are meant to deter the use and threat of use of nuclear weapons against India. "But unlike most their nuclear weapon states, India's nuclear weapons are not meant to deter the use and threat of use of conventional weapons, chemical weapons, biological weapons or a generalised formulation of protecting national interests any time anywhere. The doctrine requires that the nuclear policy should seek to deter rather than fight a war with nuclear weapons. The orientation of the doctrine is thus quite narrowly focused on the need to defend India through deterrence against nuclear weapons threat." However, India recognises that nuclear weapons cannot provide deterrence in all circumstances and limited conventional conflict remains possible even under the overhang of nuclear weapons. This was borne out by the 1999 Kargil conflict between India and Pakistan.

Secondly, India's nuclear doctrine is firmly anchored on the principle of "no first use" even against nuclear threat or use. "India's use of its nuclear weapons would be predicated on failure of deterrence, that is, if and when an adversary uses nuclear weapons against India. This severely circumscribes the potential development, deployment and employment of the nuclear arsenal."

Thirdly, India's no first use doctrine is a defensive doctrine that limits the use of nuclear weapons to retaliation only. Hence, it is only a precaution against the use of nuclear weapons against India and is in total harmony with the UN Charter. "Article 51 of the Charter under Chapter VII clearly endorses 'the inherent right of individual or collective self-defence if an armed attack occurs against a Member of the United Nations' (emphasis added)... In fact, UN Security Council Resolution 1172 is a gross violation of the UN Charter since it seeks to deny India the right enshrined in the Charter (by seeking) elimination of the capabilities that the permanent members of the Security Council themselves possess and jealously guard by disregarding their treaty obligations of nuclear disarmament."

Fourthly, the doctrine is based on the concept of minimum deterrence that implies that India's nuclear policy, strategy and posture would be guided by the minimalist principle. "The emphasis on "minimum" deterrence clearly defines this principle in relation to the capability sought, the size of the arsenal, costs involved, the level of retaliation required and the nuclear posture in peace time and in times of crisis and active threat."

Finally, "India's nuclear doctrine emphasises that global, verifiable and non-discriminatory nuclear disarmament is a national security objective. This is to be expected from a country that has pursued the goal of complete abolition of nuclear weapons for decades in order to remove its own security dilemma as well as ensure greater prospects for international peace and security."

India's desire to develop a credible minimum nuclear deterrent against nuclear blackmail and the threat of use of nuclear weapons, is an eminently justifiable national security imperative. India's no first use, retaliation-only nuclear doctrine is not only morally befitting and worthy of India's civilisational heritage, it is also operationally sound strategy. However, deterrence hinges on credibility and India is still far from demonstrating strong political resolve to execute a massive retaliatory nuclear strike. Only when India's adversaries are convinced that India has both the necessary political and military will and the hardware wherewithal to respond to a nuclear strike with punitive retaliation that will inflict unacceptable loss of human life and unprecedented material damage, will they be deterred. Only then will the nuclear monster remain tightly leashed in and around India's neighbourhood. The adoption of graduated or flexible response strategies will weaken the quality of India's deterrence and may tempt its adversaries to test India's resolve and capabilities. As long as offensive nuclear deterrence continues to be so unabashedly practised by most of the other NWS, India's defensive nuclear deterrence policies are totally justified.

NATIONAL SECURITY POLICY AND STRATEGY

The concept of national security rests mainly on the proposition that many foreign and domestic political, economic and military issues are inter-related, each with implications on the other. In India's case, this has been highlighted by insurgencies and other political events, particularly in border-states, and other outside pressures, which are brought to bear on the country's economy and technological progress from time to time. A response to this type of environment calls for a highly focussed national security policy and strategy. Effective guidance on national security and defence policy objectives is fundamental to the defence planning process. National security is a relative matter without a firm criteria but unless firm national security objectives are set and a defence policy evolved, there can be no military doctrine or balancing of defence effort with other national objectives and priorities such as maintaining a viable economy and supporting development of society.

The lack of a cohesive national security strategy and defence policy has many implications. First, it results in the absence of clear political direction regarding politico-military objectives, which is the very basis of sound defence planning. Secondly, there is inadequate coordination of defence plans and economic development. Finally, science and technology policies for defence, general industrialisation and other development programmes are not coordinated properly to achieve security goals and objectives.

Perspective Planning

A Defence Plan has to be prepared on the basis of a 15-year long perspective planning system, such that the first five years of the plan are very firm (Definitive Plan), the second five years less firm (Indicative Plan) and the third five-year term tentative (Vision Plan). There has to be a reasonably firm allocation of financial resources for the first five years and an indicative allocation for the subsequent period. Perspective planning needs to be done in the Integrated Defence Headquarters, where military, technical and R&D experts take an integrated view of future threats and challenges. This has to be based on future battlefield scenarios, and array of forecasts, evaluation of strategic options and force mixes, and analysis of potential technical and industrial capabilities. Based on this, the respective Service should work on their perspective plans and the R&D and Defence Production/Supplies experts should spell out their requirements in terms of effort, technology and indigenous production.

Integrated Planning

As stated earlier, the CDS, who would be the cornerstone of integrated operational planning for defence, has not been appointed. India's defence planning, therefore, continues to be Service based. Often, the threat perception of one Service is at variance with that of another Service. What emerges is essentially a sum of total of Service or department wise programmes. The focus is not on overall goals or priorities but on what is required by a particular Service. In its endeavour to lay the groundwork for an increased share of the budget, each Service tends to exercise its own priorities, favouring its own plans to the detriment of joint plans.

Subjects like surveillance, air defence, electronic warfare, and amphibious operations, which relate to more than one Service, do not get adequate attention. Integrated planning for defence is essential for creating balanced force structures and for the successful execution of all military missions. In fact, it is the most effective manner of ensuring effective defence. According to Charles Hitch, "the revolution in military technology has not only changed the character of our military programmes, it has also to a significant degree blurred the lines of demarcation among various Services".

Most major military missions today require the participation of more than one military service. Therefore, the principal concern now must be centred on what is required by the defence establishment as a whole to perform a particular mission—not what is required by a particular Service to perform its individual part of that 'mission'. The areas of commonality in modern weapon systems are immense and growing rapidly. Communications, guidance systems, missiles, radars, lasers—even traditional equipment such as guns, fuses, ammunition and vehicles are common. Integrated defence planning is necessary in view of escalating costs of these weapons and equipment.

Self-reliance in Defence Technology

The DRDO has a network of 51 laboratories and establishments. The Scientific Advisor (SA) to the Raksha Mantri (RM) is the Secretary of this

Department. The DRDO has a staff of 30,000, including 6,800 scientists and engineers. It receives approximately four to six per cent of the defence budget annually.

The DRDO is engaged in the pursuit of self-reliance in critical technologies relevant to defence. It formulates and executes a programme of scientific research, design and development for the induction into the Armed Forces of state-of-the-art weapons and other equipments. In April 1984, the DRDO envisaged a programme "to transform the Department into a leader of international class with the mission to capture and retain commanding heights in critical technologies". A 'mission mode' organisational structure and approach was approved by the Government with a view to increasing the element of self-reliance from the current 30 per cent to 70 per cent by 2005. This goal, however, is nowhere in sight.

The Department has developed more than 1,100 items of weapon systems and equipment with a production value of over Rs 6,000 crore. But it has not been able to make any major contribution to the state-of-art weapons and equipment. Most of its programmes, like Prithvi (sea borne version), Trishul (short-range surface to air missile), Akash (medium-range surface to air missile), Nag (anti-tank missile), Light Combat Aircraft with Kaveri engine, Pinaka (multiple-barrel rocket system), MBT Arjun, Electronic Warfare equipment, new radio sets for the Army, Sonar system for Navy, and many other items, are way behind schedule.

Despite the media hype, the costs have been heavy. MBT Arjun, when it goes into production mode, will have more than 60 per cent imported components, including several crucial components like the engine and gun control system. It will cost over Rs 25 crore a piece whereas the cost of a T-90 tank, which is as superior (if not more), is less than Rs 10 crore along with technology transfer. Matters have come to such a pass that the Armed Forces have stopped believing media reports about the so-called 'successful trials' of weapons and equipment.

Because of the failure to deliver the required weapons and equipment, defence planning and Force structuring by the Services has suffered continuously.

The DRDO's inability to deliver in time has caused a crisis of confidence and constant dissatisfaction in the Services. In order to ensure smooth progress towards self-reliance in defence technology, the Government must undertake a periodic performance audit of DRDO projects to reinforce efforts in areas of success and weed out projects that are unproductive.

NUCLEAR WEAPONS SECURITY

Since the 1998 nuclear tests, India and Pakistan appear to have accelerated nuclear weapons development and, possibly, deployments. Most observers still believe that neither Pakistan nor India has deployed warheads mated with delivery systems.

Fissile material components (pits) are thought to be kept separately from the rest of the warhead. Such a physical separation helps deter unauthorized use and complicates theft.

In the early years of the U.S. nuclear weapons program, fissile material components of warheads were physically separated; in the earliest bombs, the two were mated in the bomb-bay of the aircraft. When nuclear missiles entered the U.S. inventory, the warheads were physically separated from the missiles. In addition to physical separation, however, there need to be rules and procedures for authorized use; it is not clear what those are for India or Pakistan. India and Pakistan have been moving towards more structured nuclear command and control authority, organization, and strategic planning. However, there is no information on whether they have implemented two-man rules (a requirement for the concurrent involvement of at least two people to be able to fire a weapon) or other procedures for ensuring no unauthorized use.

There is no reliable information on where fissile material is shaped or machined into components for weapons, or where fissile cores are kept if they are separated from other weapon components and delivery systems for India and Pakistan. Some observers believe that nuclear weapons parts are "probably distributed in a number of tightly secured facilities at different locations throughout Pakistan." Physical security in the case of Pakistan is provided by the military. India has kept strong civilian oversight of the weapons program, with the military kept predominantly at arm's length. However, the details of security in both cases are unknown. In April 2000, the Indian government ended independent safety oversight at BARC, the "nerve centre" of the Indian nuclear weapons program. Some analysts have interpreted this change as an indication of accelerated nuclear weapons work at BARC. On October 2, 2001, Pakistan's Foreign Ministry issued a statement that "Our nuclear assets are 100% secure, under multiple custody." Media reported that Pakistan had moved nuclear weapons components to several undisclosed locations. Subsequently, President Musharraf reorganized elements of the Pakistan Atomic Energy Commission (PAEC) and investigated several nuclear weapons scientists who reportedly had ties to Islamic extremists.

Personnel Security

In terms of personnel security, concerns have focused mostly on Pakistan, and most recently, on the activities of Pakistani nuclear freelancer Dr. A.Q. Khan. At the end of 2003, evidence from Libya revealed that Khan had sold a variety of nuclear materials, technology, equipment, and even a bomb design, to Libya, Iran, and North Korea over two decades. Although there were reports that President Musharraf knew of improprieties regarding Khan in 1999, Musharraf took no steps to rein in Khan until 2001. At that time, Khan was "forced" to retire as director of Khan Research Laboratories and given a job as special advisor to President Musharraf. Before that, however, he had amassed millions of dollars in selling nuclear technology to rogue states. Pakistani officials claimed that they tightened controls on their nuclear weapons program with the creation of the National Command Authority (NCA) in February 2000. One of the features of those controls is the screening of key people in the Pakistani nuclear weapons program every two years by the Inter Services Intelligence Agency, Military Intelligence, the Intelligence Bureau, and the Strategic Plan Division of the NCA. However, "top-level people (including scientists) are controlled by their organizations and not psychologically screened." Much less is known about Indian personnel security. Although India set up a Nuclear Command Authority similar to Pakistan's in January 2003, there is little information on whether associated personnel screening measures have been implemented.

Nuclear Material Safeguards: IAEA Safeguards

Most of the material and facilities in India and Pakistan is not subject to international safeguards. In India, there are safeguards on 6 reactors (Tarapur 1 & 2, LEU-fuelled power reactors; Rajasthan RAPS-1 and -2, which use natural uranium; and Koodankulam-1 and -2, LEU-fuelled power reactors). In addition, the Tarapur plutonium reprocessing facility (Prefre) is safeguarded when safeguarded fuel is used in the facility and the Tarapur MOX fuel fabrication plant has safeguards when it runs safeguarded material through it. The Hyderabad fuel fabrication plant has partial safeguards.

Key nuclear weapons-related facilities in India that are not subject to IAEA inspections include the Bhabha Atomic Research Centre (BARC) in Trombay, which houses the Cirus and Dhruva research reactors for plutonium production, plutonium reprocessing plants and a pilot-scale uranium enrichment plant. These sites, as well as storage sites for weapons-grade material or for weapons themselves could be highly attractive to terrorists because they may contain weapons-usable nuclear material.

Pakistan has IAEA safeguards on a few facilities. The KANUPP power reactor, which uses natural uranium, Chasma-1, LEU-fuelled power reactor, and two research reactors at Rawalpindi that have used HEU in the past are under international safeguards. The following facilities are not under safeguards: the Khan Research Laboratories at Kahuta, which include a uranium enrichment plant and facilities for fabricating HEU into weapons; centrifuge enrichment plants at Sihala, Golra and Wah/Gadwal, the Chasma reprocessing plant, and PINSTECH and SPINSTECH facilities related to reprocessing at Rawalpindi. These nuclear material production sites, as well as weaponization, storage and assembly sites (if separate facilities exist), could be high-value targets for terrorists.

SAFETY AND SECURITY PAKISTAN'S NUCLEAR ARSENAL

Determined to retain and expand its nuclear capabilities but shaken by the reaction to A.Q. Khan's global nuclear entrepreneurship, in 2004 Musharraf's government had sharply reversed its earlier policy of keeping all nuclear matters under the wrap. It hoped thereby to assure the world that Pakistan's nuclear weapons were in safe hands. A stream of highly placed official visitors made a beeline for Washington's think-tanks and military colleges across the United States. A few years earlier this would have been unthinkable. Visits from top officials of the Strategic Plans Division (SPD), which is charged with the possession, maintenance, and safety of Pakistan's nuclear weapons became routine, and still continue.

It is especially significant that the director general of the SPD, Lt. Gen. Khalid Kidwai, is a visitor to the US. He was, for example, invited to a special guest lecture to the faculty, students, and guests of the Naval Postgraduate School in Monterey where he sought to debunk the notion that Pakistani weapons could fall into the hands of religious extremists, were on hair-trigger alert, or be used irresponsibly. Other Pakistani military officers associated with the nation's nuclear program are paid by US funding sources for writing reports and papers for US think-tanks and research institutes. Still others are in the process of writing books that will reveal the true history of the Pakistani nuclear program xlviii. To safeguard Pakistan's crown jewels is a relatively recent preoccupation that dates to the September 11, 2001 attack.

Although Pakistan's military government insisted that there was no danger of any of its nuclear weapons being taking for a ride, it did not take chances. Several weapons were reportedly airlifted to various safer, isolated, locations within the country. This nervousness was not unjustified – two strongly Islamist generals of the Pakistan Army (the head of Pakistan's ISI intelligence agency, Lt. General Mehmood Ahmed, and Deputy Chief of Army Staff, General Muzaffar Hussain Usmani), close associates of General Musharraf, had just been removed. The seriousness of betraying the progeny of Pakistan's intelligence services was something that Musharraf feared – and for good reason.

Internationally, there are widespread fears that instability in Pakistan could make its nuclear weapons and stocks of nuclear explosive material dangerously vulnerable to theft. As could be expected, Pakistan's position has been one of emphatic denial: the Foreign Ministry claims that our [nuclear] assets are 100 percent secure, under multiple custody. Soothing words, however, have not taken away a general sense of worry. Pakistan is now in the grip of a full-fledged insurgency by Islamic groups. Some of these view Pakistan's nuclear weapons as belonging to the *Ummah,* rather than Pakistan alonel. This has enhanced the feeling internationally that Pakistan's nuclear weapons, fissile materials, and other nuclear components are unsafe.

The dangers to Pakistan's nuclear weapons are potentially four-fold:

- From India and the US, separately or together. Israel is a distant possibility but not to be ruled out.
- From outside: Islamic militants attacking a nuclear storage site or facility with the purpose of capturing a nuclear weapon.
- From inside: Islamic elements in the army who have responsibility for protecting and operating nuclear sites or facilities.
- From a collaboration between insiders and outsiders.

There is concern in Pakistan of the growing Israeli-Indian strategic alliance, underscored by the supply of four Phalcon AWAC-type systems. These have the capability of tracking Pakistani aircraft over the entire geographical area. India has already acquired two Israeli Green Pine radars, capable of tracking missiles at a distance of 400 km. These are normally used in conjunction with the Arrow II anti-missile system. These early-warning systems could be effectively used by Israel to launch a pre-emptive strike at Pakistan's nuclear facilities with India's direct assistance or by using India as a base. Only an extreme crisis would result in India or the US, whether acting together or separately, to attack a nuclear armed state with all the obvious dangers this contains. Even a massive use of force is unlikely to net all of well-hidden and well-protected Pakistani nuclear weapons. Moreover, the job would be incomplete unless the major nuclear weapon facilities, reactors, and uranium enrichment plants were also destroyed completely. This would involve nothing short of total war.

On the other hand, Islamic extremists may seek a weapon for ultimate use against a US or European city. But, because it would be much easier to arrange, they may seek the destruction of an Indian or Pakistani city, with the hope of provoking total war between Pakistan and India. This would be consistent with the suicide bombing strategy followed by Al-Qaida elsewhere. In the extremist mindset, it is best if infidels are killed. But if Sunni Muslims are killed, they will simply make it to heaven a bit earlier.

Defending against other nations as well as internal enemies poses a difficult security dilemma: Pakistan would like to keep the location and details of its nuclear weapons secret in order to increase their chances of a strike by India, the US, or Israel.

On the other hand army insiders are already, by definition, in the know. Perhaps in collusion with an external Islamic group they could be plotting a move unknown to the Nuclear Command Authority (NCA), the SPD, or the Chief of Army Staff. How could such an attempt be foiled?

Only partial safety is possible no matter what the technical fix. One obvious mechanism is to reduce the readiness level. Pakistan is widely believed to store the fissile core and bomb mechanisms separately in safely guarded vaults. As early as December 1999, it had requested senior US officials visiting Islamabad for Permissive Action Links (PALs) that are directly integrated into the firing mechanism and electronics of a nuclear weapon, as well as Environment Sensitive Devices (ESDs), in order to enhance protection against unauthorized use or accidental nuclear detonations.

At that time, the US had declined for obvious reasons: these devices make it possible for the weapons to be maintained at a higher state of alert for the same level of safety, thereby increasing the threat perceived by India. But subsequent to a reversal of Pakistan's relationship with the US after 911, it is possible that the US may have acceded to Pakistan's request without demanding that Pakistan reveal the location or details of its nuclear weapons. According to an ISIS report, US Secretary of State Colin Powell had offered nuclear protection assistance to Pakistan after 911li. Pakistan found the offered technology to be quite rudimentary but nevertheless accepted it under the condition that the end point usage would remain opaque. Other aspects of the assistance included training courses for Pakistani nuclear weapons personnel in US labs where they were instructed on nuclear safety and security issues.

David Albright, a US nuclear security analyst, prescribed the following forms of additional assistance to Pakistan in the aftermath of 911:

"Generic physical protection and material accounting practices; theoretical exercises; unclassified military handbooks on nuclear weapons safety and security; more sophisticated vaults and access doors; portal control equipment; better surveillance equipment; advanced equipment for materials accounting; personnel reliability programs; and programs to reduce the likelihood of leaking sensitive information. In addition, aid could focus on methods that improve the security of nuclear weapons against unauthorized use through devices not intrinsic to the design of the nuclear weapon or through special operational or administrative restrictions. Excluded assistance would include nuclear weapons design information aimed at making more secure, reliable or safer nuclear weapons or devices, PALs, coded launch control devices, and environmental sensing devices."

While technical measures to reduce the chances of nuclear sabotage and accident must undoubtedly be implemented, there is a fundamental tension that cannot be avoided – a perfectly safe nuclear weapon is also one that cannot be used. Hence, by definition, it is useless. In times of crisis and war, when casualties and passions run high, there will be a strong urge to weaken the safety mechanisms in place.

NUCLEAR THREAT REDUCTION IN INDIA AND PAKISTAN

The Carnegie Endowment for International Peace (CEIP) published a draft report, 'Universal Compliance: A Strategy for Nuclear Security', in June 2004. The report proposes a strategic blueprint for US leadership to rethink international nuclear nonproliferation and global nuclear security. In this report, the recommended measures for nuclear risk reduction between India and Pakistan include:

- o Establishment of national risk reduction centres in both countries to administer agreed upon confidence-building measures.
- o Acommitment not to develop, produce, and use 'tactical' nuclear weapons.
- o Agreement not to flight-test missiles in the direction of the other country.
- o Agreement to flight-test missiles only from designated test ranges.
- o Provision of advance notification of the movement of missiles for training purposes.

The Henry L. Stimson Centre's report, 'Reducing Nuclear Dangers in South Asia', argues that: "The stability-instability paradox that was formulated in the West to characterise the dangers of nuclear deterrence is alive and well in South Asia. This paradox holds that, while offsetting nuclear capabilities might indeed prevent a full-blown conventional or nuclear war, the presence of these fearsome weapons could also encourage the use of violence at lower levels in the expectation that escalation would be contained by a mutual desire to avoid the nuclear threshold."

And that, "Kashmir has been inflamed since the advent of covert nuclear capabilities on the subcontinent, and tensions have grown even more pronounced with the demonstration of overt nuclear capabilities in 1998. The region is now experiencing crises with greater frequency and severity."

The report includes extensive deliberations during two workshops, November 14-18, 2002, and May 20-23, 2003, with participants from the US, India and Pakistan, convened by the Stimson Centre to discuss escalation control and scenarios that could lead to crossing of the nuclear threshold. It provides the following 'doable' steps in the near term:

- o Establishment of national risk reduction centresto serve as focal points for the administration of confidence-building measures.
- o Missile-related measures to formalise and properly implement the agreement concerning prior notification of missile launches; to formalise and extend the time-line for such notifications; to forego missile flight tests in the direction of the other country; to flight test missiles only from designated test ranges; and to provide advance notification of the movement of missiles for training purposes.
- o Clarifying terminology or developing common terminology on nuclear-related programmes, deployment, and doctrine could reduce misunderstanding and increase crisis stability.
- o Leadership declarations affirming responsible nuclear stewardshipcould help defuse nuclear dangers and facilitate an improvement in bilateral relations.
- o Increased awareness of nuclear dangers, particularly with regard to the possible acquisition of nuclear materials by terrorist groups, would be advisable.

In the Stimson Centre's report, the proposals collected in the workshops on escalation control are grouped in five categories: improving bilateral relations; nuclear risk reduction and strategic restraint; safety and security measures; and, improving intelligence through communication. Both the reports, by CEIP and the Stimson Centre, have this presumption that 'deterrence' may not work between India and Pakistan as similar to the Cold War experience.

Such assumptions are not completely invalid for the two countries did resort to nuclear rhetoric during the 1999 Kargil conflict and indulged in 'nuclear signalling' during the period of crisis in 2001-2. In addition, the absence of a doctrine without no-first-use policy and repeated calls from the Pakistani side to lower the threshold could have a certain bearing on the thinking of Western analysts. Already, the strategic debate had reached a slightly higher level than was normally prevalent in the subcontinent when the Indian Army Chief stated that a limited war with Pakistan is possible.

For any future war in the subcontinent, the two most likely scenarios discussed in the Cooperative Monitoring Centre Occasional Paper of Sandia National Laboratories, are: a breakdown along the common border in Kashmir, and failure of nuclear policy.

The authors propose an alternative approach through which India and Pakistan can begin to cooperate in managing their common border to prevent a breakdown.

The ultimate concern in the report about the existence of nuclear weapons is the possibility of their use in a time of conflict. The following are the enumerations in the Cooperative Monitoring Centre Occasional Paper that focuses on the monitoring of nuclear safety, security, and stability:

- The ability to assess the current operational and deployment status of nuclear weapons is perhaps the most critical factor in near-term crisis prevention.
- Developing measures to prevent escalation.
- National decisions to include both technical and procedural mechanisms to restrict use of weapons and delivery systems will permit more time to attempt diplomatic solutions to conflict before initiating weapons use.
- Another element of nuclear stability is determining the readiness of launch systems. There may be a number of indicators associated with launcher alert status. These include: Flight parameters loaded, other software updates (if appropriate); Vehicle fuelled (missile or aircraft); Crews readied; Delivery vehicle in launch location (moved to launch point); Transporter system in ready position (e.g., transporter erector launcher [TEL] in raised launch position); Weapon armed. While most of these indicators of launch preparation are difficult to monitor, some, such as missile fuelling and launcher movements, might be monitored through electronic sensors.
- There is the possibility of use through miscalculation or misinterpretation.

- o Sharing information on any of the concerns for safety, security or accident will require an infrastructure of capabilities and procedures. These include methods for providing timely, reliable, secure, accurate, and authenticated communications.
- o Ensuring safety of nuclear weapons and materials will primarily be a state responsibility because of the highly classified nature of most safety issues. These issues involve detailed design, as well as material and handling details. An expanded mission for hotlines between the Directors-General of Military Operations and between the Heads of State might be established to address this critical issue.

Acknowledging the fact that only the Indian and Pakistani governments can decide whether and on what basis, to establish new risk reduction measures, the 'Working Group Report of the Centre for Strategic and International Studies (CSIS)' recommends the following steps for nuclear risk reduction:

- o A new communications mechanism-nuclear risk reduction centres (NRRCs) in India and Pakistan-should be established to complement existing bilateral channels.
- o The main functions of the NRRCs would be to provide each party a dedicated, secure means of: (a) notifying the other side about activities or events on its territory that might be wrongly perceived or misinterpreted that could lead to conflict, (b) sharing information that the two countries are obliged to exchange under existing security agreements, and (c) seeking and receiving clarifications about ambiguous events on the other' sterritory. Other functions could include the conduct of joint exercises of certain NRRC notification procedures, technical back-up during crises, and support for consultations on the implementation of existing confidence-building measures (CBMs).
- o Adequate infrastructure already exists in South Asia to support a wide range of secure communication options, including data, voice, video, or a combination of these.

  The approximate cost for a dedicated cable permitting teletype and voice communication would be US$10,000-50,000 annually. For a dedicated satellite channel permitting teletype, voice, and video, the annual cost would be roughly US$560,000.
- o The centres would operate on a continuous, round-the-clock basis. Written messages using agreed formats would be the norm, although voice and video capability would also be desirable. It would be the prerogative of each government to decide where it would institutionally

house its NRRC and to determine how its NRRC would relate to other government organisations. The Indian and Pakistani solutions to these questions need not be symmetrical.

The Working Group Report concluded, that "the circumstances in South Asia today are very different from the circumstances surrounding the current US-Russian relationship and the relationship that existed when the US-Soviet Centres were brought into being. To tailor a new communications mechanism to the needs of South Asia, the mechanism could appropriately take on a wider range of functions than the US and Russian Centres."

Rodney W.Jones assumes that there lies intense political conflict over Kashmir and that the escalation in South Asia has the potential of becoming a nuclear war. In one of the papers presented during the fourth nuclear stability roundtable during March 12-13, 2002, in Washington on 'Military Asymmetry and Instability in Emerging Nuclear States: India and Pakistan,' he suggests the following conditions of nuclear stability in the region:

- o High nuclear threshold (strong conventional defence)
- o Secure second strike capabilities (robust C4I)
- o Rough parity in size and defence space
- o Neither falling behind the other's first strike edge (good early warning?)

  Supposing that "nuclear deterrence might provide the security that allows a general improvement in security relations" in South Asia, the UNIDR (United Nations Institute for Disarmament Research) research paper depicts various aspects of nuclear confidence-building measures between India and Pakistan. Commenting on the current conflict situation between the two countries, the authors of the paper subscribe to developing CBMs in connection with the 'central issue-Kashmir'. An interim suggestion is made to work on the possibilities of addressing the 'central sore-cross-border terror raids' from Pakistan.

With regard to nuclear CBMs, according to the UNIDR paper, India and Pakistan should share the development of respective nuclear doctrines and security concepts to have clarity over 'red lines'; develop mechanisms on notification of ballistic and cruise missile tests; create nuclear risk reduction centres with robust safety systems to deal with the issues of accidental or unauthorised use; and install a secure and dedicated line of communication including safe command and control systems between the national authorities (the nature or constitution of national authority remains undefined). The paper categorically puts the 'Kashmir issue' to be discussed as in the final stages of CBMs between the two countries.

The UNIDR study concludes that the two countries should seize the ripe moment (that has begun since the two countries agreed to peace talks during the sidelines of the SAARC summit in January 2004) in the context of possibility of conflict.

"Any future terrorist incident might provoke India into punitive action, which in the worst case might lead to uncontrolled or accidental responses, all the way to a nuclear exchange. This suggests that, although the nuclear aspects will have to be part of the general discussions on security, it might also be worth considering whether they can be made separable, in case the moment passes too quickly."

The aspect of geographical proximity of the two countries is also discussed in one of the reports dealing with nuclear threat reduction measures. Based on some hypothetical South Asian launch point-target combinations, the missile travel time between India and Pakistan is estimated between 8 to 13 minutes. Taking account of the danger of false alarms and miscalculations, the Pugwash Discussion Paper of 2002 suggests that a posture of De-alert (most basic measures would be to keep the weapons de-mated from delivery systems; use of locking devices), and installation of best available safety measures into the weapons, like use of Insensitive High Explosive (IHE) and fire-resistant pits would significantly reduce the risk of inadvertent or unauthorised use of weapons.

From the above discussed strategic policy recommendations, there emerge two sets of proposals that could draw attention of the diplomats and strategic planners of India and Pakistan. In the first set, one can identify mechanisms for escalation control and nuclear force management within each state. The second set includes possible measures of nuclear CBMs by the two countries to work towards long lasting stability in the region.

Control and Nuclear Force Management

- o Leadership declarations affirming responsible nuclear stewardship (avoidance of shrill rhetoric).
- o Developing strategies to avoid escalation of conventional confrontation to nuclear exchange level.
- o Avoiding sensitive targets in the event of a conventional war.
- o Raising the level of nuclear threshold (strong conventional defences).
- o Securing second strike capabilities.
- o Review of decision-making to develop, produce, and use 'tactical' nuclear weapons.

- o Regular assessment of each other's current operational and deployment status of nuclear weapons (missile fuelling and launcher movements might be monitored through electronic sensors).
- o Determining the readiness of launch systems.
- o Improvements in intelligence to avoid miscalculation or misinterpretation.
- o Acquisition of technology to help provide prompt and accurate information concerning missile launches and nuclear detonations.
- o Advancement in respective command and control mechanisms including establishment of effective early warning systems.
- o Refraining from giving pre-delegation of authority to use nuclear weapons.
- o Effective physical safety of nuclear materials and installations.
- o Ensuring safety and security of nuclear weapons and materials.

Steps Required for Nuclear CBMs

- o Improving bilateral relationship.
- o Sharing knowledge of decision-making processes.
- o Agreement on advance notification of missile testing and movements.
- o Flight test missiles only from designated test ranges.
- o Provision of advance notification of the movement of missiles for training purposes.
- o Review of policy decisions related to tactical nuclear weapons (including development, production, or use).
- o Establishment of multi-layered, reliable, secure, accurate, and authenticated communication mechanisms.
- o Establishment of Nuclear Risk Reduction Centres (NRRCs).

Most of the above-mentioned studies on South Asia suggest that problems related to Kashmir may be the spark to trigger a nuclear exchange between India and Pakistan. Linking of the Kashmir issue with Indo-Pak nuclear strategy is quite complex. In fact, such an assumption indirectly endorses (and is born out of) Pakistan's nuclear blackmailing. In reality, it is the Pakistani military that has crossed the Line of Control (LoC) in the past to provoke Indian defence. Pakistan does not adhere to no-first-use (NFU) and keeps making frequent calls to lower the nuclear threshold in the apprehension of India taking reprisal measures to stop Pakistan-sponsored terrorism in Indian territory.

Pakistan insists on Kashmir being the 'core' issue of stability/instability between India and Pakistan. India maintains that the scourge of 'terrorism' in South Asia has adverse implications for both regional and international security.

In between the two exclusive views, remains a pertinent question unanswered-who is to guarantee that if the issues related to Kashmir remains resolved, towards which India has already been making significant efforts, Pakistan's military-ISI sponsored terrorist activities in other parts of India would end? In such a complex security environment, bilateral confidence-building measures alone would keep the escalation under manageable limits.

6

Defence Budgeting System of India

DEFENCE BUDGETING OF INDIA

The Union Budget 2010-11 has raised the defence outlays to Rs. 1,47,344 crore (US $31.9 billion). This represents a growth rate of a mere 3.98 per cent, in nominal terms (or 0.3 per cent in real terms) over the previous years' allocation of Rs. 1,41,703 crore, and far below the 34 per cent nominal increase witnessed in the budget for 2009-10. The sudden dip in the defence budget's growth rate follows two related steps taken by the government. While the first one is related to the government's resolve about fiscal consolidation, the second is on account of the acceptance by the government of the recommendation of the Thirteenth Finance Commission (TFC). This commentary analyses the latest defence budget as well as the likely impact of TFC's recommendation on India's future defence spending.

BUDGETING PROCESS AND SOME ISSUES

This budget as usual was prepared under limited space available to Finance Minister and his team the current political equation with Left-parties sharing the policy platform with congress. In some way it has kept check on runaway liberalization euphoria, which has till date proved to be anti-poor, if we go by various indices of socioeconomic welfare and growth. The same old beaten practice of cut and paste technique and lowering taxes on a few things and then increase on some other things has been adopted. Nowhere concept of zero-base budgeting, setting growth targets and addressing distortion in economic and social administration systems is evident. This way you can always favour 2-3 industries by turn every year and collect moneybags for party funds and favours to politicians and their cronies.

Taking past budget as a base and then trying to mobilize more taxes is an idiotic approach. It is not 'budgeting' as a policy instrument. It is merely routine accounting of {Munims}. There is hardly anything radically different in 2006 budget. I don't understand what government wants to achieve by varying taxes on umbrella and lipsticks? Is this the job of Union government? How it affects economy and productivity of country? Does it really matter if excise duty is 4% or8% on lipsticks or writing chalks? What government should do is have simple three slabs 4 % 8% and 10% in all kinds of indirect taxes and duties and straight two slabs of 10% and 20% in Income tax with dividing income line of Rs 1 million per annum. All incentives and rebates should be withdrawn except for Provident funds and pension plans for social security and interest paid on housing purchase. We are not addressing viability of a product industry by building its fundamental strengths and removing structural weaknesses, but merely through tax regulation of government by giving tax relief and grants. This is old and outdated model of economics management and has no relevance left. Politicians are still functioning in 1956 mode. In fact all tax manuals should be 4-5 page booklets with simple procedures and automated formats so that corrupt tax officials are taken out from scene and put on monitoring and recovery process in cases of tax evaders. They should be given tough targets and thrown out if not successful.

Middle class is again under attack this time through different route. Service taxes have been hiked which is bad decision.12% is too high a rate. You can't tax everything. Tomorrow you will tax housemaids and tutorial services and public toilets. It is absurd and stupid. It will result in now more tax evasion. It is unjustified too.{now 95 services will be under service tax- existing 81+15 new proposed including ATM withdrawal}. The argument to tax ATM use is bizarre and reflects old mindset of bureaucrats to try to regulate systems through taxation route. It is odd that you have to pay for taking out your own cash put in banks at virtual no returns on savings bank. Banks can charge overheads but how government can tax this? An average Indian pays out almost 60% of his expenditure amount on account of various taxes only. So he gets merely 40% component as real value i.e. labour, material, design and benefits of products required in his average life routine. India is one of the most unproductive, mismanaged and highly taxed country. Still the funds collected by government annually in range of just Rs 4 lac-crores {INR 4000 Billions or US $ 82 Billion} is just peanuts.

This works out to only INR 3800/-per year per citizen. What any Government can do by this meager amount and plan for citizens? And imagine almost 50% out of this being siphoned off or spent on government officials and clerks themselves, their salaries, perquisites and pensions etc. All welfare schemes are meant for public servants only and not for people whom they are to serve.

Average Per capita income of a government (public servant in India currently) is 10 times that of per capita income of India. This is ridiculous. Is this country working to feed corrupt, unproductive public servants? 98% of Indian people are feeding a package of luxury to just 2% civil servants at cost of their two time meals. There is need to contain the rot of corruption, slim down government machinery and freeze their salaries and perks which are umpteen numbers. The productivity of public servants is very poor and they are generally corrupt and misbehaved because of job security and lack of accountability. This is anti thesis in model of democracy.

Why government has so small collection? Reason is simple-Mass scale rampant tax evasion and parallel economy running in country. Actually India's GDP is at least double of official figures {may be close to three times}. This has direct impact on inflation, hidden currency circulation, *havala* transactions and pressure on resources. People who consume most services actually pay least as percent of their real income. Widespread theft of basic services and energy is causing havoc in economic and social welfare planning. Only middle class is squeezed out every year more and more.

Politicians are party to this game. Income gap is increasing between rich and poor. Prostitution, illegal affairs and now organized crimes are increasing in bigger cities and also small too, just because cost of living has gone up tremendously and there are virtually no jobs. Police force is totally criminalized and ineffective reduced to brokerage centres. Over last 15 years of so-called reforms and competition being encouraged, the prices of general use household items and even simple OTC medicines have gone up by in at least 3-5 times range excepting for auto and electronic goods, meaning average 20% annual escalation in Consumer prices. And every year government data lie about actual inflation rate.

Against this double-digit inflation rate we have fixed 6% FDR rate and are reducing Provident fund interest thereby impoverishing old citizens who will die of deprivation and penury. There is no social security net in India. Government is virtually forcing people to divert to stock markets whose operations are highly shady at the moment and illogically elevated prices are ruling in stock markets. These prices defy all theories and concepts. Greed and manipulation is behind this. Mutual Funds are dumping common men's money there. Who is going to loose? Warning signals are clear.

The budget is not at all a long term or even mid-term planning document. It is based on very poor intellectual and expertise inputs. Problems like employment generation, increasing of productivity in economy, investment in long overdue judicial reforms and expansion, social security schemes like old age homes, effective logistics for commodities and goods distribution and storage facilities and a good infrastructure have not been addressed. India badly needs large number of decentralized new townships that are self contained with housing, hospitals, utilities, business centres and industries to release pressure on real estate and bring down soaring prices of land. Where black money is dumped too. Housing loans should be provided at low interest rates of 7-8% to encourage people to invest in housing and bring down prices of houses and commercial property. Stamp duties are too high in States forcing people to convert property into black assets. But knowingly politicians continue this.

Higher education is unnecessarily under control of State governments whereas most universities should now be privatized with well-defined UGC aid criteria, tighter quality control by setting up autonomous college councils and fixing of fair fees by an empowered panel in Ministry of HRD for private sector to meet expenses of quality education and seriously enter here. Same way allocation of funds in absolute terms for the schooling sector is peanuts despite charging of education *cess.* The biggest drain is government salaries and perquisites on unproductive, corrupt and unfit employees recruited by bribes, political connections and caste and reservations basis. This is of immense concern. Coupled with corruption in bureaucracy and siphoning off of almost 50% of public expenditures to the coffers of politicians, bureaucrats, engineers and contractors, hardly anything is left for actual public investment and welfare. Some new approach to public administration system coupled with fast automation and slimming down of civil services with moderate salaries to them should be implemented. There is need to tame corruption in civil services and defense services too. Defense outlay should be reduced by India and Pakistan sitting together and resolving issues. Education, healthcare, social security and basic services are lacking seriously in the country. We are moving towards chaos and crisis after about a decade's time. India is going to be largest polluting nation including local colony level pollution. There is going to be acute shortage of housing, land, water and electricity.

Selling cheap cars is not priority of this nation, nor to sell mobile phones and boast about highest growth rate of this sector in world. This is idiotic.

These sectors are a liability and expenditure of resources with shortage of petroleum. In a country Where 1.5 crores people are added every year and you go and fight in WTO for Agriculture Market Access for exports of agro-goods, you should be talking about agriculture growth rate and not auto-sector and electronic equipment growth rate. Condition of agriculture in India is pathetic. The growth rate is too low. Farm productivity is poor. Basic commodities are not available to poor citizens and not at all affordable. What you will export?

India has no petroleum. So expansion of auto sector is foolish. Instead we should focus on mass rapid transport and decentralization of self-contained townships in massive drive to reduce land scarcity, which is causing meteoric, rises in property.

Basic and radical reforms are required to make country a healthy society to live where people feel safe, get two times square meals, have opportunities for employment and where honest can work productively Nothing of this sort has been addressed in the mere accounting jugglery of figures called Union budget. This certainly is not budgeting. I fail to understand why so many rebates and clauses are there in all tax manuals. Why can't they have simply a 4-5-page manual with simple procedures and all types of taxes pegged below 10% cap? No one wants to pay taxes in two digit rates? It is psychological barrier and there is no need for high taxes. But then how black money will be generated, how politicians and corrupt bureaucrats will thrive. From 1991 to 2005,economic planning and public administration in India are more or less failure. Current budget is on beaten track and will lead to more misery to people in coming times. It is mediocre exercise without application of brain and not with good intents and future focus.

Conclusions: The budget document should first list budgeting premises, the indicators used and the targets of growth and reforms set for next 5 and 10 years period, shortcomings identified in economy and the methods of budgeting adopted so people can critically evaluate proposals after approving the budgeting premises of government. Economic survey is not adequate document for this purpose and why it is put only one day in advance? It should come out at least 30 days in advance for people and experts to digest and comment and send budgetary proposals. Finance minister and his team should not think that they have got a unilateral license to impose whatever they think good or right just because they have been elected and empowered to do this. They are answerable to people and should consult in major issues before bringing out laws and budgets. This is how democracy should function. Indian politicians and bureaucrats are still living in British colonial era just mentally replacing British and acting like them instead. That is how an IPS or IAS behaves when you visit him or her. Arrogant, superior, elite and unaccountable with little indications of humility and realization that s/he is public servants and paid by visitors to work for their welfare and for general service of humanity. Their only qualification is that they have slogged and passed one UPSC examination with little proven background. It is imperative to reduce Government establishment expenses of union and state governments to less than 10% of their annual budget or 2% of India's GDP. It is much more directly and indirectly. In fact corrupt nexus of Businessmen-politicians and bureaucrats drains off 50% of India's official GDP.

Citizens' satisfaction and feedback survey on an ongoing basis through Internet portals: In the end I would suggest FM to come out next year with Draft budget after economic survey of India and circulate it. Ministry of Finance or Planning Commission should setup a portal where public suggestions and opinion about draft budget should be invited. These information and objections should be compiled and then incorporated in Final Budget document.

Citizen's satisfaction survey should be started in India for all major government services including police and judiciary as is done in several countries like US, Canada, Australia, Singapore to get broad public feedback about required reforms rather than from only a handful of psuedo-experts and opinion makers in power corridors.

INDIA'S DEFENCE BUDGET 2008-09

Union Budget 2008-09 has allocated Rs. 105,600 crores for India's Defence. Crossing the one lakh barrier for the first time, and accounting for nearly 14.1 per cent of total central government expenditure, the Defence Budget looks quite impressive. But when seen in the context of India's expanding interests, this allocation remains as moderate as ever. Moreover, an in-depth analysis reveals problems in defence and budgetary management, none of which show signs of abating.

For fiscal year 2008-09, India's defence allocation has increased by 10 per cent over the previous year's allocation of Rs. 96, 000 crores, and by little over 14 per cent compared to last year's revised allocation of Rs. 92,500 cores. In the last five years, the defence budget has increased by nearly 37 per cent from Rs. 77,000 crores in 2004-05, which represents over 8 per cent growth per annum. Notwithstanding the current allocation and growth of the defence budget over the years, the question remains whether India's defence spending is compatible with its economic and security interests.

A brief survey of the Indian economy reveals its great potential and global reach. The economy registered an average growth of nearly 8 per cent a year during the 10th Plan, and seems set to continue the growth momentum in the 11th Plan period. What is more important is that much of this growth is driven by the external sector, mainly growing trade with the rest of world. India' total trade (exports plus imports) has increased by more than five times in the last decade and now accounts for over 35 per cent of its gross domestic product (GDP). This testifies to the fact that the economy is much more globalized than, say, 10 years ago when trade accounted for less than 20 per cent of GDP. The growth of the Indian economy and its global character has also infused confidence among international investors who see India as an attractive place for investment. The growing inflow of foreign direct investment is testimony to this fact. This process of greater integration with, and concomitant acquisition of greater stakes in, the international economic system is likely to continue in the coming decades. Military capability is necessary, for instance, to protect the country's sea lines of communication – 90 per cent India's trade by volume and 70 per cent in value moves by sea.

A survey of the regional military balance shows India's unfavourable position vis-à-vis its neighbours. China's relentless military modernisation, backed by double-digit growth in military expenditure for more than a decade, is a case in point. Its military modernisation, exemplified by the recent demonstration of IT-and space-based capability, has expanded its military reach from the traditional battlefield into the 'space and cyber-space domains'. This is besides the other 'anti-access/area denial capabilities' developed through a range of modern weapons systems that, according to a 2008 Pentagon Report, have left even the United States worried. Given the long-standing India-China border dispute, China's war preparations for winning "local wars under conditions of informationalization" together with its massive infrastructure development along the border, have certainly given it a definite military advantage.

At the same time, the sharpening of Pakistan's armoury, especially with the help of US military aid, is no less worrying. Since 9/11, Pakistan has received more than US $10 billion worth of military assistance from the United States. Such assistance, which includes F-16 fighter aircraft, air-to-air missiles, cluster bombs, air defence radars and surveillance technologies, has direct security implications for India, since it narrows the advantage in conventional warfare that has been in India's favour.

The moderate nature of India's defence spending, the question arises as to how much India should spend on defence. Though an answer lies in a complex set of issues ranging from the nature of threats, the fiscal health of the government and the kind of diplomacy it chooses to pursue, yet some statistical references can be drawn from other countries that are devoted to building or have attained world-class military capability.

While the United States, with a military budget (for Fiscal Year 2009) of more than $700 billion and a share of nearly 50 per cent of global military expenditure, remains the largest military spender in modern times, India's defence budget estimated roughly at $26.5 billion for 2008-09 constitutes a mere two per cent of the global total.

In terms of proportion of economic resources devoted to defence, India's latest defence budget, which accounts for 1.99 per cent of expected GDP in the coming Fiscal Year, is less than the global average of around 2.5 per cent, and lags behind America's 4.1 per cent and Pakistan's 3.5 per cent. In absolute terms, India's defence spending, ranked 10th in the list of major spenders in the world, constitutes a fraction of the American military budget and less than half of China's 'under-reported' but official defence budget of $57.22 billion for 2008.

Given the higher proportion of economic resources being devoted to defence in these countries, should India raise its defence allocation, say, to 3 per cent of GDP? The answer lies in the adequacy of the present budget to meet the country's security requirements. As the evidence shows, the proportion of financial allocations made available to the defence establishment vis-à-vis its demand has increased to nearly 95 per cent in recent years, even though its share in GDP has decreased significantly in the same period.

This indicates that there is hardly any shortage of funds to meet the defence establishment's financial requirements irrespective of its share in GDP. In any case, the fixing of defence allocation to a certain portion of GDP is not theoretically a sound proposition, given the volatilities in economic growth rates and threat perceptions in the long run. What is more important is that the security requirements, which ultimately get translated into the annual defence budget, need to be adequately financed.

A close look at the formulation of the Indian defence budget, however, reveals little evidence of the country's security concerns being properly addressed or financed. The annual defence budget, which follows from the Defence Capability Plan, 15-year Long Term Integrated Perspective Plan, 5-year Services Capital Acquisition Plan and Annual Acquisition Plan, is handicapped in terms of catering to the true security needs of the country because of the poor formulation and execution of, and inordinate delays in, planning. In other words, the security needs of the country are poorly reflected in the budget, and the capability requirements of the Armed Forces either get delayed or come to possess a short shelf-life. As a result, the Armed Forces are under-prepared to meet any worsening in the security scenario as well as technological upgrades by adversaries.

Another major problem in defence management, as reflected time and again in successive budgets, is the inability of the defence establishment to fully utilise the allocated funds, especially those meant for the modernisation of the country's security infrastructure.

Though the modernisation expenditure, credited under the 'capital expenditure' of the budget, has increased considerably from nearly 25 per cent in 2000-01 to over 45 per cent in 2008-09, the problem of timely utilisation of allotted resources continues to haunt the defence Services.

As the latest budget reveals, out of Rs. 41,922 crores earmarked for 'capital expenditure' for 2007-08, Rs. 4412 crores, or over 10 per cent, remained unutilised. These unutilised funds, which mean opportunities lost or delayed in acquiring needed capability, have become a regular feature despite reforms in the acquisition structures/procedures.

An examination of the capital acquisition structure/procedure reveals several weaknesses in the system: poor planning; deficiency in formulation of qualitative requirements; lack of motivation for indigenisation efforts; single-vendor approach towards selection of weapon systems; poor human resource and information management; 'large number of submission and approval points'; and 'multiple agencies with dispersed centres of accountability'.

The cumulative effect of all this is a gap in the capabilities sought by the Armed Forces; under-optimisation of the huge resources spent over the years; and a poor self-reliance index.

The Indian acquisition system defies the best international practices prevalent in counties such as France, the UK and Australia. In contrast to the Indian system, the acquisition process in these countries is undertaken by an integrated body encompassing all the stakeholders – Armed Forces, Industry, R&D organisation, quality assurance organisation, civilian bureaucrats and other skilled workforce.

This integrated body is responsible for all acquisition functions, right from the planning level to the disposal of equipment, and thus owns the responsibility of the whole life-cycle process of any equipment or system. The advantage of this integrated body lies in its single-point accountability to provide timely solutions to the Armed Forces' requirements and, in the process, it provides the best value for money and also a thrust towards self-reliance. Keeping the above merits of the integrated acquisition organisation in mind, India could possibly adopt a similar institutional arrangement for expediting its acquisition process.

As regards self-reliance in critical military technology and production of advanced weapons systems, India, despite decades of effort, has remained import-dependent. The poor self-reliance index of 30 to 35 per cent against the target of 70 per cent by the end of 10th Plan testifies to this fact. Inadequate budgetary provision for defence research and development (R&D) is the major reason behind India's poor defence industrial production and heavy outflow of financial resources to foreign suppliers. Overdependence on foreign suppliers not only has its costs and industrial disadvantages but also provides opportunities for corruption and delays in procurement. The present allocation of Rs. 6,486.35 crores for defence R&D constitutes a mere 6.1 per cent of the defence budget. In contrast, major military powers spend a much higher proportion of their budgets on military R&D. For instance, the United States spends around 16 per cent of its defence budget on R&D. American dominance in military technology and production of sophisticated weapons systems is the result of higher allocation, concerted efforts in the right direction and involvement of industries in research activities.

In India, almost the entire defence R&D activity is undertaken by the DRDO (Defence Research and Development Organisation), with little budgetary or technological support from the defence industry, which largely comprises of state-owned Ordnance Factories and Defence Public Sector Undertakings (DPSUs). The private sector, which is a key contributor to civilian technology and a key driver of economic growth since liberalisation began in the early nineties, is still kept out from contributing to military technological advancement.

The absence of R&D efforts by the defence industry has forced the DRDO to concentrate on every aspect of military technology, many of which could be undertaken by the industry itself. As a result, a very small proportion – 8 to 10 per cent of R&D budget – is percolated down for fundamental research. If India wants to be self-reliant in critical military technology and defence production, it needs to enhance its R&D spending. At the same time, increased allocations need to be channelled in the proper direction, and industry, including in the private sector, needs to be engaged in R&D activities so as to make DRDO focus on key and critical technologies.

Considering its economic and security imperatives, India's defence spending is not only moderate but also fails to capture the true security needs of the nation. The defence budget, because of the problems in the acquisition system, is constrained to translate budgetary resources into required military capability in the given time and at optimal cost. To augment defence spending, what India needs is an efficient defence planning mechanism, backed by an integrated acquisition organisation. Also, given its poor self-reliance index, India needs to enhance R&D spending. Enhanced budgetary allocations should be channelled in the right direction, with the industry (including private sector) taking a lead in technology development.

DEFENCE FINANCE AND MANAGEMENT

The contents of the general, as well as, the defence budget of the Government of India have normally been widely discussed and debated. However, the focus mostly has been on the magnitude of the budget rather than the system of budgeting. Yet it is the system that needs to be the focus of discussions and requires reforms. Over a period of time, the budget documents had become quite static in terms of structure, content and communication of results. With the demands of those needing information from the budget changing with time, reforms in the structure and content of the defence budget had become overdue.

A budget is an instrument of policy. Through the annual financial statements it can translate a long term or medium term plan into action. The questions that arise are: what do we expect out of the budgeting system? And does it facilitate a meaningful translation of the intended objectives as reflected in the budget estimates? The perception about what the Defence Budget: Towards an Outcome and Programme Based System 709 defence budget should contain also depends on various categories of users. The institutions/ persons looking into the budget can be divided into the following three main categories:

- Parliament, which votes the budgetary appropriations and also reviews the performance through the appropriation accounts and audit reports. Preceding the vote on the budget, Parliament has the report of the Standing Committee on Defence, which examines the demands for grants in detail.
- The administrative ministry, the executive arm and supporting institutions working with it. The administrative ministry formulates the budget and, after necessary backing of the Finance Ministry, gets the approval of Parliament to enable it to operate.
- A mix of users such as experts in the field, institutions, beneficiaries, academics and the common citizens who are interested in the

information, especially the value for money derived from the actual expenditure.

To meet the changing needs of the diverse sets of users, the defence budger needs to change both its format and contents with time. Yet systemic changes in structure, form and content of the budget have been slow to come about in India. Changes have been made from time to time but essentially in amplification of contents or deletion of certain items, or addition of new service relating to expenditure. We, therefore, need to know how far and why it has not been feasible to introduce new concepts.

The Defence Services Estimates (DSE) have an amalgam of outlays that can be converted in terms of outcomes into tangibles and some intangibles. As far as the defence budget is concerned, it is clear that the Parliament, the executive, defence analysts and the tax payers would be interested to know the outcomes.

They would be keen to know the quantum of funds provided for air defence, the cumulative total of such allocations in the budget over a period of time and the results achieved in providing protection against potential air attacks. While evolving any modifications in systems, it is necessary to know what is needed in the Indian context by various users.

Having recognized the inherent advantage of a budget that can reveal what it has achieved in terms of intended objectives, the question arises as to whether the existing structure and content need a total substitution, partial modification or supplements in order to serve as a conclusive document for evaluation of the outcomes.

The past legacy also needs to be tackled in any overhaul or change in the existing system.

The legacies are located in the content of the basic administrative and accounting data generated from the source levels, the mode of transmission, the organisational entities involved in the processing of the data, the relationships between these entities, the command and control, the technology used and, most important, the manpower resources, both in terms of skills and the numbers at the appropriate levels.

Other relevant factors are: reluctance to exchange information in an institutionalised manner and an exaggerated sense of secrecy in publishing and disseminating information.

This chapter attempts to delineate feasible reforms to make the budget speak for itself in terms of intended objectives and the outcome or value for money realised out of the expenditure incurred.

The Existing System

The Defence Services Estimates (DSE), as a document, has evolved over a period of time to its current structure. Though its structure has largely remained the same in form and contents, it has had modifications. It is believed by many that, as a public document, its existing format is adequate to convey the objectives of the government. The comments/reactions to a budget presentation are made in terms of judgement on magnitude of allocations for army, navy, air force, DRDO and for new services, etc. However, a growing number of people, especially in the ministry and service headquarters, well-informed defence experts and academics have persuasively argued for a change. Many Members of Parliament have often sought more information, than what is available in the existing document.

The criticism of the present system is that it is largely input oriented. Specifically this means that it focuses on expenditure in generic terms, i.e., in terms of pay and allowances, stores, transportation, etc., and not in terms of targets and its actuals. The budget is also devoid of details in a number of major components of expenditure. The figures of expenditure on certain categories such as 'stores', 'works', etc., are such that it is not clear as to why and for what the funds are provided.

The budget is divided in terms of 'revenue' and 'capital'. Even in this regard, the classification was until recently carrying legacies of the past and did not reflect the basic nature of certain items. In several areas, assets of a capital nature were being classified under revenue. Consequently, capital assets were underpitched, especially in respect to the army. The omnibus nature of items under capital expenditure indicated as 'other equipment', 'aircraft', etc., do not reveal adequate information on specific items of expenditure, even where these are of large magnitude. The word 'maintenance' nowhere figures under Revenue Budget but is covered under 'pay and allowances', 'stores', etc.

With substantial increase in funding for defence, the need for adequate information has become of great importance for interpretation of the budget. At present, information on the budget is available to the executive/parliament through the following three main reports:

- The Appropriations Account
- The audit report of Comptroller and Auditor General
- Reports of Parliamentary Committees – especially those of the Standing Committee on Defence and, in certain cases, the reports of the Public Accounts Committee, based on the audit reports.

The Appropriation Accounts signed by the Controller General Defence Accounts (CGDA)/Secretary Defence (Finance) and by the Defence Secretary gives the actual expenditure against allocations under various minor and sub heads.

The reasons for variations of actuals against allocations are also indicated. However, it does not throw adequate light on physical achievements (outputs) in respect to a bulk of the items since the document is not intended to be an account on performance. However, there are exceptions. For two organisations-military farms and military engineering services-assessment of performance is given in separate sections.

Under the present system, getting an overall picture of budget in financial/ physical terms and the actual performance is not easy and requires a lot of derivation, collation of data/information and enormous effort on the part of the ministry/services/departments. A document reflecting outcomes of at least major items provided in the budget would make the whole task easier apart from serving the basic and very important task of effective management of schemes and achievement of objectives.

By and large, the existing structure of the DSE with classification and sub-heads such as 'stores', 'works', etc., cannot facilitate the understanding of what is the outcome intended from the money spent on various items of expenditure related to defence. Even in an important area of maintenance of aircraft, it is difficult to derive from the budget that if Rupees "X" have been allocated for maintenance of an aircraft type "A", whether the required level of maintenance has been achieved.

This information becomes available much later when an Audit Para is raised and even becomes an item in the report of the Public Accounts Committee (for example MiG-29). The existing budgetary system has another deficiency. For instance, allocations made for a gun are spent and the expenditure reports also reflects this position but the guns may still not be inducted for the purpose for which they were procured.

The existing system may show good financial progress with almost entire payments having been made in respect of an item, but the crucial phase of testing, which is vital towards achieving the final outcome, could drag on.

Successful tests of many systems do not necessarily lead to a successful outcome or their timely induction into the armed forces. The DSE reveals very little about allocations even of a non sensitive nature. There are only one line entries in the budget documents for amounts running up to a few thousand crore of Rupees.

There are a number of other weaknesses in the system. The time taken for transactions does not get reflected in the financial information reports pertaining to a budget, and a continuous update of information on liabilities incurred by various sanctioning/spending authorities is not available An equally serious shortcoming is the inability to fully disseminate information to the concerned authorities and the absence of a synergised effort among various wings under the MOD for creating a comprehensive integrated report that would reflect the financial-cum-physical programmes.

Steps have been taken from time to time to make the existing DSE and the annual compilation of accounts more meaningful.

In 1987, a reform was initiated in segregating pension from the DSE and ordinance factories from the army budget, with the objective of making this production organisation into a separate cost centre. Further reforms took place in 1992, based on the report of the task force (under A. K. Ghosh) which added over 150 categories in the classification of accounts, revealing more on the content of the expenditure, so that certain specific activities could be made transparent. It is clear that a well evolved coding section, in vogue since the 1930s and subsequently enhanced by computerisation in 1971, has enabled further expansion of codes, meeting the growing need for giving information on expenditure related to an item.

DEFENCE BUDGET ESCAPES ECONOMIC SLOWDOWN

The new defence budget comes at a time when the performance of the Indian economy is under stress and the prospect of recovery is tenuous. As the *Economic Survey 2011-12*,presented to the Parliament a day before the Union Budget, puts it, GDP growth is projected at 6.9 per cent in the present fiscal year and at 7.6 per cent in 2012-13.

These growth rates, which are significantly lower especially in comparison to the nearly 10 per cent growth registered in 2006-07, has however not forced the government to tighten its purse. Instead, it has resorted to what can be termed as fiscal profligacy, by increasing the overall central government expenditure by a hefty 18.54 per cent, with little regard for the fiscal situation.

Consequently, the fiscal deficit, which the Finance Minister had promised in his previous budget speech to reduce to 4.1 per cent of GDP in 2012-13, is now projected to increase to 5.1 per cent. This expansionary fiscal policy has been the prime mover for the large increase in the budget of the defence ministry, which would otherwise have come under severe budgetary pressure if the Finance Minister had chosen a tight budget.

Key Aspects of the Defence Budget 2012-13

Although the latest defence budget has witnessed an increase of 18 per cent, the growth rate is only 13.15 per cent over the revised estimate of the now concluding fiscal year.

In other words, the defence budget for 2011-12 has been revised upward by Rs 6,521.32 crore to Rs. 1,70,936.81 crore. However, unlike the revised estimate for 2010-11, in which both the Revenue Expenditure and Capital Expenditure were higher than their respective budget estimates, the revised estimate for 2011-12 shows an increase in Revenue Expenditure (by Rs. 9,576.32 or 10.06 per cent) and decline in Capital Expenditure by Rs. 3,055 (or 4.41 per cent).

The large increase in the defence budget notwithstanding, its impact on various components has been different. From the perspective of resource allocation, while the share of the defence budget in the GDP has marginally increased, its share in central government expenditure has fallen.

One noticeable aspect of the new budget is that in comparison to Capital Expenditure, the Revenue Expenditure has increased faster. This growth has however been driven primarily because of the increase in pay and allowance of the armed forces, which has increased by 27 per cent to Rs. 63,182.46 crore, accounting for around 46 per cent growth of the total defence budget.

Table: Comparative Statistics of Defence Budgets, 2011-12 & 2012-13

	2011-12	*2012-13*
Defence Budget (Rs. in Crore)	164415.49	193407.29
Growth of Defence Budget (%)	11.59	17.63
Revenue Expenditure (Rs. in Crore)	95216.68	113828.66
Growth of Revenue Expenditure (%)	9.01	19.55
Share of Revenue Expenditure in Defence Budget (%)	57.91	58.85
Capital Expenditure (Rs. in Crore)	69198.81	79578.63
Growth of Capital Expenditure (%)	15.33	15.00
Share of Capital Expenditure in Defence Budget (%)	42.09	41.15
Share of Defence Budget in GDP (%)	1.83	1.90
Share of Defence Budget in Central Government Expenditure (%)	13.07	12.97

Note: Rs. 1.0 crore = Rs. 10 million = US$ 209,105.39

Shares in Defence Budget

The Army with an approximate budget of Rs. 97,302.54 accounts for 50 per cent of the latest defence budget, followed by the Air Force (Rs. 48,191.16; 25 per cent), Navy (Rs. 37,314.44; 19 per cent), Defence Research and Development Organisation (Rs. 10,635.56 crore; six per cent) and Ordnance Factories (Rs. 135.13 crore).

It is noteworthy that compared to the previous year's budget, Navy is the only service which has increased its share in total defence allocation (from 15 to 19 per cent). The Air Force's share has decreased the most (by four percentage points), whereas the Army's share has declined by one percentage point.

The 15 per cent increase in the Capital Expenditure has resulted in an additional amount of Rs. 10,379.82 crore. Given that most of the Capital Expenditure is incurred on modernisation of the armed forces, it is vital to see how the increase would affect each of the services.

It is however to be noted that the three services (Army, Navy and Air Force) account for 94 per cent (Rs. 74,439.95 crore) of total Capital Expenditure in 2012-13, with the Air Force at the top with a share of 38 per cent (Rs. 30,485.35 crore), followed by the Navy (31 per cent or Rs. 24,766.42 crore) and the Army (24 per cent or Rs. 19,188.18 crore). Of the total Capital Expenditure of the three services, around 89 per cent (Rs 66,459.43 crore) is earmarked for capital acquisition or modernisation.

These impressive figures do not however reveal the complete story. A closer look at the growth of the modernisation budget of 2012-13 would reveal that the focus is entirely driven by the Navy, which has got a 72 per cent hike (to Rs. 24,151.51 crore) in its modernisation budget. The Air Force's modernisation budget has increased marginally (by 0.5 per cent) to Rs. 28,503.9 crore, while the Army's has declined by three per cent to Rs. 13,804.02 crore.

The marginal increase in the Air Force's modernisation budget and the decrease in the Army's do not seem to be in sync with their modernisation requirements. This is more so given the pending signing of some of the big-ticket contracts (including the multi-billion dollar Rafael), and the sharp devaluation of the Indian rupee against the US dollar.

As regards the latter, although the rupee has appreciated from its lowest point in mid-December 2011, the present exchange rate, which is around fifty rupees to a dollar, is still high and, if it remains at the same level could further erode the import capacity of the acquisition budget.

Return to Under-spending

When the defence budget 2011-12 was presented in February 2011, it gave an impression that the years of effort put in by the defence ministry to fine-tune its procurement process has finally yielded dividend. This impression now seems to be premature, as the defence ministry has once again come back to under-spending its capital budget. As the new budget reveals, of the total Capital Expenditure earmarked for 2011-12, Rs. 3,055 crore (4.41 per cent) has been surrendered at the time of revised estimate. The unspent amount could have been much higher if the Navy had not been allowed to overspend its allotted capital budget by Rs. 2801.25 crore (the Air Force and the Army together have surrendered Rs. 5,727.15 crore).

While the surrender in the Air Force's modernisation budget is mostly from the head of 'aircraft and aero-engine', in the case of the Army the surrender is from a number of heads, including 'aircraft & aero-engine', and 'other equipments'.

The surrender of funds under such critical heads and of such magnitude not only reflects poorly upon budgetary management and the procurement system, but is also a cause of concern given the huge gap in national military capability and the rapid modernisation in neighbouring countries, particularly China which is pursuing an unprecedented level of military modernisation with a double-digit annual increase in defence expenditure for two decades. Given this scenario, the least that needs to be avoided by the services is the surrender of allotted funds. The defence establishment including the service headquarters therefore need to introspect and arrive at solutions that expedite procurement in a time-bound manner.

INDIA'S DEFENCE BUDGET 2012-13

The Union Budget 2012-13, presented to the Parliament on March 16, 2012 hiked the defence outlays to Rs. 1,93,407.29 crore (US$ 40.44 billion1). This represents a growth of 17.63 per cent over the previous year's outlays – one of the highest increases in recent years excluding that for 2009-10 when the budget was increased by over 34 per cent, mostly to accommodate the pay hikes caused by the implementation of the recommendations of the Sixth Central Pay Commission.

The increase in the latest defence budget was made possible by the expansionary fiscal policy adopted by the government in general. Further, although the increase looks impressive at first glance, it is not however driven by the modernisation needs as much as by manpower needs.

DEFENCE BUDGET 2010-11

Although the defence budget for 2010-11 has been increased by less than four per cent over the previous year's allocation, it has nonetheless been increased by a modest 8.13 per cent over the revised estimate for 2009-10. In other words, the Ministry of Defence (MoD) has surrendered (at the time of revised estimate) Rs. 5,439 crore from the original allocations made in 2009-10. The surrendered amount could have been more if the Revenue Expenditure-which accounts for running expenses of the defence services-had not been revised upwards by Rs 1,561 crore over the original estimates. On the other hand, the Capital Expenditure-most of which is accounted for acquisition of defence hardware-has been revised downward by Rs. 7,000 crore.

The marginal increase in the defence budget has a negative impact on almost all key components. On the positive side, however, the ratio between Revenue Expenditure and Capital Expenditure has been improved towards the latter. The improvement is largely due to the marginal increase in Revenue Expenditure, which itself was inflated in last year's budget by salary increases and one-time arrears due to implementation of Sixth Central Pay Commission recommendations. Among the defence services, the Army with a budget of approximately Rs. 74,582 crore in 2010-11 has the largest share, distantly followed by the Air Force (Rs. 40,462 crore), Navy (Rs. 21,467 crore), DRDO (Rs. 9,809 crore), and Ordnance Factories (Rs. 1,015 crore). However, in terms of Capital Expenditure, the Air Force with a budget of Rs. 25,251 crore holds the largest share (42 per cent) among the three services, followed by the Army (Rs. 17,255 crore; 29 per cent) and the Navy (Rs. 12,138; 20 per cent).

From the modernization point of view, out of Rs. 60,000 crore, nearly 78 per cent (Rs. 46,521) crore will be available to the three services for procurement of Aircraft and Aero-Engine, Heavy and Medium Vehicles, Naval Ships, and Other Equipments (Armaments, Electronics, Ammunition, Missiles, etc.) among others. Within each service's acquisition budget, the Air Force will have Rs. 15,206 crore for procurement of Air Craft and Aero-Engine; while Rs. 10,464 crore have been provisioned for procurement of Other Equipments for the Army. The Navy will get Rs. 6,950 crore for procurement of Naval Fleet.

Why Meagre Growth in Defence Budget?

While presenting the Union Budget, the Finance Minister (FM) emphasised that "Secure border and security of life and prosperity fosters development." The 3.8 per cent increase in the defence budget (in comparison to the 8.6 per cent increase in total central government expenditure) does not however seem to be fully in sync with the above emphasis. This is more so when India's more troubling neighbours have increased their defence spending at a sharp pace. Of particular interest is China, whose double digit increase in defence spending over the past twenty years and resultant military modernisation in both qualitative and quantitative terms has been taken 'note' of by the Ministry of Defence. (China's 2009 official defence budget of $70.37 billion is 2.2 times that of India's 2010 budget.) However the above 'note' does not seem to be backed by adequate growth in India's defence budget. In fact, in the last 10 years, India's defence budget has grown by 10 per cent and more only in three years.

Notwithstanding the seemingly 'direction-less' growth in India's defence budget, the reasons for the small increase in the latest defence budget is not so difficult to fathom. There are in fact two clear reasons for it.

The first is related to the government's resolve to "come back to the path of fiscal consolidation at the earliest." It is noteworthy that the central government had announced several stimulus packages to fight the economic crisis which was harsher in 2008-09. As a result the fiscal deficit had increased to an unsustainable level.

Now with the crisis less severe, the government has made an attempt to bring down the fiscal deficit for 2010-11 to 5.5 per cent of GDP, as against 6 per cent in 2008-09 and 6.7 per cent in 2009-10 (revised estimate). The fiscal tightening means limited the scope for accommodating more resource demands from the MoD which accounts for over 13 per cent of total central government expenditure.

The scope has been further limited by the government's focus on 'inclusive growth', by way of increased agricultural, social and infrastructural spending. For instance, in the Union Budget, the Finance Minister has increased the Central Plan Outlay on Agriculture, Rural Development, Transport and Social Sector by 14 per cent to Rs. 2,97,065 crore.

If the imperatives of fiscal consolidation and 'inclusive growth' have limited government spending capacity, the MoD's inability to spend the resources allocated in the previous year's budget has also not helped its cause. As mentioned earlier, the MoD has so far surrendered. Rs. 5,439 crore from its 2009-10 budget. This inability to spend has no doubt strengthened the Finance Ministry's justification for a smaller increase with the customary promise that "any additional requirement for the security of the nation will be provided for." The Finance Ministry is fully aware that the MoD has difficulties in spending the allocated resources, especially the amount given in the capital account.

INDIA'S DEFENCE BUDGET 2010-11

As per the Budget Estimates (BE) proposed for the year 2010-11, the total expenditure of Central government will be Rs. 11,08,749 crore, which is an increase of 8.6 per cent over total expenditure in BE of 2009-10. The Plan and Non Plan expenditure in BE 2010-11 are estimated at Rs. 3,73,092 crore and Rs. 7, 35,651 crore, respectively. While there is a 15 per cent increase in Plan expenditure, the increase in Non Plan expenditure is only 6 per cent over BE of 2009-10. The fiscal deficit has been projected as 5.5 percent of GDP in 2010-11 against 6.9 per cent during the preceding year.

The fiscal year 2009-10 was a challenging year for the Indian economy. The significant deceleration in the second half of 2008-09 brought the real GDP growth down to 6.7 per cent, from an average of over 9 per cent in the preceding three years. However, due to implementation of broad based counter cyclic policy package, the negative fallout of the global slowdown has been arrested. Although due to fiscal expansion and liberal monetary policy, the Indian economy is showing some signs of stabilization, unless there is consolidation of gains achieved during the last fiscal year the economy may take longer to revert to the high GDP growth path.

The Thirteenth Finance Commission has recommended a calibrated exit strategy from the expansionary fiscal stance of the last two years. As a part of the fiscal consolidation process, the Finance Minister in his Budget speech on February 26, 2010 proposed to reduce the domestic public debt-GDP Ratio. In the Medium Term Fiscal Policy Statement, the Government has proposed a rolling target for fiscal deficit in the next two fiscal years. It is proposed to bring down the fiscal deficit from 5.5 per cent of GDP in 2010-11 to 4.8 per cent in 2011-12 and to 4.1 per cent in 2012-13.

The expenditure on Defence comes under Non Plan expenditure. As per the Budget Estimates for the year 2010-11, Defence has been allocated Rs. 1,47,344 crore, i.e. a marginal increase of 3.98 percent over the BE of 2009-10. The outlay for Defence comprises of Rs. 87,344 for Revenue expenditure and Rs. 60,000 crore for Capital expenditure. Keeping in view the requirement of Defence for modernization of forces, the Capital budget has been given an increase of 9.44 per cent over the BE of 2008-09. The revenue allocation has increased only by 0.5 percent. However, there is a net reduction in allocation of Rs. 1096 crore in Revenue budget in comparison to the Revised Estimates of 2009-10. Last year, the Revenue budget was increased by 50.85 per cent over the BE of 2008-09 due to implementation of the Sixth Pay Commission's recommendation.

Since part of that was a one time expenditure, thus no additional funds were required under the Pay and Allowances head this year. However, considering the fact that a substantial part of Revenue expenditure is incurred on Stores & Equipment, Transportation, Revenue Works, Maintenance of Buildings, Installation, etc. and there is a danger of double digit inflation, thus the proposed allocation under these heads of expenditure will require extra effort on the part of defence functionaries to prioritise expenditure without compromising the operational readiness of the forces.

Due to rising social and political tensions in different parts of the country, there is far greater need for inclusive growth. To achieve this goal the government has to allocate more resources for infrastructure development, health and education, etc. Thus Plan expenditure is bound to rise in the coming years and consequently the Government will have to take steps to reduce Non Plan expenditure to achieve reduction in the fiscal deficit. Considering the security environment in and around India, the government will have to provide more funds under the Capital budget required for modernization of forces. Thus, Defence authorities will have to work out how to function with a minimal increase in the Revenue budget. The Thirteenth Finance Commission has observed that there exists considerable scope to improve the quality and efficiency of defence expenditure through increased private sector engagement, import substitution and indigenization, improvements in procedures and practices and better project management, within the parameters of Government of India's policy. Efforts in this direction will further expand the fiscal space available for defence spending.

The Standing Committee on Defence in its report on Demand for Grants (2009-10), placed in the Lok Sabha on December 16, 2009, also recommended that there is an urgent need to curb wasteful expenditure. The Committee has consistently been raising this issue in its earlier reports as well. In pursuance thereof, the Ministry had constituted a Defence Expenditure Review Committee (DERC) to comprehensively review all aspects of defence expenditure. The committee has already submitted its report. However, the action taken report on DERC recommendations indicating the areas where expenditure can be curbed is awaited. Since tax payer's money is spent on such committees it is essential that the outcomes of their recommendations be placed in the public domain.

The Ministry of Finance had projected a growth rate of 7 per cent per annum for defence revenue expenditure. Capital expenditure is projected to grow at 10 per cent per annum. The resultant projection for overall annual growth rate of defence expenditure works out to 8.33 per cent. However, due to the economic slowdown and the compulsion of providing more funds for inclusive growth, the allocation for Defence is less (particularly for revenue expenditure) than what was projected by the Ministry of Finance. This situation is likely to continue into the near future.

Thus, Defence Mangers need to initiate immediate measures to control the rising revenue expenditure. The Revenue expenditure of Defence has grown from Rs. 10,194 cores in 1989-90 to Rs. 87,344 crore in 2010-11, i.e. an increase of almost nine times during the last two decades. A look at the graph below shows that Revenue expenditure is growing at a much faster pace in comparison to Capital expenditure.

The revenue expenditure trend for the last three years shows that about 46 per cent of expenditure is incurred on pay and allowances, 35 percent on stores and equipment, 10 per cent on revenue works, 4 per cent on transportation, and 5 per cent on Miscellaneous Charges. To check the rising revenue expenditure, the following measures could be considered:

1. Since more than half of revenue expenditure is spent on pay and allowances, to reduce expenditure on this account in the short term is not possible. However, considering the fact that the nature of war has changed, there is a need to develop force structures that are capability based and not threat based. Defence transformation through technological improvements is the need of the hour. Further, the three Services need to be integrated through reorganisation of higher formations and through joint training and joint procedures, which will ensure coherence and synergy. All this will facilitate the downsizing of the armed forces and result in a reduction in revenue expenditure.
2. A substantial portion of expenditure is incurred on stores and equipment. It also comprises of expenditure on maintenance of equipments. It is a well established fact that the cost of arms acquisition is only a small fraction of the life cycle cost and logistics and maintenance management is a far more important activity. Consequently, countries like the United States and United Kingdom have adopted a performance based logistics (PBL) strategy for system support as a result of which the availability and reliability of systems have improved. Under this strategy, the original manufacturer or its nominated contractor maintains the weapon system at the specified level of operational readiness and usage, and is paid a graded incentive for exceeding the specified levels of system maintenance. The PBL has been found to be a far more cost effective solution than in-house logistics and maintenance management. The requirement of existing service logistics and

maintenance infrastructure could be reduced by adopting this strategy. Further, modern supply chain management techniques need to be employed to reduce storage echelons and inventory holding, by making more use of ICT.

3. The process of implementation of outcome budgeting in Defence needs to be expedited. It will bring accountability into the system and authorities will be required to define and identify the objects for which funds are required and then intimate what outcome(s) have been achieved. It will reduce ad-hoc decision making and thus reduce wasteful expenditure. Some of the service-specific organizations and establishments, such as workshops, repair organizations, naval dockyards and depots, should immediately be brought under the regimen of outcome budgeting.
4. In the case of transportation, expenditure could be reduced by making more use of railways facilities instead of road transport. There are some coordination problems with the Railways which need to sorted out since it is in the interest of both the departments. Now large numbers of Defence Personnel are entitled to fly by air. There is a tendency to go for full fare ticket (even in normal circumstances) when cheap air tickets are also available. The total expenditure on this account may be negligible but the issue is not that of amount. In fact, it reflects the fact that while spending Government money the canons of financial propriety are not being adhered to in letter and spirit.
5. The revenue expenditure is regulated by the principles and procedures contained in the Defence Procurement Manual (DPM)-2009. With a view to improving the quality of expenditure, the Ministry of Defence has delegated substantial powers to Services Headquarters and lower formations. This delegation has certainly helped in improving the speed of the expenditure but the same cannot be said about the quality of expenditure. There are instances of procurement of items without adequate justification and in excess quantity. To reduce wasteful expenditure the system of allocation of some grants every year without ascertaining the actual requirement needs to be reviewed. For example, every year funds under Hot Weather Grants are allotted which is not required since many units do not need Matkas (earthen wares) as they have made provision for water coolers.
6. Moreover, the units get a number of grants and in many cases the amount is a few thousand Rupees only. These grants are received by units through different directorates of Service Headquarters. Since

processing and intimation of these grants involves a lot of manpower, it needs to be considered whether units should be given a lump sum amount for Miscellaneous expenditure and be authorised to use the same as they deem fit for the defined purpose. It will improve quality of fund utilisation and reduce manpower requirement of Headquarters, thereby resulting in savings in expenditure.

7. While delegating financial power to lower formations it was assumed that Local Purchases would be more economical. However, it is difficult to say that the desired purpose has been achieved. To bring economy in local purchases it is essential that Central Authorities ensure that as far as possible Rate Contracts for the items required by field units are concluded.
8. Presently Units/Formations prepare procurement plan (except for ACSFP & TAG Grant) after funds are received. Presently, the endeavour is to ensure that all allotted funds are utilised and in the process many items are procured which are not required or purchased in excess of requirement. To overcome this situation it should be made mandatory for units/formations to prepare Priority Procurement Plan for all types of purchases in advance and no new items shall be included unless unavoidable. The present system compels officers to spend the allotment even though it may not be essential or urgent.
9. Defence should adopt Project Management approach for inducting complete systems or setting up facilities to enhance operational readiness on a life cycle basis. By adopting new methodologies along with Information Technology, optimal control of the projects at each phase of the project life cycle is feasible. Effective Project Management will facilitate achievement of desired outcome and time and cost over-runs could be minimised, resulting in substantial savings in expenditure.

INDIA'S DEFENCE BUDGET 2009-10: AN ASSESSMENT

In its interim budget for 2009-10 the Union Government has allocated Rs. 1,41,703 crores for the country' Defence Services that include three Armed Forces (i.e., the Army, the Navy and the Air Force), and other Departments, primarily Defence Research and Development Organisation (DRDO) and Defence Ordnance Factories. This is apart from Rs. 24,960 crores which have been earmarked to defray civil expenditures of Ministry of Defence (MoD) and its affiliated organisations, including, the Coast Guard, and for defence pension (Rs. 21,790 crores). In other words, the total resource available for the MoD and its various establishments is Rs. 1,66,663 crores. By convention, only budgetary provisions for the Defence Services constitute India's defence budget. Though the allocations made in the interim budget are not binding for the next government to follow, it is unlikely that the new government will make any major changes in the allocation, given the mandatory increases in certain components of the defence budget, the worsening security situation in the country's neighbourhood and the gap in the country's defence preparedness.

This commentary examines the various components of the defence budget, analyses the impact of the budget on the modernisation requirements of the Armed Forces, and the problem of under-utilisation of resources under the capital head.

Vital Components

The defence budget for 2009-10 has increased by 34.19 per cent over the previous year's budget estimate (BE) of Rs. 1,05,600 crores. However, BE of 2008-09 has been scaled upward by 8.52 per cent (Rs. 9,000 crores) to Rs. 1,14,600 crores at the revised estimate (RE) stage.

This means, this year's allocations has increased by 23.65 per cent over the RE of 2008-09. Of the total defence budget, revenue expenditure, which caters to the 'running' or 'operating' expenditure of the three Services and other departments, is pegged at Rs. 86,879 crores. Capital expenditure, which mostly caters for modernisation requirements, accounts for Rs. 54,824 crores. Of these two, revenue expenditure has been increased-in comparison to its last year's growth of less than 7 per cent-at a much faster rate of 50.85 per cent (Rs. 29, 286 crores). The growth of capital expenditure has however declined, over the previous year's growth, to 14.20 per cent (Rs. 6,817 crores). The sharp rise in revenue expenditure has taken its share in the defence budget to 61.31 per cent, from 54.54 per cent a year before. In other words, the share of capital expenditure has gone down by nearly 7 percentage points in these two years.

The faster growth of revenue expenditure is primarily due to the hefty increase in pay and allowances flowing from the implementation of Sixth Central Pay Commission (CPC).

To put the figure in perspective, total budgeted pay and allowances debited from the Services' budgets has more than doubled from 21,891.67 crores in 2008-09 to Rs. 44,500.69 crores in 2009-10.

Service-wise, the Army accounts for the largest share of the 2009-10 budget with an approximate allocation of Rs. 76,680 crores, followed by the Air Force (Rs. 34,432 crores) and the Navy (Rs. 20,604 crores). While the

Ordnance Factories (OF) have a budget of Rs.1,505.45 crores, the DRDO's budget is Rs. 8,481.54 crores.

Impact on Modernisation

The Indian Armed Forces are on a modernisation drive. The shopping list of the Services includes virtually all types of weapons and systems, including big-guns, fighter aircrafts, armoured vehicles, radars, missiles, naval vessels, among others. The most pertinent question is whether the latest budget makes necessary provisions to meet these requirements. Given the fact that the modernisation programme of the armed forces largely depends on capital acquisitions, it boils down to how capital budget is allocated.

Assuming that nearly 80 per cent of the capital budget is meant for capital acquisitions, the latter consisting of 60 per cent of committed liabilities and 40 per cent of new schemes, the main sub-divisions of the capital budget are as below:

- Total Capital Budget: Rs. 54,824 crores
- Capital Acquisition: Rs. 43,859 crores
- Committed Liabilities: Rs.26,316 crores
- New Schemes: Rs.17,544 crores.

Moreover, over Rs. 17,500 crores (nearly 30 per cent of the capital budget) will be available for new weapons and systems that the Armed Forces have planned for induction. While this augurs well from the modernisation point of view, much depends on how much and how the resources are spent in the coming fiscal.

Higher Allocation and Under-utilisation of Resources

The growth of over 34 per cent in India's defence budget is one of the highest in the country's history of defence spending (the last time the defence budget was increased by over 30 per cent was in 1987-88 when allocation was increased by 43.4 per cent to Rs. 12,512 cores). In the recent past, the defence budget, despite registering modest growth rates, has been subjected to criticism in view of its declining shares in total central government expenditure and gross domestic product. In fact, the defence budget had decreased to below two per cent of GDP in the last fiscal year.

The new budget, defying all criticism, has made a substantial increase in allocations. From the perspective of resources allocation, the defence budget for 2009-10 represents 14.87 per cent of total central government expenditure, and 2.35 per cent of gross domestic product (GDP). However, accompanying the growth in defence budget is the problem of utilisation of resources under the capital head. As the latest budget reveals, the budgeted capital expenditure for 2008-09 has decreased by Rs. 7,007 crores (15 per cent) from Rs. 48, 007 crores to Rs. 41,000 crores at the RE stage. Its implication is also seen in the wide variation in the growth of the capital budget. If the defence establishments had fully spent the entire 2008-09 capital budget, the 2009-10 capital expenditure would have seen only 14.2 per cent growth instead of 33.72 per cent rise (Rs. 13,824 crores) that has been registered over the previous year's RE.

It is ironical that while capital expenditure has been increased substantially over the years, not sufficient attention has been devoted to spending those resources in a time-bound manner. As a result, under-utilisation of resources has increased with the growth in each year's capital expenditure. In absolute number, under-utilisation has increased by over four-and-a-half times between 2004-05 and 2008-09. In percentage terms, it has increased from 4 per cent to 15 per cent in the same period. As the defence preparedness of the country largely depends on the firepower it possess, which in turn depends on capital expenditure, the latter's timely and efficient utilisation deserves due consideration. Though MoD in recent years has tried to improve acquisition procedure, it appears inadequate to expedite the process. The recurring underutilisation of resources is a case in point to seriously examine the weakness in the system. If necessary a complete overhaul of the acquisition system may be considered to ensure that funds are utilised in a proper time frame and for the purpose it is envisaged for. India's defence budget 2009-10 has no doubt registered an impressive growth of over 34 per cent. However, much of the growth is accounted for by the increase in revenue expenditure, which, in turn, has been inflated by the surge in pay and allowances necessitated by the implementation of the recommendations of the Sixth Pay Commission. The impact of the increased provision for pay and allowances is such that the revenue budget's share in the defence budget has increased to more than 61 per cent, compared to its previous year's share of less than 55 per cent. The consequent decrease in the share of capital expenditure has resulted in its modest 14.2 per cent growth amounting to an additional provision of Rs. 6,817 crores over last year's allocations. Nonetheless, the allocation of Rs. 54,824 crores under the capital head is still substantial in absolute terms.

Considering that around 80 per cent of the capital budget would be available for procurement of weapons and systems, including some new ones, the defence establishment would be under pressure to spend the resources in a time-bound manner. Experience in the recent past shows that under-utilisation of capital budget has increased with each year's allocations. This necessitates a critical examination of the acquisition system to ensure that the Armed Forces are equipped with the right equipment at the right time.

INDIAN SERVICES ARE THE NET LOSERS

As per the figures released by Defence Offset Facilitation Agency (DOFA), offset agreements worth Rs 8125 crores had been signed by the end of 2009. The share of aero systems is 94 percent at Rs 7645 crores and that of naval systems 6 percent at Rs 480 crores. While bulk of the export orders have gone to the public sector (mostly HAL Ltd), some orders have been placed on the private sector companies for the supply of goods and services. To generate offset contracts worth Rs 8125 crores, the value of main contracts would be close to Rs 17000 crores (assuming offset percentage to be mere 30 percent). Again, considering the standard cost penalty of 10 percent, the Indian defence budget has already suffered an extra outflow of close to Rs 1550 crores on account of offsets-only to facilitate export orders of sundry items for some select Indian companies.

It will not be incorrect to state that the Indian offset policy is designed to obtain export orders for the public sector at the cost of the defence budget. Take the case of 126 fighter aircraft that India proposes to buy at an indicative cost of 11 billion dollars. The proposal carries an offset liability of 50 percent, resulting in a likely cost penalty of 10 percent. It implies that India could save one billion dollars if no offset obligations are imposed or buy up to 15 additional aircraft with the same budget. It is certain that extra outflow of one billion dollars will finance export orders for HAL. Worse, HAL would manufacture and supply low-tech items like doors and windows of aircraft and not systems/sub-systems that may boost its technological prowess. On the whole, offsets are not contributing to the upgradation of indigenous technological base but adding to the woes of the services and taxing the defence budget. Indian policy makers have failed to appreciate the full potential of offsets and trivialised a powerful instrument of industrial growth for transitory gains for DPSU and other entities.

The Way Forward

The offsets cost a country considerable extra expenditure. The question therefore arises whether they are desirable. It is universally accepted that offsets make sound business sense only if the trade-off results in extraordinary economic or technological gains. Technologies that industrially-advanced countries are reluctant to sell can only be obtained through the leverage of offsets. Over 130 nations are demanding offsets in defence purchases today.

Despite knowing that the seller is bound to amortise the offset expenditure by suitably factoring it in his price quote, the countries find the proposition appealing.

India has an unusual knack of inserting provisions in a policy that are totally contrary to the stated objectives of the policy itself. Self reliance is a stated aim of DPP-2008. Yet, India does not accept technology under offsets. It is a dichotomy that the services fail to understand. The common reason given by the Government functionaries is that they are unable to price technology. It is a totally specious and hollow excuse. India purchases technology as a part of 'Buy and Make' deals-either contracted as a part of the main deal itself or negotiated separately at a later stage. Apparently, no ToT contract can be entered into without pricing the technology involved.

There is no standard price of technology in the world market. It is purely need-based and determined by the degree of desperation of the technology seeker. DRDO can be asked to identify technologies that it needs. Normally, DRDO should seek technologies in which it has made considerable headway but not mastered-commonly referred to as lacking 'last mile connectivity'. Thereafter, DRDO can work out the anticipated expenditure on indigenous effort to master the said technology as also urgency of its application. These two factors help decide fair, reasonable and acceptable price of technology.

Many knowledgeable observers are of the opinion that MoD has been pressurised by the public sector to disallow ToT against offsets as the public sector wants to perpetuate its monopoly on receipted technology through the current system of 'Buy and Make' deals. The public sector fears that acceptance of ToT against offsets would make the private sector preferred partner of foreign vendors. Therefore, opposition of the public sector is purely to safeguard its exclusive turf. It is time MoD rises above extraneous considerations to ensure that the benefits accruing from offsets do not get outweighed by the cost penalty. Transfer of technology should be made the preferred form of offsets. Through a well-evolved system of application of multipliers, irresistible incentives should be provided to foreign vendors to offer technologies that India needs the most.

FUTURE DEFENCE SPENDING UP TO 2014-15

If the Finance Ministry's emphasis on fiscal prudence and inclusive growth has resulted in a smaller increase in the latest defence budget, the Report of the Thirteenth Finance Commission, tabled in Parliament on February 25, 2010, also does not paint a very optimistic scenario for India's future defence spending.

The Constitutional Commission, which has recommended on specific aspects of Centre-State fiscal relations, has also proposed a roadmap for defence spending for the period 2010/11-2014/15. As per the roadmap, defence spending is to grow by an annual average of 8.33 per cent during this period, with the revenue and capital components slated to increase by an annual average of seven per cent and ten per cent, respectively. As a percentage of GDP, defence spending is to be progressively decreased to 1.76 per cent in 2014-15. The fiscal consolidation part outlined by the Commission. More importantly, the Finance Ministry, which is in charge of implementing the Commission's recommendations, is not only in agreement with the path but also tries to better the fiscal roadmap suggested by the Commission. This means that MoD's future spending as outlined in the TFC could come under further stress in coming years.

The Road Ahead

While projecting the MoD's budget through 2014-15, the TFC took into account the projections made by both the Finance Ministry and the MoD. The final projection by the TFC however turned out to be the same as made by the Finance Ministry-possibly to the dissatisfaction of the MoD, which argued for "the need to provide adequately for enhanced force multipliers." The TFC however stuck to its guns, saying "the Finance Ministry's projections address these needs [of the MoD]" and further added that:

"we [the Thirteenth Finance Commission] are of the view that there exists considerable scope to improve the quality and efficiency of defence expenditure through increased private sector engagement, import substitution and indigenisation; improvements in procedures and practices and better project management, within the parameters of Government of India's policy. Efforts in this direction will further expand the fiscal space available for defence spending."

The Finance Commission needs careful consideration, given the indication that India's future defence budget may not grow as desired by the MoD. In this regard, the Defence Ministry needs to carve out a plan as to where it can bring efficiency in its spending.

At present, the defence budget is broadly divided into Revenue and Capital expenditures, with the former accounting for nearly 60 per cent of total budget. However, given the cost-intensive nature of capital acquisition, the MoD, as argued rightly before the Finance Commission, needs more resources for 'enhanced force multipliers'.

This makes a case for rationalisation of revenue expenditure, if the overall budget is to grow by a fixed 10 per cent annually. The MoD has therefore to revisit its spending on major revenue components such as Pay and Allowance; Stores and Equipment; and Transportation, among others. Of particular focus should be Pay and Allowances, which has increased significantly from Rs. 24,690 crore in 2007-08 (budget estimate) to approximately Rs. 46,767 crore in 2010-11.

The way defence Capital budget is spent has been major a source of major concern, expressed by various authorities, particularly the Comptroller and Auditor General of India (C&AG). Besides, the repeated surrender of capital funds and India's heavy import dependency have probably attracted the maximum attention for remedial measures.

Although the MoD has taken a keen interest in alleviating the problems by way of revising the Defence (Capital) Procurement Procedure (DPP), some lacunae still persist. The biggest problem perhaps is the lack of an integrated acquisition structure, as brought out by the Reports of Group of Ministers (2001) and C&AG (2007).

In the absence of accountability at one place, various acquisition functions, carried out by different agencies, lack a mission-oriented approach, often at the cost of optimum time-cost trade offs and indigenisation/self-reliance. This not only raises the acquisition cost but also delays or hampers defence preparedness. It is high time the MoD looks deep into this issue.

7

Indian Navy for the 21st Century

NAVAL HELICOPTERS, BOMBERS AND RECONNAISSANCE AIRCRAFT

The Ka-31 AEW (airborne early warning) helo has a modernized cabin, the Kabris system of global navigation and landing made by the Kronstadt firm of Moscow at the Kumerstan production plant.

The system is located on the right side of the cabin. Ramenskoye instrument designers designed the pilot's equipment. The chopper is effective in sea and coastal patrol missions. The first five Ka-31s were supposed to have joined the Indian Navy during 2001-2002. A $100 million deal with Russia will see induction of ten more of these helos into our navy.

The navy is also interested in leasing four TU-22M3 long-range bombers, or 'Backfire-C'. It was introduced in 1984 in the Soviet arsenal. This TU was fitted with ramp inlets for higher dash performance and armed with a single 23-mm Gsh-23L two-barrel cannon in a tail barbette. It can carry an internal rotary launcher for six RKV-500N (AS-15 'Kickback') short-range attack missiles. A further four may be carried under the wings. In naval use, the strategic bomber uses free-fall weapons, including nuclear and high explosive (HE) bombs, and cruise missiles for anti-shipping attacks, besides carrying out electronic recce. Maximum speed: Mach 2 at 36,090 feet, its service ceiling being 59,055 feet. Ferry range: 6,476 nm. President Putin's early October 2000 visit to India brought in its wake confirmation of the TU-22M3 as well as the Gorshkov deals, among others.

Besides, the Indian Navy has evinced interest in acquiring U.S. maritime patrol aircraft, the veteran P-3 Orion. Pakistan already has the P-3s, as noted.

In mid-June 2003 there were reports that some progress had been made by India in acquiring them from the USA. A U.S. team was scheduled to visit India in March 2004 to hold talks inter alia on the Orions. The Indian Navy wants to have a fleet of 30 maritime recce aircraft; currently it has 13, mostly Russian Il-38 and Bear-D TU-142s. Two of the current inventory, however, were lost in accident in Goa. According to navy chief Madhvendra Singh in February 2004, the Indian Navy was "scouting" the world market for aircraft of this type. India's Soviet-supplied Bear-D Tupolevs can already fly from the country's largest naval air station, INS Rajali, off east coast at Arakkonam, which is located about 70 km from Chennai, to the Persian Gulf and back. Arakkonam has been in operation since 1992 and serves as India's long-range maritime recce station. Nevertheless, the navy feels it lacks in adequate and effective intelligence, surveillance and recce platforms. Pakistani Orion-threat has to be tackled by India's naval MiG-29K combat aircraft. Since March 2003 the USA is supplying our navy with spare parts for its Sea King helos.

The Air Defence Ships (ADS)

The day India acquired the Gorshkov from Russia, India's indigenously designed ADS, or small aircraft carrier, left the "drawing board stage". Defence Minister George Fernandes was quoted as declaring that India could start operating two of the ADS by 2011. Navy chief M. Singh had stated much the same. Construction is expected to begin by the end of 2004 or early next year at Kochi.

European firms are entering India's defence sector. The French MBDA received in 2003 our navy's orders for air defence system for the P 17 ships (Nilgiri or Leander-class, 2,962-tonne frigate), which are being constructed in Mumbai. Bharat Dynamics Ltd. (BDL) will build these systems.

Stealth, Nuclear Submarines

Though a submarine is by itself a stealthy weapon, sonars (a kind of underwater radar, one might say) from various platforms— under sea, maritime recce aircraft, land and from surface ships and other submarines—can detect its propeller, vibrations and other noises under water. When sonar 'pings' a submarine, it is operating in the 'active' mode. The advantage here is that when the 'ping' returns to the transmitting platform, often a submarine itself, the presence of the target submarine is confirmed. The downside is that the submarine 'pinged' can become aware via its own sonar that it has been pinged, thereby alerting it to the presence of the pinging sub. On the other hand, sonar may operate in the 'passive' mode when it is merely 'listening' to the noises generated by the propeller, vibrations, wake and other types of noise of a submarine. If these noises are cut down, minimized, then the hunter-killer submarine will have a hard time detecting a hostile submarine, unless the hunter switches its sonar to the 'active' mode. A 'stealth' submarine is built to reduce a submarine's normal noises, or 'signature' in jargon, to the barest minimum.

Scorpene

Having an ongoing deal with Islamabad on their Agosta-class submarines firmly in place since 1978, including the advanced Agosta-90 B, Paris merrily went about rectifying the 'imbalance' it helped create on the Indian subcontinent. The French consortium of the state-run DCN and Thales, which had supplied the Agostas to Pakistan, offered New Delhi their most advanced conventional submarine, a generation ahead of Agostas, the Scorpene.

According to a rediff.com report of 16 February 2001 India, the submarine arm of which had been established late, on 8 December 1967, had failed to build a nuclear-powered submarine after spending two decades and Rs.20 billion in the attempt. In mid-2001 the French sent to India their most advanced stealth naval units to showcase and impress.

A deal was struck in June 2001 by a submarine-hungry India, since its mostly Soviet-made underwater vessels were already ageing beyond repair. The deal was expected to be cleared over two years later by India's Cabinet Committee on Security (CCS), an ample tribute to red tape! The Mazagon Docks Ltd. (MDL) in Mumbai would produce at least six of these stealth diesel-electric subs, which have the capability of fitting a small nuclear reactor in their hull as well. This last bit of capability seemed to fit India's ambition to command nuclear-powered—-and eventually armed-—submarines as well. In October 2000 India held talks with both France and Russia on indigenous production of the Scorpene and the Russian Amur. As of that year, i.e., at the turn of the millennium, no Indian submarines were equipped with missiles, unlike rival Pakistan's Agostas. Hence, New Delhi rushed to buy Barak missiles from Israel for its prized carrier, Viraat, to begin with!

The first of three Agostas had been inducted into the Pakistani Navy in 1999; in December 2003 Pakistan managed to produce its own Agosta at its Karachi shipyards. The Agostas have advanced command, control and communications (C^3), torpedoes, anti-ship missiles, anti-submarine warfare (ASW), anti-surface, intelligence-gathering capability.

But the 1,670-ton Scorpene boasts of the Tavitac NT, a new combat management system, fully automated, digital radar videos, threat evaluation and weapon assignment. Its Mesma air-independent propulsion system enables it to remain submerged for a longer period than its predecessors. Earlier submarines would have to frequently surface in order to re-charge their batteries. Its range is 6,400 nautical miles (nm.) at 8 knots speed. Among its armaments are six 21-inch bow torpedo tubes with a total of 24 wire-guided torpedoes. The Scorpene has a number of 21-inch weapons. It also has popup anti-ship missiles. Alternatively, it can carry 30 mines. The submarine has a complement of 32.

India has in place a 30-year perspective plan to indigenously produce state-of-the-art submarines, mostly at MDL. The latter is expected to produce 24 submarines in phases, and of two types. The other type will probably be the Russian submarines. A Far Eastern Economic Review report of 15 August 2002 had already noted that Asian states, including India, Pakistan, Southeast Asian states but especially Japan seemed to be falling head over heels to acquire stealth submarines in a hurry.

Akula, Amur, ATV Submarines

The navy wishes to lease two nuclear-powered Akula submarines (Type 971), also known as 'Bars' in NATO parlance, from Russia for five years from 2004. The Indian Navy had already gathered experience in handling nuclear submarines, as noted earlier, during 1988-91 when operating a Soviet-leased Charlie-class submarine, dubbed the INS Chakra, equipped with SS-N-7 cruise missiles. The Soviet collapse in 1991 upset the navy's plan for building 4-6 nuclear-powered submarines. No blueprint could be expected from Russia for these vessels since such tech transfer would violate the nonproliferation treaty (NPT). As navy chief Madhvendra Singh observed in February 2004, any navy today would like to have nuclear submarines. They are quiet, need little fuel, and can remain long submerged, features, which give them a distinct edge over more conventional submarines. Hence, said Singh, India would also like to acquire them, but he remained evasive on the steps India might be taking in that direction. At least two more Russia-supplied nuclear submarines for the Indian Navy are said to be to be in the pipeline.

The Akula II, built at Severodvinsk, is quieter, more advanced than its predecessors, e.g., it has better sonars, can do 35 knots submerged, dive up to 600 metres, carry twelve 3,000 km-range Granat cruise missiles (SLCMs) which can be fired from its ten 533mm torpedo tubes and also against land targets.

The navy is also interested in the Russian Amur-1650 submarines and funding two Project 09170 nuclear-powered submarines in Russia with a view to acquire them. The Amur-1650, produced since the 1980s, is a fourth-generation diesel-electric boat designed by Russia's oldest submarine designer, the Rubin Central Marine Design Bureau in St. Petersburg. It can be converted into air-independent propulsion and keep submerged thrice longer. While earlier Amurs of the Types 530 and 950 had four torpedo tubes, the 1650 has six; it is two to three times heavier than the earlier models, displacing 1765 tonnes and is equipped with advanced cruise missiles, mines and torpedoes. As already noted, India's 30-year submarine-building plan was focused on opening, as of 2000, two separate assembly plants for the Scorpene (24 planned) and the Amur. The DRDO was engaged in developing the maritime, nuclear-capable Sagarika missile though, as we shall see later, it remains shrouded in mystery. A similar missile, the Dhanush, had failed an initial test.

It should be noted in addition that the navy in 2000 was planning to indigenously produce five Advanced Technology Vessels or ATVs, a code-name for nuclear submarines. The Times of India quoted Navy chief Singh on 3 April 2003 to the effect that the strongest arm of India's nuclear triad should be under the sea, i.e., SLBM/SLCM-carrying submarines. However, Singh skirted all further questions related to that topic.

Moscow is also interested in selling more diesel submarines to India and has already sold Project 977 EKMs. Diesels are more useful than nuclear submarines in inland seas and coastal waters. The late 1998 Indo-Russian cooperation agreement on military technology during then Russian Defence Minister Primakov's India-visit stipulated India buying $10 billion worth of Russian arms during 2000-2010, including diesel submarines.

Moscow has no reason to be unhappy with such "strategic partnership" with India, a phrase used with somewhat alarming frequency by its leaders, not least by President Putin himself during his two visits to India in 2000 and 2001, both times in October. Already in March 1999 then Soviet Defence Minister Igor Sergeyev had hurried to India and assured that Indian military personnel would be trained in his country. China and India are the two largest arms importers from Russia which help keep its sluggish defence industrial wheels turn. The Moscow Times since the 1990s have been giving vivid description of Russia's defence fund crunch and the pathetic condition of its Far Eastern Fleet and its personnel quite frequently (vide, e.g., 26 March 1996 issue, online ed.). Since the mid-1990s India bought an average of $400 million-$800 million arms from Moscow.

France showcased her hi-tech navy in India on 22 May 2001 by sending inter alia reportedly the world's first stealth surface combatant, the 3,600-tonne La Lafayette frigate to Mumbai. Its equipment, including four 5,000 hp engines, is suspended from poles to minimize sonar-detectable vibration. The frigate has advanced automated information and combat-management systems.

It is armed with eight Exocet missiles (MM 40 SSM), Crotale SAMs, one 100 mm gun, two 200 mm guns, and one 10-tonne heavy helo called Panther armed with anti-ship missiles. Besides, the Lafayette-class has 3D multi-function and 2D long-range radars. The frigate reportedly can take direct hits, yet remain combat-capable. Highly automated, it can speed at 25 knots, its range being 9,000 km. It is 125 metres long with a complement of 164. An Indo-French deal in June 2001 envisaged India building five of the Lafayettes with French knowhow, probably at MDL. Paris insisted that while the vessels may be built in India, its weapons and sub-systems must be bought from France. The latter country also suffers from a defence budget crunch, so the deal comes, like with Russia's deals, as a godsend to Paris. The same holds true of the Indian Navy in general, neglected as it was for a whole decade during mid-1980s-mid-1990s, and for MDL.

Krivak (Project 1135.6)

Earlier, in November 1997, India signed a $ 931.5 million agreement with Moscow for the supply of three 4,000-tonne Krivak III-class frigates, to be followed by indigenous production. In June 2003 it received two, the Talwar and Trishul (not to be confused with the latter's earlier Whitby-class namesake which served during 1960-92).

The third, Project 1135.6 named INS Tabar, was commissioned on 19 April 2004. Like its two predecessors, it was scheduled to visit foreign ports, about a dozen, en route to India. The Indian Navy wants 3-4 more of these. The Krivak-IIIs are dubbed Talwar-class in India. Another recent acquisition by the Indian Navy is the Nilgiri-class combatant, also called Project 17, or P 17, mentioned above. In 1997 the government had approved their design and indigenous production.

The Talwar is also supposed to be stealthy. It has sound isolators to cut down vibrations and a protective heat shield to defend against heat-seeking missiles and thermal imagers. It is armed with over 200km-range vertical-launch Club N and Club S anti-ship and ASW missiles. It has a wide array of weapons. The frigate can hit land, sea and air targets. Newer versions are expected to be armed with Yakhont and BrahMos missiles, the supersonic speed of which makes them difficult to intercept. A Talwar frigate can carry either a Ka-28 ASW helo or a Ka-31 AEW helo. The frigate has four gas turbines and can speed at 30 knots. These frigates are expected to tackle Pakistan's Agosta-90B submarines.

However, there was much delay in delivery, totalling about 18 months. The Russian-supplied surface-to-surface (SSM) Shtil missile was found to be faulty. Of 12 test-flights only seven were successful. About 500 Indian naval personnel sent to St. Petersburg to take possession of the two initial frigates had returned empty-handed after languishing in sub-zero temperature for months. The Russians had assured the Indian Navy that the fault would be rectified later, but Indian Navy chief Singh refused to take delivery of the frigates till the glitches were corrected. The Talwars are to be inducted in 2005, said Singh. Subsequently, they would be fitted out with the BrahMos missile. En route to India from builders Baltisky Zavod in St. Petersburg, the Talwar and Trishul (home port Mumbai) separately showcased themselves in the Americas, Europe and Africa by making port calls.

INS Delhi

Three modern Delhi-class destroyers, including the Mysore and Mumbai, were commissioned respectively in 1997, 1999 and 2001. The latest Delhi destroyer should not be confused with its older namesake. The latter had been decommissioned in 1978 after seeing 30 years of service.

INS Shivalik

Meanwhile, on 18 April 2003, the indigenously built frigate, also supposedly stealth, began trials in Mumbai, according to the BBC (online). Its speed is 32 knots, has SSMs and SAMs, torpedo tubes, rocket launchers, and indigenously designed sonar. At $ 140 million it is expected to be commissioned in December 2005. Navy chief Singh observed on the occasion of the trials that a developing country like India could not afford to buy warships abroad, hence, indigenous production was a necessity.

The navy had submitted its long-term plans like Vision-2025, 15-year shipbuilding and an aviation masterplan to the Defence Ministry. The navy had already obtained the government's green light for its 30-year submarine-building plan, including the Scorpenes and Russian submarines. The navy was expected to induct soon, according to the same report, Ka-31 early-warning helos, Israeli unmanned aerial vehicles (UAVs), Prabal and Kora-class missile corvettes, and Brahmaputra-class frigates. It also has plans for mid-life up gradation of Ranbir-class destroyers and Godavari-class frigates.

The Russian-built submarine INS Sindhushastra arrived in Mumbai in October 2000 and soon joined the DGX-2000 war exercise in the Arabian Sea the following month. It added a new dimension in the subcontinental warfare with its Club supersonic cruise missiles. The Club is a shorter-range (300 km) version of the Granat, dubbed 'Tomahawksi' in the West due to its similarity with the US Tomahawk cruise. However, the missile technology control regime, or MTCR, bars the Granat from export since it exceeds MTCR-permissible limits of maximum 300 km and a 500-kg warhead.

The Club can hit both sea and land targets. This means it can help in land warfare as well, as UK and US cruise missiles had demonstrated in the campaigns in Afghanistan and Iraq at the beginning of the 21st. century. A submarine can fire the Club while submerged. The Club can also be configured to carry a nuclear warhead.

The DRDO plans to develop its strategic Brahmastra cruise on the basis of club technology. MDL was scheduled to build three Bangalore-class destroyers in 2002 armed with the Club. The latter missile uses fuel-efficient turbojet engine to approach target, then in the terminal phase its warhead detaches from the fuselage at over 30 km (16.2 n.miles) from target.

A second rocket propels the warhead at Mach 3 speed towards the target, posing great difficulty for the latter to intercept it. The small Club is versatile. It can be launched from torpedo tubes or a warship's vertical launch cells. The three modern Russian Talwar-class frigates are also equipped with the Club.

The Delhi-class destroyers and newer missile corvettes like the Kora-class, one-helo-equipped INS Karmuk (the 4th. and last), built in Garden Reach shipyards (GRSE) of Kolkata are also equipped with Russian-built Uran cruise missiles with a range of 250 km. GRSE is expected to deliver nine more corvettes and frigates over the coming decade.

BrahMos

The anti-ship, supersonic BrahMos is the product of yet another Indo-Russian joint venture. According to the navy chief Singh in February 2004, at least one Indian combatant would be fitted out with the BrahMos by the end of 2005. The end of 2004 expects 'user trials'. The Russian-supplied Talwar-class frigates are expected to be equipped with the BrahMos eventually.

Barak

Two of the Israel-supplied Barak missile systems have already been installed as of February 2004. More are expected.

Dastan

The navy has reportedly been holding talks in acquiring these 'heavy' torpedoes in, of all places, landlocked Uzbekistan!

Sagarika, Dhanush

The Indian Navy is going for cruise missiles as weapons of the future. Developmental work of naval cruise and possibly SLBM missiles began late, in 1992, compared to missiles for the other two armed force services, which began about as decade earlier.

The ability of naval cruise missiles to hit both sea and land targets, as demonstrated repeatedly in the US-led wars in West Asia in recent years, has been an eye-opener for all navies.

However, there seems to be two controversies surrounding the 300-km Sagarika missile.

First, does it exist at all? Admiral Bhagwat of the Indian Navy reportedly denied outright the existence of the project in the late 1990s. The other one is equally baffling. If there were a Sagarika, is it an SLBM or an SLCM, a ballistic or a cruise missile? The US Air Force, according to one commentator , considers the Sagarika an SLBM with 290 km range, expected to become operational in the current decade. It reportedly benefited from Russian assistance in 1995, denied by Moscow.

It is known that the Aeronautical Development Establishment (ADE) in Bangalore has been working on naval missiles since 1992. One of its aims is the capability to launch missiles from submerged submarines like the ATV, also under development, as noted earlier.

This capability acquires urgency since China's YJ 8-2 anti-ship and land-attack cruise missile has already been at an advanced stage of development. There is also a land-attack version of the ADE missile. India, as already noted, handled the Soviet-supplied SS-N-7 aboard the nuclear-powered submarine Chakra.

That radar-evading missile could fly just 30 metres above the surface, was small, relatively cheap to produce, and difficult to detect, the typical characteristics of a cruise missile.

Dhanush, on the other hand, is marked as an SLBM, the naval version of the Prithvi, has one-tonne payload, either conventional or nuclear. Its propulsion system is liquid fuelled. But the first test in 2000 failed, as noted. Its unstable sea platform was posing a major problem.

Meanwhile the Indian Navy's electronic warfare (EW) system covering surveillance and combat has deteriorated. This has restricted its operations in the Indian Ocean. The government is reviewing extensive modernization requests. The navy's Kashin-II destroyers, a Brahmaputra-class, three Godavari-class, five Leander-class and two Petya-class frigates are suffering from EW shortcomings.

The Russian-built EW systems have outlived their life-cycles. The navy is in a hurry to replace them, initially with EW systems from Israel's Rafael Armament Development Authority Ltd. in Haifa. Seven such systems would cost the navy $ 107 million. The navy wishes to spend $ 500 million for longer-term modernization. DRDO is shifting R&D from tactical electronic support measure (ESM) to more strategic electronic intelligence (ELINT) systems. The latter tracks ships and aircraft passively. But there is criticism also of the DRDO's piecemeal approach rather than the more desirable integrated development.

The navy's procurement problems have been well known. Delays in both domestically built weapons and foreign purchases have been adversely affecting the navy's ambition to turn into a blue-water force.

The media reported in August 2001 that a high-power Defence Acquisition Council (DAC) was being set up to smoothen defence procurement, minimize infighting among the three armed services over allocation of resources, and clear all long-term defence deals. DAC will sit on top of the Defence Production and Defence Procurement Boards. Its members would include the top brass of the three armed services, besides the envisaged Chief of Defence Staff (CDS) meant for handling nuclear weapons, and civilian secretaries from various defence-related branches like Defence Production, Defence Finance and Defence Acquisition.

India's Joint Naval Exercises

The Indian Navy with a large number of states, including those from neighbouring Southeast Asia, routinely holds a number of joint naval exercises. Between February 1993 and 2001 eight annual exercises took place between the Indian and the Singapore Navies, the one in 2001 was scheduled off Kochi on the Kerala coast. In 2003 there was a joint naval exercise scheduled with the Iranian Navy for March 2003. The first ever Indo-Russian joint naval exercise was scheduled for two months later, in May, off both India's eastern and western coasts. The Indo-French 'Varuna-2003' exercise took place soon thereafter.

On 4 July that same year a big joint exercise dubbed 'Summerex' was planned with the US Navy involving our navy and the Coast Guard along with their helos and aircraft. Both Eastern and Western Commands were to have participated off the Chennai coast. India's helos might have included the indigenous advanced light helicopter ALH built by HAL.

It was still undergoing tests at Kochi before being inducted into the navy. INS Rajali at Arakkonam, India's largest naval air station mentioned before, was to play an important role, too. US Navy special operations forces, known as SEALs, were also planning to hold joint marine commando exercises with their Indian counterpart, the Marine Commnado Force, or Marcos, off Goa and Mangalore earlier in March 2003.

Such joint naval, and other inter-service, exercises have become part of the routine in Indo-US defence relations, a far cry from the earlier decades when New Delhi openly opposed US naval and other military presence in the Indian Ocean. 'Summerex' was yet another in a series of joint Indo-US naval exercises.

In late September 2002 the US Pacific Command fielded an ultra-modern, AEGIS-equipped Ticonderoga-class destroyer and a Spruance destroyer, an SSN (nuclear) submarine and a maritime recce aircraft in an Indo-US naval exercise dubbed 'Malabar-4'. Often such exercises also have had exotic Red Indian names like Iroquois. These exercises often involve sub-surface, surface and air operations.

Even more startling was the first ever-joint naval exercise with China scheduled for November 2003, preceded by Indian Premier Vajpayee's Beijing-visit from 22 June. This was to have been a three-day SAR (search and rescue) manoeuvre but without combat simulation. India had proposed anti-piracy exercise near the pirate-infested Malacca Strait, as it had carried out with the US and the Indonesian Navies. But China had replied that such operations are carried out its border guard units, not its navy, carry out such operations. Hence, a SAR exercise was chosen instead.

India and China have been exchanging port calls with one another, notwithstanding their silent rivalry. An Indian naval contingent was scheduled to visit Shanghai in November that year. This contrasted with India's worries about the Chinese naval, other military and intelligence-gathering presence in the Cocoa Islands of neighbouring Myanmar and growing naval activities in the Indian Ocean.

Such worries notwithstanding, joint exercises are also being held with the Pakistani Navy. Talks with Islamabad started on 16 February 2004 on countermeasures against arms smuggling to India's Gujarat and Maharashtra coasts. India's Coast Guard is to play an important role here. It has a 15-year plan to acquire 146 vessels and 100 aircraft and helos to discharge its mission of guarding our long coastline against smugglers and poachers. A hotline dedicated to Indo-Pakistani maritime patrolling was also reportedly on the anvil.

The "biggest ever" joint Indo-French naval exercise dubbed 'Varuna-2004' involving half-a-dozen warships was scheduled to be held off Goa during 6-15 April 2004. Joint naval exercises between Paris and New Delhi had started since 1998.

France will again field its nuclear-powered attack submarine. In the international fleet review in Mumbai held in February 2001 it had already sent one. Varuna-2004 will involve wide-ranging naval activities, including anti-air, ASW, air combat drills and cross-deck-landings of aircraft. Indian and French officers would take turns in commanding the vessels. A UK destroyer, HMS Gloucester, was scheduled to join the French contingent.

The Record of India's Naval Operations

Here are a few examples of the Indian Navy's combat and patrolling operations since the country's independence. In mid-December 1961 The Indian Navy, then in its rudimentary shape barely a little over a decade following independence, nevertheless successfully carried out its task of backing the army's land operations against the Portuguese colonizers in Goa.

It stood guard over the Bays of Marmagao and Aguada against any Portuguese attempt to send reinforcements. It also sank an enemy warship off Diu and neutralized Portuguese-controlled airport and its control tower by bombardment.

An anti-aircraft Portuguese frigate, the Albuquerque, was damaged and abandoned by its crew off Marmagao. Naval assault teams, under cover fire of 4.5-inch guns from friendly ships, ultimately took Anjadip and forced the enemy garrison there to surrender.

Ten years later, again in December, came the Bangladesh war with Pakistan. The carrier Vikrant and its escorts blocked Pakistani seaborne supply routes to then East Pakistan.

Chittagong, Cox's Bazar and other port facilities were cut off, thereby leaving over 90,000 Pakistani troops to face major Indian land and air assaults with rapidly depleting resources. Vikrant's Seahawk and Alize ('Chetak') squadrons wrought havoc on East Pakistan's vital installations. "Very shortly" the Indian Navy's Eastern Fleet was in total control of the sea and surrounding air space. The Pakistani force had no other option but to surrender. The war had lasted less than two weeks, 3-16 December 1971. Our navy also sank, as already mentioned, a Pakistani submarine off Vizag. In addition, the Western Fleet achieved brilliant results in devastating the Karachi port and sinking both Pakistani naval and merchant vessels to our west, as noted. We lost a frigate.

'Operation Pawan'

On 29 July 1987 India and Sri Lanka reached an agreement involving our navy's peacekeeping role in Colombo's uphill struggle against the Tamil Tigers, or LTTE. Ethnic strife was rampant, especially in the Jaffna region of the island republic. The Indian Navy played a multi-purpose role in this. It monitored movement of vessels carrying refugees and that of fishing boats. Its role of transporting and maintenance of the Indian Peace-Keeping Force, or IPKF, was crucial.

The 'milk run' from south Indian ports to Sri Lanka involved transporting 200,000 men in both directions, 100,000 tonnes of stores and 8,000 vehicles. Our merchant fleet also chipped in to help. In October the Eastern Naval Command, backed by our Coast Guard, put a cordon sanitaire in place. Ships and aircraft constantly patrolled the 300-mile long line of control. A blockade of all supplies to the militants was implemented. Smaller vessels like landing and coastal craft also played an important role. The navy's ability to sustain such a large body of troops for a long time attracted special attention in military circles.

More recently, in 2001, the new Indian Marine Special Force and Army commandos denied use of shallow lagoons to the LTTE insurgents. Further, they carried out clandestine attacks on the latters' hideouts and training camps.

Today's standard operating naval procedure in a Sri Lanka-type situation involves combat landing on beaches, aerial surveillance, and support to the troops by helos and aircraft. Pilots of the ageing Alizes, which have seen service since 1961 (No.310 Cobra Squadron), nevertheless showed valour.

'Operation Cactus'

Among other Indian Navy operations away from Indian shores was 'Operation Cactus' in 1988. When mercenaries overwhelmed Abdul Gayoom's armed force in the Maldives, the President of the island republic turned to India for help.

Within hours the navy flew aerial recce missions over the island while the army and the air force inducted troops to put down the armed coup there. The mercenaries then abducted a merchant vessel, Progress Light, took hostages, including the Maldives Transport Minister and his wife, and set sail for Colombo. Indian naval combatants intercepted the abducted ship. But since hostages were involved, the situation required more than use of brutal force. The Maldives government's attempts to negotiate failed. Thereupon two

Indian Navy warships fired warning shots and went for what looked like graduated use of force. The rebels finally surrendered on 6 November. The Indian Navy had successfully fought terrorism at sea and was given 'tumultuous welcome' at Male. There are several other episodes involving our navy's peacekeeping missions under UN auspices, e.g., in Africa.

During 26 June-13 July 2003 the Indian navy, upon receiving a request from Mozambique's president J.A. Chissano in preceding May, sent the guided missile cruiser Ranjit and an offshore patrol boat, Sukanya, to Maputo. Their mission was to safeguard the 53-head of state summit of the African Union there. The navy also imparted training to 100 native naval personnel.

Since 1995 the navy holds the biennial event called 'Milan' with the aim of increasing maritime cooperation among the neighbouring littorals of the Bay of Bengal. In mid-February 2003 Milan-2003 was held at Port Blair, for the first time after the latter acquired its unifed Andaman and Nicobar Command.

Participating navies included units from Australia, Indonesia, Malaysia, Singapore, Sri Lanka and Thailand. Seminars, sports, professional exercises and other elements engaged the attention of all these navies as well as our Coast Guard. The Indian Navy's theme for the occasion was: 'Building Bridges Across the Seas'.

NAVAL MOUNTAINEERING

Besides scaling Mt. Everest way back in 1965, Saser Kangri I and IV (7,672 metres) in fall 2003 as part of its 'naval mountaineering', and flying its ensign in Antarctica in 1981, the Indian Navy was reportedly helping Mauritius in mid-2003 to guard its EEZ. This is billed as being of strategic importance, not least because this operation opens up another dimension of our navy's activity. There are states like Mauritius, which have large EEZs but inadequate means of guarding them. If India starts 'helping' them guard their territorial waters, this means it will wield influence over these states in the future. Something which Islamabad, and even China, would not enjoy witnessing.

Summing Up

The Indian Navy, the fifth largest in the world, has to maintain its own in the face of potentially hostile Pakistan and China, and the danger of the two acting in collusion against India's maritime interests at times of crisis. As noted at the outset, our navy was given the lowest priority among the three armed services. For a decade since the mid-1980s it faced unadulterated neglect. Currently, however, the government has been paying greater attention to its needs, especially modernisation, in more recent times. In February 2000 then Finance Minister Yashwant Sinha had announced a quantum jump in defence expenditure, a whopping 28.2 per cent increase over the last FY (BBC.co.uk, 29 Feb.2000).

In FY 2003-04 the navy's share went up to 18% of the total defence budget. That amounted to about $ 357 billion. Percentage-wise, this was a big jump for the navy, which had hitherto been allotted not more than 11-14 per cent of the defence budget. In early 2004 Finance Minister Jaswant Singh declared Rs. 25,000 crores as non-refundable grant for defence outlay. Surely, the navy would have its share of it.

India's long coastline jutting out, its central location in South Asia and far larger maritime assets than Pakistan's, or those of any other South Asian littorals, automatically bestow upon the country a significant naval role in the Indian Ocean and beyond.

This also includes precluding Islamabad from playing an important peace-keeping role—and thereby an interfering and influential role in other littorals. This also means living up to India's stature as the outstanding South Asian state. Out of the seven countries of the region, India easily stands out in size, population, and economic, cultural and military prowess. In case a war breaks out on land, for instance, over Kashmir, India's naval superiority, if the latter can be established beyond dispute, can hurt Pakistan badly by intercepting its sea-borne trade, including oil imports, and its naval forces.

India's decision to maintain aircraft carriers, it should be noted, remains controversial. There is a school of thought which maintains that an aircraft-carrier is a white elephant and a developing nation like India cannot really afford a carrier.

The latter is vulnerable to enemy air and sea attacks and would eat up a huge chunk of defence outlay. If lost to attack, the cost would not be worth it. The pro-carrier school, which is linked to plans for blue-water navy and force projection far from India's shores, would like to have ideally three carriers(one for retrofit, and one each for the Eastern and Western Naval Commands), and long-range recce and bomber aircraft.

The pro-carrier, blue-water force arguments may be summarised as follows. Firstly, these assets can intercept hostile forces far away from the Indian coastline. The potential Pakistani and even more, the really potent Chinese naval threat cannot be ignored, notwithstanding periodic surface bonhomie. The Chinese, besides supplying Islamabad with naval combatants and technology, not to speak of their nuclear and missile cooperation, have been helping build Pakistan's naval base at Gwadar. It will provide access to the Persian Gulf for the Chinese. That is something the Indian Navy must watch out for.

Second, by the same token, long-range naval forces, including their air wing, will safeguard India's trade, especially oil from West Asia, which are of vital importance to the country's economic well-being.

Thirdly, modernization has become a must. According to Jane's Defence Weekly (11 March 1995, online), nine of the navy's 36 major ships were due to retire by 2000, including six of 18 submarines. The navy's declining share of the defence budget, according to Jane's, was preventing it from replacing these combatants as of the mid-1990s. Today, the modern naval assets will also help keep the peace in the South Asian region, as proven by past experience. Fourthly, a powerful Indian Navy would be a factor of deterrence for Pakistan, given the latter's vital sea-borne trade. India has a 5:1 advantage over the Pakistani Navy in terms of combat vessels, air assets and manpower. The Indian Navy seems to consider the Pakistani Navy rather as an "irritant" with limited sea-denial capacity. It is more concerned about the growing Chinese influence in the Indian Ocean. It would like to counter it partly by increasing its own presence in eastern South China Sea.

India is concentrating, among others, on developing the much-delayed, futuristic naval base at Karwar in Karnataka. Originally it was to have been completed by 1995 but now the earliest time it will become functional seems to be 2005-6. Dubbed 'Operation Seabird', the new naval base will come under the navy's Western Command, its 'sword arm'. Karwar will gain in strategic importance and also help decongest existing bases at Mumbai, Cochin and even Vizag.

Project Seabird will be allotted 8,000 acres of land along the west coast. It will be designed to handle a large number of warships and aircraft. Besides, it will have a dockyard for repair, retrofit and modernization of surface combatants and submarines. The Defence Ministry is roping in international firms, e.g., Rolls Royce, to lend a hand in developing this hi-tech facility. Way back in 1995, when the project had obtained the green signal from the government, it would have cost Rs.1, 294.41 crores.

India's blue water ambitions are obvious. Its size, position in the Indian Ocean with two large water bodies of the Arabian Sea and the Bay of Bengal on either side along with their critical importance for national and international trade, the composition of its naval force, which includes carriers, long-range recce aircraft and bombers, and the stated ambition to acquire SLBM-submarines, are among the pointers in that direction. Important SLOCs criss-cross the Indian Ocean.

Long-haul maritime cargo from the Persian Gulf, Africa and Europe transits it, especially oil. This cargo affects the daily lives of most peoples on earth. The Southeast Asian chokepoints of Sunda, Lombok and the 960 km-long Malacca Straits had half of the world's merchant fleet capacity and a third of the world's ships passing through them as early as 1993. The shipping through the Malacca Strait easily exceeds those transiting through the Suez and the Panama Canals combined. India lies between the Straits of Hormuz and Malacca.

Both these choke points can become volatile, fears the Indian Defence Ministry cited above. While there are alternative routes to Malacca, there are no such alternative sea routes for the Persian Gulf oil except via overland pipelines which, however, would be vulnerable to insurgencies, terrorism and war. So, any crisis in the Hormuz region would impact on India and numerous other states. India's geographical location dominates the SLOCs from the Persian Gulf before they round off south of Dundra Head in Sri Lanka. This SLOC also runs close to India's Andaman and Nicobar Islands before entering the Malacca Strait. Merchant traffic transiting the latter passes close to India's area of maritime interest. So, like Hormuz, any problem at or near Malacca affects India's interests, too.

Training with nuclear submarine revealed the navy's ambition for long-range, blue-water operations. By 2010 India is expected to become a strategic force centred on two carrier battle groups, or CVBGs, nuclear-powered submarines, or SSNs, and strategic/ maritime strike aircraft, all of which will play a dominant role in the Indian Ocean region. As an analysis from the Virtual Information Center (vic-info.org, 10 Nov.03) in the USA puts it, the Indian Navy will become primarily an ocean-going navy by the end of this decade, with few ships of less than 1,200-ton displacement.

Thus, in a nutshell, India's 'sea-control' strategy in the Indian Ocean region is sound and perfectly logical, given its geographical location and concomitant political and economic factors. It is time that the government keenly monitors the modernization of our navy and attaches the importance to it that it rightly deserves.

INDIA'S SEAWARD DEFENCE INVOLVES PROTECTING THE 7,000-PLUS

India's long peninsula jutting out into the Indian Ocean, some 1,280 islands and 2.2 million sq.km of exclusive economic zone, or EEZ. India's territorial waters extend to 12 nautical miles (nm), contiguous zone to 24 nms, continental shelf to 200 nms but this could be increased to 350 nms, and 200 nms of EEZ. India's 2.2 million sq.km of sea area is equivalent to about two-thirds of its total land area. Yet, traditionally, the Indian Navy has been given almost a step-child treatment compared to the other two major branches of the armed services, the Army and the Air Force.

India's Bombay High offshore oil installations meet 14 per cent of the country's oil needs. Bombay High accounts for about 38 per cent of the country's oil output (The Times of India, Kolkata, 31 March 2004, p.1. Henceforth TOI). The bulk of our overseas trade is sea-borne, including oil. Hence, the significance of naval role in India's defence cannot be overerstimated. But while the army and the air force each has five commands at its disposal, the navy has to be satisfied with three. Its major bases are: Mumbai (HQ, Western Command, the navy's 'sword arm'), Goa (HQ Naval Air), Karwar (under construction in the late 1990s), Cochin (HQ, Southern Command), Visakhapatnam (HQ, Eastern Command and Submarine Command), Kolkata, Chennai, Port Blair (now under unified Andaman and Nicobar Islands Command), and Arakkonam (Naval Air). A new Coast Guard station has been set up on the Lakshadweep islands. Four more are envisaged in 2004 in Jafarabad in Gujarat, Ratnagiri in Maharashtra, and one each in Kerala and Pondicherry.

India has had a rich maritime tradition. The spread of Hinduism and Buddhism overseas, e.g., Indonesia and Japan, was possible partly due to our rich maritime tradition. Same holds true for our trade with ancient Rome and other old civilisations.

Several centuries before Christ, the Maurya and Andhra dynasties devoted attention to becoming the 'Lords of the eastern seas'. Sailendra's maritime empire lasted a full five centuries. More recently, Calicut and the Marathas fought valiantly against the hordes of Europeans pouring into our subcontinent. But it was the British Navy, which outfoxed all others and helped establish the Raj for two centuries here.

After independence, India depended on the UK for its maritime security till London decided to pull out of the east of Suez at the turn of the 1970s. Cold War circumstances oriented our navy, and much of the other defence services, to the USSR from the 1960s.

In 1964 a defence team had approached the USA for help in defence matters. But Washington after Kennedy had its own Cold War calculations and seemed inclined to favour India's rival, Pakistan.

The same team later went to Moscow, straight into the welcoming Soviet bear hug! Former Indian Navy chief A.K.Chatterjee gives a vivid description of the teething troubles that our navy faced in switching over from British orientation to Russian orientation. Problems posed by different technology, naval customs and the formidable language barrier had to be overcome.

In the 1965 war, Pakistan surprised India by a daring naval attack on Dwarka. It was more of symbolic than strategic value. Six years later the Indian Navy paid back.

With compound interest. It improvised two huge raids with towed, short-range coastal Osa-class fast attack patrol boats firing SS-N-2 Styx missiles which devastated Karachi-based oil storages.

India lost the frigate Khukri, however, while Pakistan's US-supplied submarine Ghazi justified its name by meeting its watery grave under our naval attack off Vizag. It was surreptitiously looking for our prized aircraft carrier, INS Vikrant. Pakistani destroyer PNS Khaibar, the minesweeper Muhafiz and several merchant ships were also sunk off Karachi harbour.

These skirmishes pointed to a key factor. Both Pakistan and India would like to threaten each other's sea lanes of communication (SLOCs) in war; neither can afford that threat since both sides depend heavily on their SLOCs for trade, including oil supply. Babriet.tripod.com reports that as much as 97 per cent of Pakistan's trade moves by sea. India's, and for that matter China's, corresponding figures rate also above 90 percent.

But besides war, the navy has other, enormous tasks. These include policing the 200-km exclusive economic zones (EEZs), protecting our high-value Bombay High offshore oil installations, our aircraft-carrier, joining UN-mandated missions abroad, helping neighbouring countries like Sri Lanka and the Maldives when threatened and seek help, and intercepting piracy, smuggling and terrorist transits in cooperative ventures with other navies.

As India's Ministry of Defence Annual Report 2000-20001 observes, "Given the size, location, trade links and extensive EEZ, India's security environment extends from the Persian Gulf in the west to across the Strait of Malacca in the east and from the Central Asian Republics in the north to the equator in the south…".

Pakistan's Naval 'Threat'

Following its defeat, both on land and sea in 1971 by Indian forces, Pakistan began to beef up its navy. Pakistan cannot hope to match India in numbers, be it the navy, army or air force. So, its naval strategy is based on 'sea denial' as contraposed to India's more ambitious strategy of 'sea control'. Islamabad started phasing out its mainly vintage British combatants and some US auxiliary ships like minesweepers.

French Daphne submarines had already joined the Pakistani Navy in 1970. After the 1971 war with India, Islamabad started moving towards Beijing, both being India's antagonists.

During the late 1970s-early 1980s, six US Gearing (FRAM I) destroyers arrived to form the bulk of Pakistan's surface fleet. A fourth Daphne arrived from Portugal in 1975 while two French Agosta submarines joined the fleet three years later.

In the 1980s a County-class UK destroyer, renamed Babur, and two Leander-class frigates also joined. By the end of the 1980s the Pakistani Navy also leased a total of eight Garcia and Brooke-class US frigates. The four Brookes were guided-missile frigates. The US also supplied various ASW and air-defence systems. China provided Soviet-designed Osa-class patrol boats for better coastal defence. Islamabad seemed paranoid after its shattering experience with attacks from the Indian Osas in 1971. In 2001 reports suggested that China was also supplying Pakistan with a warship and the know-how to build three others.

The US-supplied Harpoon missiles installed aboard the Gearing destroyers considerably enhanced Pakistani anti-ship capability, much to the consternation in the Naval Headquarters in New Delhi. The US military aid to Pakistan during the 1980s, of course, must be seen against the backdrop of Islamabad siding with Washington in opposing the Soviet military presence in neighbouring Afghanistan.

But to supply Pakistan with anti-ship Harpoons, apparently to fight the Soviets in landlocked Afghanistan, seemed the height of absurdity! Anyone could guess that they would be used against the Indian Navy in any future conflict, and not against the Soviets. Islamabad also acquired Bofors wire-guided, electrically powered, and lightweight Tp45 torpedoes for use against quiet submarines in shallow waters.

When these combatants started ageing, too, there was international competition among arms suppliers. The French DCN won the contract in 1994 for delivery of three Agosta-90B submarines, renamed Khalid.

The latter class was inducted in September 1999. These were able to launch anti-ship missiles. India did not have sea-borne missile-launching capability at the time.

In early March 2001 Pakistan successfully test-fired two different Exocet versions, the air-launched version AM-39 and the sea-launched SM-39, the latter from the submerged Khalid. Both reportedly scored success. They hit a decommissioned destroyer, which sank (Dawn, 11 Mar 01, online).

The end of the Afghan war and Pakistan's involvement in nuclear arms development triggered the Pressler Amendment in the USA against it, which banned all arms supply and required pulling out inter alia the eight US frigates on lease. But other supplier nations filled the vacuum.

The UK supplied six Type-21 frigates, renamed the Tariq-class. These could carry Lynx helos. Their main mission is defensive, reaching a little beyond the narrow continental shelf, and have AsuW (anti-surface warfare) and ASW (anti-submarine warfare) tasks.

Given Pakistan's dependence on maritime oil deliveries, the perceived threat from the Indian submarine force, largely Kilos, and the bitter devastation of 1971 in the Karachi port area, this acquisition was understandable. France sold a Tripartite-class mine-hunter and the three Agosta-90B submarines, mentioned before.

While the first submarine would be built at the Cherbourg shipyards in France, the other two would be assembled at Karachi dockyards. Pakistan was to gradually acquire the know-how to build these boats, too. Paris simply ignored Indian protests over this sale.

The Agosta-90Bs, or Khalid, were significant since they were scheduled to have MESMA air-independent propulsion (AIP), replacing diesel-electric propulsion system, which needs periodic surfacing of the vessel to periscope depth so as to recharge batteries.

The AIP system allows the submarine to remain submerged three times longer than the diesel-electric system. The Agosta-90B has the fully integrated SUBTICS combat system and four bow 533-mm torpedo tubes.

The Khalid would be carrying the SM-39 Exocet S939 submarine-launched missiles. These are sea-skimming missiles with their own inertial guidance, active radar homing, with the speed of 0.9 Mach and the range of 50 km. The submarine can also carry the Aerospatiale Matra missile.

Pakistani sources claim that even their older Daphne-class submarines were quieter than the Soviet-supplied Indian Kilos and Foxtrots, not to speak of their more recently acquired French Agostas. India, rather belatedly, is catching up at the beginning of the twenty first century and even surpassing Pakistani submarines with its French Scorpenes, supposedly a generation ahead of the Agosta-90B.

All Pakistani subs and some frigates were reportedly equipped with Harpoons by the turn of this century. The main target for these Harpoon-armed combatants is India's carrier(s). Two Harpoons can finish off a 'small', 28,700-tonne full-load displacement carrier like the Viraat. Possibly India's latest carrier, the 44,500-tonne Gorshkov will need a few more to sink.Further, the Vulcan Phalanx close-in weapons systems (CIWS), MK36 SRBOC (super rapid bloom, offboard, countermeasures) decoy launchers and other electronic suits are being installed on combatants like the frigates.

These are largely to compensate for Pakistan's poor air defence capability. Even marines might be aboard frigates carrying portable surface-to-air missiles, or SAMs, like the Stinger to fight off an air attack! Meanwhile, the Pressler Amendment had been modified by the Brown Amendment in the USA which reopened the arms flow, including more of the much coveted Harpoon anti-ship missiles and the P-3C Orion maritime recce aircraft, to Islamabad.

These two sophisticated items added to the Indian Navy's woes. At the turn of 2000, some destroyers were scheduled to be fitted out with the Harpoon Block IC missiles (124 km range). These have greater capabilities than (older) Exocets, including the capacity for indirect attack, reacquiring the target and greater range.

Besides, two new naval facilities were being built in the mid-1990s. Port Qasim at the Karachi dockyard was being modified to accommodate the new Agosta-90B submarines, while Ormara in Baluchistan would also be developed with Belgian and Turkish help to decongest the Karachi naval piers.

The cost for the new base would be Rs.4 billion. There is scope for uncertainty whether industrially backward Pakistan would be able to support production of advanced vessels under license where other, more industrially developed Third World countries have had great difficulties.

Gwadar on the Makran coast of Baluchistan was another potential naval facility, which might be developed not only to take the congestion at Karachi out but also to be relatively safe from an Indian attack. Islamabad probably still has periodic nightmares of the devastation of Karachi shipyards in its 1971 war with India.

In June 2003 US President George Bush granted Pakistan a five-year, $3 billion package, half of which was meant to bolster that country's defence, though the coveted F-16s were excluded. Bush at the same time also okayed an Indo-Israeli deal for transfer of the advanced Phalcon radar system, thereby overriding Islamabad's objections. The US had long held up the Phalcon transfer to India since Tel Aviv needed Washington's clearance as US technology was involved in the system.

The Pakistani naval air arm had already been operating older Alouette IIIs for recce missions. The US Orions were a godsend, surely to New Delhi's consternation. The elderly Alouettes had been given ASW capacity by providing depth-charges.

The naval air was also strengthened with Sea King helos. These were armed with Exocet missiles. From 1993-94 the navy stepped up even further its efforts at 'sea denial' vis-à-vis India. Five Mirage-5 fighter-bombers, armed with two Exocets each, are based in Karachi. These are operated by the Pakistani Air Force but under Naval Command and have anti-shipping role. The navy's Atlantic aircraft were also being fitted out with modern gadgets.

The Pakistani Navy also has a small special operations unit based at PNS Iqbal, Karachi. It operates a few 110-tonne Italian-made midget submarines.

There is also a para-military Maritime Security Agency, mostly equipped with older craft. It patrols the EEZ. A small Coast Guard is also present, with a few patrol boats, and reports to the Ministry of the Interior.Islamabad has not hidden its ambition to acquire SLBMs.

Its three latest Agostas are also nuclear-capable. At the turn of the twenty first century the Indian and Pakistani naval balance sheet looked like the following, according to Pakistani Navy source with inputs from other sources mentioned in the following chart :

The Potential Chinese Naval 'Threat'

At the beginning of the twenty first century, China's PLA Navy (PLAN) was about six times larger than the Indian Navy. Increasing and long-range Chinese naval aspirations and activities in the Indian Ocean region are a source of concern for New Delhi. The Chinese claim to the Spratlys and Paracel Islands are disputed by several Southeast Asian nations, which worry over rising Chinese naval activities in the South China Sea. Taiwan, it goes without saying, shares similar concern. The South China Sea and the Taiwan Straits are regions where China is most assertive, its interests clashing here with several littorals as well as the US.

China applies its laws in areas of South China Sea though these remain disputed areas. Beijing also uses Hong Kong as an intelligence-gathering facility.

India's joint naval exercises with Japan, Vietnam and Singapore, hence, may not be entirely confined to anti-piracy drills but may, at least potentially, have the greater, potential danger of China's assertive naval activities in the future within their visor.

So, from New Delhi's viewpoint, adequate safeguards must be developed to deter Beijing, and any potential Beijing-Islamabad axis, be it in the arena of nuclear-powered SLBM (ballistic missile) or SLCM (cruise missile) submarines, or force projection in distant regions. Sea, air and land power often merge. Hence, air cover for naval fleets is as much needed as amphibious forces to seize a beachhead, long-range recce aircraft to alert friendly fleets and shore facilities regarding enemy activity far ahead.

Long-range maritime bombers like the Backfire TU-22M3, which India wants from Russia, can attack a distant naval enemy formation before it can start damaging Indian mainland. The recent US-led wars in Afghanistan and Iraq have shown what today's naval forces, which are hardly purely naval but rather frequently a mix of sea, air and land elements, can achieve. These have only whetted the appetite for a modern navy in many countries.

Chinese naval activities have been on the rise in recent years. This has caused headaches in our naval HQ. A 'friendly' Chinese naval visit in 2000 to Tanzania to play football (!) probably sent a chill down Delhi's spines! There are other PLAN activities dedicated to Myanmarese ports/navy facilities in the Bay of Bengal. Our navy presumably abhors the term 'cocoa'; the Chinese station to monitor our missile tests from Chandipur-on-sea in the Ganjam district of Orissa is located on Myanmar's Cocoa Island nearby. Pakistan also did not exactly contribute to our euphoria when it conducted joint naval exercises with the Myanmarese navy in summer 2001. Of course, the Indian Navy has not been inactive either. It sent a flotilla to the South China Sea littorals in 2000, thereby showcasing its blue-water navy ambitions, not least for Beijing's benefit.

India also has to take into account China's potential strategic SLBM-submarine threat, however remote that threat may appear at present.

India's 'minimum credible deterrence' doctrine pertaining to nuclear deterrence also includes sea-launched nuclear-tipped missiles as part of the country's nuclear triad. China's two or three 8,000-ton Xia-class nuclear-powered SLBM-submarines are reportedly based at Hainan Island. The Xia has six 533-mm bow torpedo tubes. But reportedly, they rarely prowl around.

Besides, The PLA Navy plans to launch its second-generation attack submarines in 2005. This is dubbed 'Project 093' and is based on Russia's 1980s Viktor III-class submarine technology. PLAN, like its Indian counterpart, is also interested in Russia's very capable Akula-class.

It already has four and is expected to acquire eight more of the Kilo 636 by 2007, armed with 288-km Club-S anti-ship missiles. As of mid-2003, India was the only other state to possess these. Five of PLAN's indigenous diesel-electric SONG submarines are also being produced. The figure may hit ten subsequently. The SONGs are superior to the earlier Mings, which number around 20.

PLAN's Aegis-type, large phased array radar-equipped destroyers, with the number 170, pose a formidable threat, too. 48 new type of vertical-launch anti-aircraft missile systems, either Russian or locally produced, will enable long-range air defence, including against attacking aircraft and missiles. In early 2002 PLAN had ordered two more of Russian-built Sovremenny-class destroyers equipped with supersonic anti-ship missiles like the Yakhont or a newer version of the 200-km Moskit. PLAN reportedly obtained the latter missile along with the two destroyers. The Moskit is a large, supersonic missile with a distinctly anti-carrier role.

In stealth frigates, too, the PLAN is moving ahead. 'Type 054', which is the French Lafayette-type stealth frigate, is being serially produced. The first one was expected to be launched in 2003. The frigate is superior to the existing Jiangwei-class.

All this is hardly cheerful news for the Indian Navy. The latter simply cannot gloss over their presence or upcoming induction.

China's second-generation '09-4' boats, about 4-6 in number, are expected to deploy by 2010. Each submarine will carry 12 potentially MIRVed (multiple warheads) JL-2 SLBMs with the range of 8,000 km. China, however, faces severe engineering problems with these complicated missiles, but that is hardly much of a consolation for the Indian Navy. Today's problems can be solved tomorrow! Besides the Xias, PLAN has Han-class, nuclear-powered attack submarines and the Mings and SONGs. As of early 2001, PLAN's major naval combatants numbered, by weapons systems, as follows:

Six destroyers and 10 frigates with anti-air missiles, -Around fifty destroyers and frigates with anti-ship missiles, -Six destroyers and 11 frigates with ASW helicopters, and -Seven destroyers and one frigate with anti-sub torpedo tubes.

However, China's naval ambitions and growing activities in India's neighbourhood did not stop the first ever Sino-Indian joint naval exercise scheduled for November 2003, like the exercises with Indonesia and Singapore. This was part of the Indian Navy's two-pronged strategy of cooperation as well as competition, as explained later. A key mission of these exercises is better understanding of each other's operating procedures and thereby enhance coordination, be it in missions like intercepting terrorists and smugglers, or search-and-rescue (SAR).

The Indian Navy's Modernisation Drive

A sea change has taken place in our government and its policies with the change of world politics since the 1990s. While being in the backburner during 1985-95, the Indian Navy is now conducting regular joint exercises with its US counterpart, towards which New Delhi had been outspokenly hostile in the 1970s—especially over the threatening gesture of its Hawaii-based Seventh Fleet in the 1971 Indo-Pakistani war, its SLBM-submarine patrols in the Indian Ocean and its growing base in Diego Garcia. A U-turn in Washington since Reagan's days also facilitated such eventual military partnership. At the same time, India is trying to modernize its navy. In the pipeline are, inter alia: the burnt-out but now retrofitted Russian carrier Gorshkov (this has been on the anvil since the last two decades; its pricing remained problematic for long!) and its air complement of MiG-29Ks; advanced French submarine Scorpene and stealth frigates; and the induction of the Indo-Russian BrahMos anti-ship supersonic cruise missile (range kept limited to 300 km to comply with the MTCR missile control regime) with impact power nine times greater than subsonic ones like the Russian Moskit. China had inducted the Moskit. India already possesses the Russian Club subsonic cruise with supersonic impact; the Dastan heavy torpedo that Defence Secretary Ajay Prasad was scheduled to negotiate last November (2003) in, of all places, landlocked Uzbekistan!

Currently, the Indian Navy's missions include certain apparently contradictory elements. The key areas of its interaction with other navies in the Indian Ocean and adjoining regions can be grouped under the following heads: Cooperative: Those touched above, viz., territorial defence, policing EEZ, providing protection, with other navies, of maritime commerce from pirates – especially in the Malacca Straits region, which handles forty per cent of world sea-borne traffic. A Jane's Defence Weekly report of 28 May 2001 stated that in the year 2000 alone, there were 108 pirate attacks in Southeast Asia. The waters around Indonesia accounted for 47, Africa 41, and South America 30. About half the attacks, however, go unreported. The International Maritime Bureau based in Kuala Lampur monitors the piratical activities.

Hence, naval cooperation between the Indian Navy and those of other states involve today the effort to curb terrorism, protecting the sea lines of communication and the EEZs, search-and-rescue (SAR) missions, and others. Add to these the actual and potential threats by terrorists of various political hues, and one immediately realizes the India's gargantuan task of defending its maritime interests. Joint exercises with a large number of navies have become routine for our navy, as detailed later. Strategic: While such cooperation in an ongoing process in the activity areas mentioned, India at the same time has to prepare for a low profile, yet palpable, Sino-Pakistani naval threat, both separately and jointly. India has to be prepared for Pakistan's strategy of 'sea denial'.

Our navy is reportedly considering the option of going for SLBM-submarines; after all, the potential strategic threat from China, especially from its Xia-class and later-generation SLBM-submarines (the Xias, as noted, are mostly based in the Hainan Island) cannot be ignored even while exchanging pleasantries and shaking hands! Nuclear-powered and –armed submarines seem to be on the anvil. Nuclear reactors enable far longer patrol time and keep the submarine quiet. Already our navy had hands-on experience in running the Soviet-leased nuclear-powered submarine dubbed INS Chakra. It had been leased on 5 Febrary 1988 for four years and returned in 1991.

India's long, navigable coastline and large overseas trade by sea also demands the ability to project blue-water force; hence the need for—undoubtedly controversial— aircraft carriers. Our sole carrier, Viraat, is fast approaching its predecessor, Vikrant's senility. Rapid technological changes make induction of stealth technology, cruise missiles, hi-tech radar, missile-defence and satellite communication systems a must. A thorough overhaul is needed.

In November –December 2003, the Public Accounts Committee pulled up the Indian government for delays in inducting approved weapons; Premier Vajpayee demanded that our Defence Research & Development Organisation (DRDO) itself be revamped. The Indian Navy has to put up with such red tape and yet make bold strides.

India's Latest Aircraft Carriers

India is the only country of the seven in South Asia to boast of an aircraft carrier. It is also one of the few in the world to possess one.

It's INS Vikrant, the very first one, was decommissioned on 31 January 1997, after 36 years and 11 months of service. India's current carrier, INS Viraat which, like Vikrant, was UK-supplied, had seen action in the Falklands war over two decades ago, then known as Hermes. Viraat is also expected to end its service life in about the next six years.

Enter Admiral Gorshkov

The USSR never had a carrier force anywhere comparable to the US carrier battle groups (CVBGs). In the 1970s, however, Moscow did design the relatively small, 44,500-tonne Kiev-class carriers but, according to The Moscow Times (12 October 2000), these were "scrapped" in the following decade. The largest US carriers like the Nimitz-class exceed 90,000-tonnes in displacement. The 1,200-crew Kievs making 32 knots were basically helicopter-carriers, and did not have enough deck space or takeoff catapults, unlike their US counterparts, to operate combat aircraft, especially loaded with heavy ordnance. The Yak-38 'Forger' vertical- takeoff-and-landing (VTOL) aircraft they were meant to carry turned out to be ineffective. However, the Kievs carried significant missile capability like SS-N-12 anti-ship, SA-N-3 and SA-N-9 SAM missiles forward of the superstructure. Its ASW ordnance included RBU-6000 mortars. But as far as catapults were concerned, even the 'real' Soviet aircraft carrier, Admiral Kuznetsov, did not have them. The Moscow Times (12 Oct.2000) called it a "miracle" if the Gorshkov, renamed after the modernizer of the Soviet Navy, could operate combat aircraft on its deck.

The Gorshkov, originally called Baku, was the fourth and last of the Kievs. It was launched in 1982 and served initially as a development platform for various command-and-control technologies. This work delayed its commissioning for a full five years. Both India and China evinced interest in acquiring the Kievs in the 1990s since they were retired in 1992 due to fund crunch in post-Soviet Russia.

China apparently also eyed the larger Varyag carrier, which was being built in Ukraine when the USSR collapsed. The result was that the Varyag remained in the doldrums, unfinished, chiefly due to lack of funds. Meanwhile, in 1994, the Kiev-class Gorshkov, (re)built in 1987, caught fire and became just an empty shell. It was retired next year. In July that year, 1995, an Indian team visited Moscow and held talks inter alia on acquiring the burnt out carrier. Hard bargaining started.

The Russians offered for 'free' the empty shell, provided the Indians paid Moscow for its obviously needed retrofit. It was like offering the mere cover of a book for free but then extracting a price for the pages inside separately! The Indian side must have demanded a discount since Gorshkov was a burnt out shell. Also, the Kiev-class's four steam turbine propulsion engines needed much purified water. But the Gorshkov's on-board water-purification plant turned out to be faulty. Impurities in water could cause clogging, rupture, leakage of fine copper turbine pipes and other headaches. The haggling over price lasted nearly a decade. A $ 1.5 billion deal was eventually struck. India was to pay $650 million for the retrofit and another $ 730 million for the carrier's air wing, including helos.

The air component of the Gorshkov was to consist initially of 16 MiG-29K (naval MiG-29s) supersonic combat jets and 8 Kamov Ka-27 and Ka-31 helos. These helos could either carry out anti-submarine warfare (ASW) or airborne early warning (AEW) missions, depending on their types. Eventually, 60 MiG-29Ks would comprise the combat air wing of the Gorshkov. India had insisted that the Russians extend the flight deck of the carrier and also install takeoff catapults. TOI reported on 28 June 2003 (p.7) that our navy wished a bow ski-jump take-off ramp at a 14-degree angle for the MiG-29Ks.

Whether with or without the catapults, the flight deck must have been extended to operate the MiGs. The Russians meanwhile were trying to extract maximum price for their carrier. They knew that New Delhi was desperately looking for a carrier to replace the ageing Viraat. They had even linked India's wish to acquire long-range TU-22M3 strategic bombers and nuclear-powered Akula submarines with the Gorshkov deal.

While India financed the retrofit, which, along with other Indian naval orders, came as a shot in the arm of Russia's fund-starved Far Eastern Fleet, I New Delhi also negotiated hard. It let Moscow know that India was also considering buying the Israeli Barak or the French Aster anti-missile systems in lieu of the Russian offer of their Kashthan system. Even three months before handing over the Gorshkov to India, Russia stated that the possibility of introduction of foreign anti-missile elements had been causing uncertainty over the deal. However, finally on 9 March 2004 India acquired the Gorshkov at the Severodvinsk shipyards from SEVMASH, Russia's machine-building plant.

There is a humorous side to the Gorshkov story. After it had burnt off in 1994, a US firm approached the Russians with the offer to buy the Gorshkov and turn it into a floating casino off southern Florida! That must have outraged Russia's sense of self-respect and former superpower status!

Gorshkov's Air Wing

The MiG-29K is the naval version of the MiG-29 combat jet, also dubbed in the West as 'Fulcrum D'. The naval version is a single-seater, similar to the U.S. F/A Hornet, F-15, F-16 and the SU-27 'Flanker'. The MiG-29 is an all-weather, counter-air weapon. Its maximum speed: 2.3 Mach/1,520 mph; ceiling: 18,400 metres; payload: 4,000 kg; range: 1,100 km without refueling; armaments include Gsh-30L cannon and six air-to-air missiles (AAMs). The carriers Vikrant typically carried six aircraft and nine helos; for the Viraat the respective figures were 12 and 7. Initially, 14 aircraft will form the Gorshkov's air wing but ultimately the target is 60 aircraft. The Indian Navy proposes to counter Pakistan's US-supplied maritime recce Orions with these MiGs. The Sukhoi SU-MKI is meant for the air force but has a naval version which may replace India's ageing Sea Harriers.

Bibliography

Ajey Lele: *Strategic Technologies for the Military : Breaking New Frontiers*, Sage, Delhi, 2009.

Alperovitz, Gar. *The Decision to Use the Atomic Bomb*. New York: Vintage Books, 1996.

Anil, K.C.: *Military and Democracy in India: Challenges, Politics and Power*, Sumit Enterprises, Delhi, 2009.

Banerjee, Sumanta: *In the Wake of Naxalbari: A History of the Naxalite Movement in India*, Calcutta: Subarnarekha, 1980.

Bellamy, C.: *Knights in White Armour: The New Art of War and Peace*, London, Random House, 1997.

Benjamin, Joseph : *China-Pak Relations : Prospect and Retrospect*, Reference Press, Delhi, 2004.

Bhat, T.P. : *India and China : Trade Complementarities and Competitiveness*, Bookwell, Delhi, 2008.

Budge I: *The New Challenge of Direct Democracy*, Oxford, Polity Press, 1996.

Chitkara, M.G. : *Indo-Pak Relations Challenges Before New Millennium*, APH, Delhi, 2001.

Clinton, William J. *A National Security Strategy for a New Century*. Washington, DC: Government Printing Office, 1998.

Damrosch, L.F.: *Law and Force in the New International Order*, Boulder, Westview Press, 1991.

Dasgupta, B.: *The Naxalite Movement*, Bombay: Allied Publishers, 1974.

Dixit, Prabla: *Defence Economics: A Struggle for Power*, New Delhi, Orient Longman, 1981.

Fletcher, Arnold: *Afghanistan, Highway of Conquest*, Ithaca, New York, Cornell University, 1965.

Friedman, G.: *The Future of War of Cyber Crimes*, N.Y., Random House, 1996.

Gaur, Mahendra : *Indian Policy of Neighbour*, Delhi, Kalpaz Pub., 2006.

Ghosh, Ajoy : *China-Pak Conflict : Threat to South Asian Security*, Reference Press, Delhi, 2003.

Hays, Peter L. and others: *Countering the Proliferation and Use of Weapons of Mass Destruction*, New York, NY: McGraw-Hill, 1998.

Huntington, P. : *The Soldier and the State : The Theory and Politics of Civil-Military Relations*, Natraj Pub, Delhi, 2005.

Huntington, S.P.: *The China Modernisation Military and the State*, N.Y., Vintage Books, 1964.

James Campbell: *Excursions, Adventures and Field-Sports in Ceylon : Its Commercial and Military Importance*, AES, Delhi, 2006.

John M. Seidl: *Politics American Style: Race, Environment and Central Cities*, New York, Prentice-Hall, 1972.

Jones, W.H.: *The Government and Politics of Indian Military*, London, Hutchinson, 1971.

Juvale, R.P. : *Military Strategy and Diplomacy*, Cyber Tech Publications, Delhi, 2010.

Kala, G.K. : *Demystifying Military Leadership*, Manas Pub, Delhi, 2003.

Karolides, N.J. and Karolides, M.: *Focus on Fitness*. Santa Barbara, CA: ABC-CLIO, 1993.

Kumar, Raj : *Weapons and Military Technology*, Sumit Enterprises, Delhi, 2009.

Laura Brav: *The Practical Guide to Humanitarian Law,* Lanham, MD: Rowman & Littlefield Publishers, Inc., 2007.

Leena Parmar: *Military Budgeting: Global Perspectives*, Rawat, Delhi, 1999.

Martin H. Greenberg: *Studies in Nuclear Terrorism*, Boston: G.K. Hall & Co., 1979.

Mary, W.: *Asian Power and Politics: the Cultural Dimensions of Authority*, Cambridge, Belknap Press, 1985.

Morris Janowitz, *The Professional Soldier: A Social and Political Portrait,* Glencoe: The Free Press, 1960.

Nayyar, K K : *National Security : Military Aspects*, Rupa, Delhi, 2003.

Peter G. Tsouras: *Dictionary of Military Quotations*, Manas, Delhi, 2006.

Posen, B.R.: *The Sources of Indian Military Doctrine*, Ithaca, 1984, Cornell Univ. Press.

Radhakrishna: *Handbook of Military and Defence Services*, Sumit Enterprises, Delhi, 2009.

Rita Raj: *Global Encyclopaedia of Military Education and Training*, Global Vision, Delhi, 2010.

Rosen, P.: *Societies and Military Power: India and its Armies*, Ithaca, Cornell University Press, 1996.

Rudolph, Heimanson: *Dictionary of Military*, N.Y.: Oceana Publications, 1967.

Simon, D. : *Public Administration and Policy of Indian Military*, New York, Knopf, 1950.

Singhal, D. P.: *India and Afghanistan: 1876-1907. A Study in Diplomatic Relations*, St. Lucia, University of Queensland, 1963.

Strange, Susan: *The Retreat of the State: The Diffusion of Power in the World Economy,* Cambridge: Cambridge University, 1996.

Sutton, J., *Technology and Defence Market Structure*, MIT Press, Delhi, 1998.

Index

S

W

❑❑❑